Tom,

Merry Christmas
2014

Judy

AMERICA
AT WAR
IN COLOR

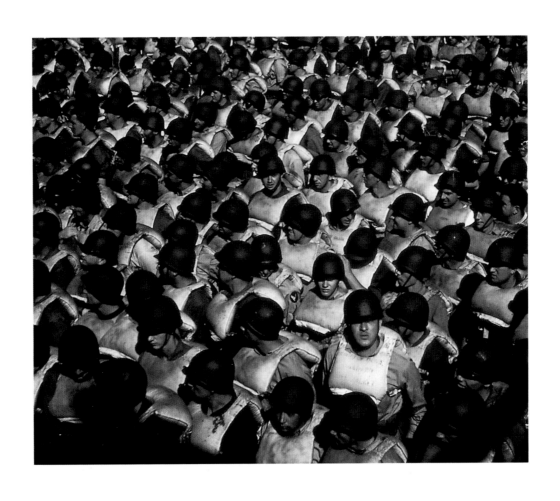

ACKNOWLEDGEMENTS

To all those at TWI, Carlton Television, Carlton Books and IMG Literary
who helped make this book happen. In particular, our personal thanks go to
Tanya Underwood, Zoë Payne, Claire Richardson, Sally Claxton and Robert
Divine for their help in making the book as good as it is, despite our
inadequacies. We would also like to acknowledge the work of the late Jeffrey L.
Ethell and the inspiration it gave us, and to thank James Bradley for his foreword.

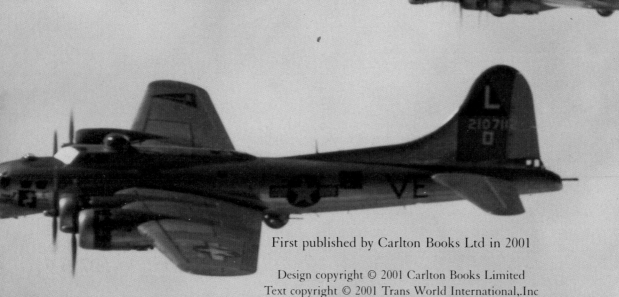

First published by Carlton Books Ltd in 2001

Design copyright © 2001 Carlton Books Limited
Text copyright © 2001 Trans World International,.Inc

This edition published in 2012 by
CHARTWELL BOOKS, INC.
A division of BOOK SALES, INC.
276 Fifth Avenue Suite 206
New York, New York 10001
USA

ISBN-13: 978-0-7858-2947-8

Printed in Dubai

A CIP catalogue record for this book is available from the British Library.

Art direction: Diane Spender
Design: Michael Spender
Commissioning Editor: Claire Richardson
Picture Research: Adrian Wood and Sally Claxton
Production: Garry Lewis

AMERICA AT WAR
IN COLOR

UNIQUE IMAGES OF THE AMERICAN EXPERIENCE IN WORLD WAR II

STEWART BINNS & ADRIAN WOOD

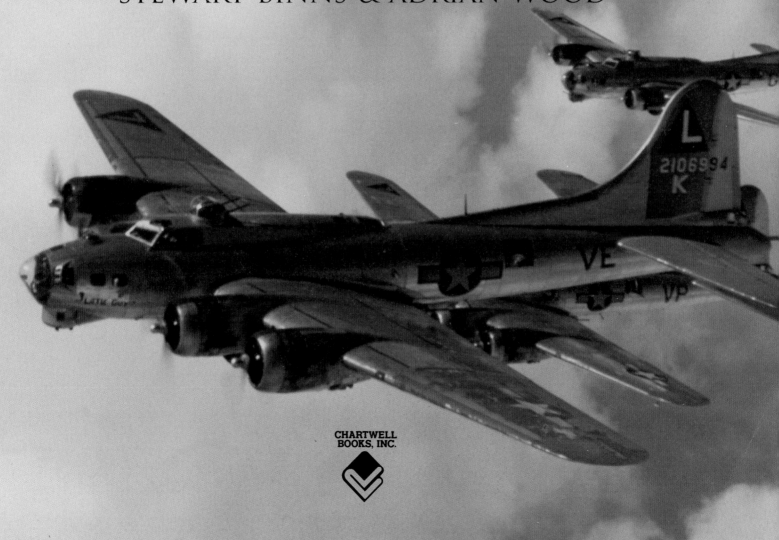

CHARTWELL
BOOKS, INC.

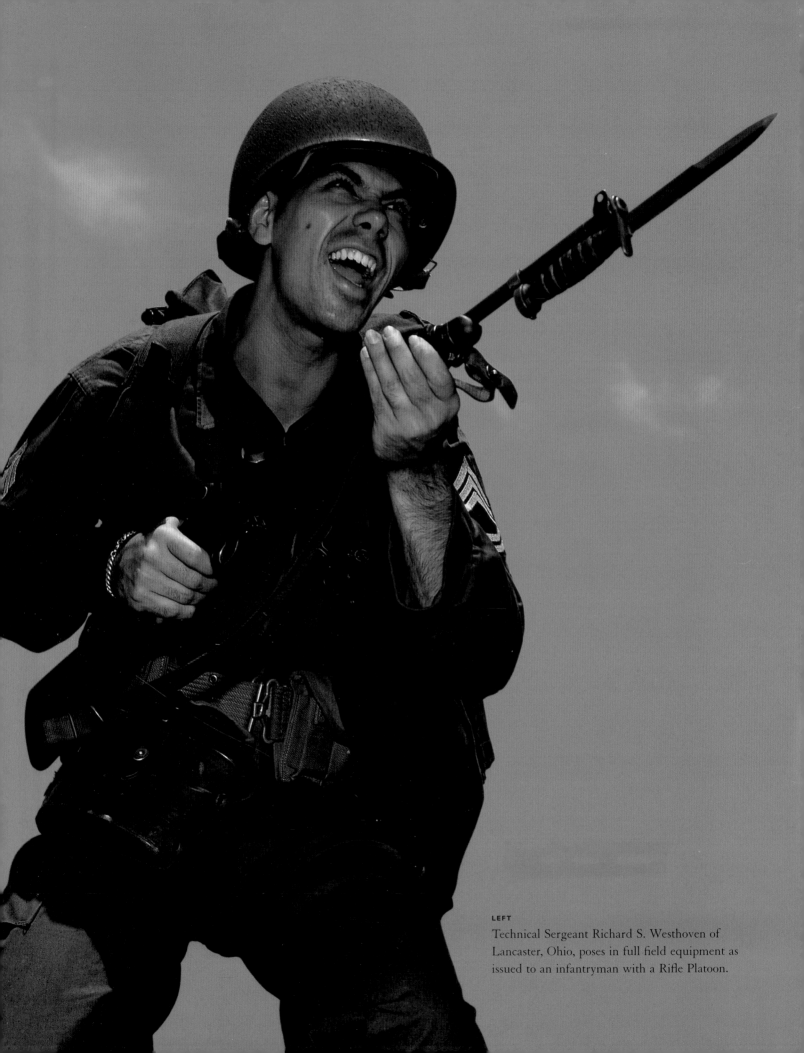

Technical Sergeant Richard S. Westhoven of Lancaster, Ohio, poses in full field equipment as issued to an infantryman with a Rifle Platoon.

CONTENTS

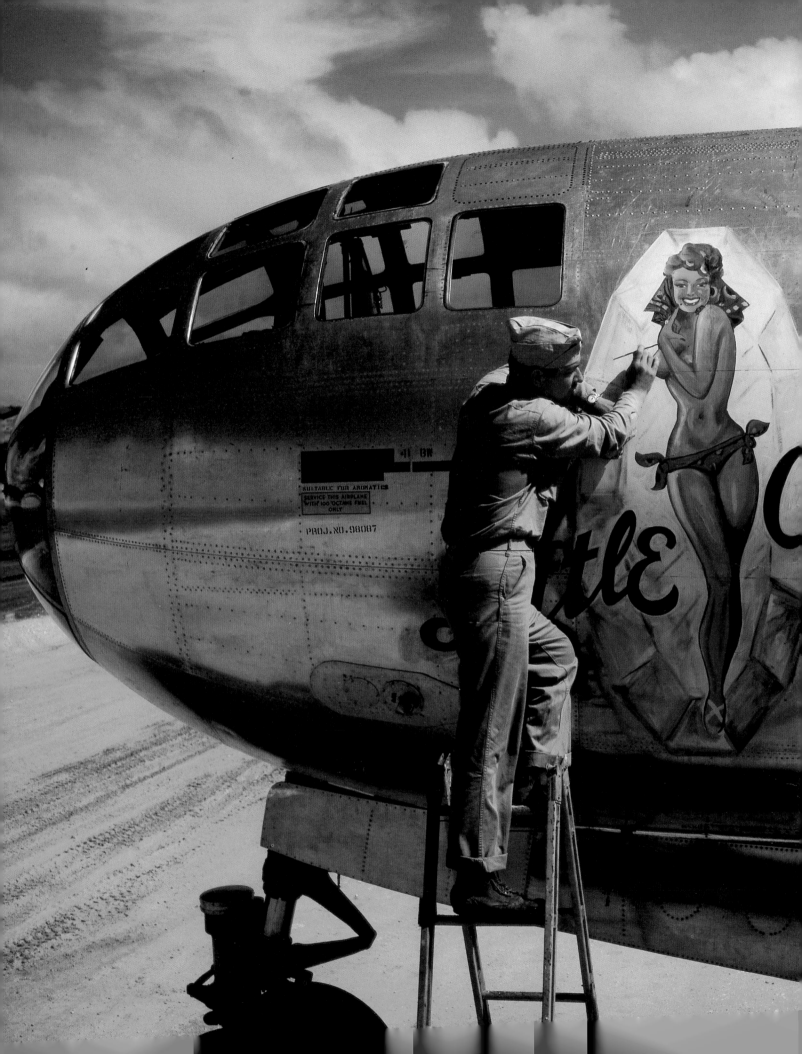

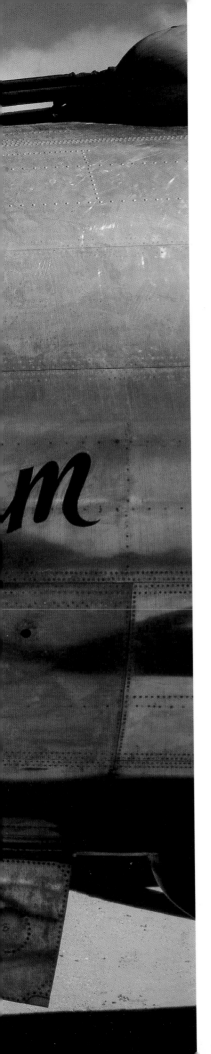

FOREWORD

BY JAMES BRADLEY
author of *Flags of Our Fathers*

MY FATHER STANDS IN THE MIDDLE OF THE MOST REPRODUCED PHOTO IN THE HISTORY OF PHOTOGRAPHY, THE FLAGRAISING ON IWO JIMA. HE WAS MOSTLY SILENT ABOUT THAT MOMENT AND LEFT HIS EIGHT CHILDREN ONLY EIGHT SIGNED COPIES AS A MUTE TESTAMENT AT HIS DEATH. THE ORIGINAL PHOTO WAS BLACK AND WHITE. BUT THE COPIES HE CHOSE TO LEAVE AS HIS LEGACY TO HIS FAMILY ARE IN COLOUR. MY AUTOGRAPHED COPY HANGS IN FRONT OF ME ON MY OFFICE WALL AS I WRITE THESE WORDS.

Joe Rosenthal shot the famous photograph, but standing next to him was Bill Genaust holding a movie camera loaded with colour film. (A frame is reproduced on page 229.) My dad had seen Bill's film countless times. All America had; it was used as "sign off" footage for the television networks at night, a patriotic visual for the playing of the national anthem. The copies my dad left us represented Joe's photo colourized according to Bill's film.

I always wondered why dad chose to leave us colourized versions of the photograph. Looking through *America At War In Colour*, I now understand. My father remembered the moment in colour—the red, white and blue of the flag he was hoisting; the low banks of white clouds against a pale blue sky; the emerald Pacific stretching away from the black sands of Iwo Jima. How much more real and personal the colour version of that photo must have been to him.

For sixty years we have become accustomed to seeing World War II in shades of gray, drained of the hues of reality. Now Stewart Binns and Adrian Wood, both award-winning documentarians, have scoured the world's libraries to present the war as the participants saw it. This would be a fine book if it were in black and white. In colour, it is a great book.

LEFT

Marine Private First Class Handsall W. Sprenger of Louisville, Kentucky, became known as the Michelangelo of the Marianas for his ability to adorn the nose of B–29 bombers with his Petty-like illustrations.

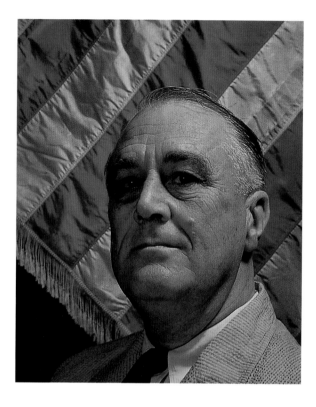

LEFT
President Franklin D. Roosevelt.

RIGHT
The crew of B-17G ride to their aircraft somewhere in England.

Those who participated in World War II not only lived in colour; they spoke in the language of colour. When you enlisted you were "called to the colours." Red-blooded Americans in army gray or navy dress blues went off to fight. Brownshirts forced Jews to wear yellow Stars of David. The Red Army was our ally. If an American serviceman was injured he got a Purple Heart; if he was captured he hoped for a Red Cross package; if he was killed mom became a Gold Star Mother.

The power of colour speaks for itself. Look at the photo on page 48 of the U.S.S. *West Virginia* aflame at Pearl Harbor. In black and white, the image merely documents an event. But in colour it transports us there: we can almost feel the heat of the orange flames and smell the oily acrid black smoke strangely juxtaposed against the beautiful sunshine hues that are Hawaii. The colour shots throughout this book similarly close the gap between us and the drama of World War II. We realise that familiar black and white photographs have come to distance us from the war, while colour makes it part of our reality.

The authors have chosen their materials judiciously to bring us the entire war. The fetid South Pacific jungles, the snowy fields, silver airplanes gleaming in the sunlight, cramped landing boats, the supportive home-front workers, the wounded and the winners—it's all here. The chapter introductions are sharp and accurate and could stand alone as excellent summaries of the Yankee experience in history's largest conflict.

From the flesh-tones of the locker room pin-ups to blood-soaked bandages to F.D.R.'s progressive pallor, this book allows you a peek at the war as the participants saw it. Follow ruddy-cheeked youths going off to war and see how battle turned them gray, old before their time. See the war as it really was. Experience *America At War In Colour.*

James Bradley

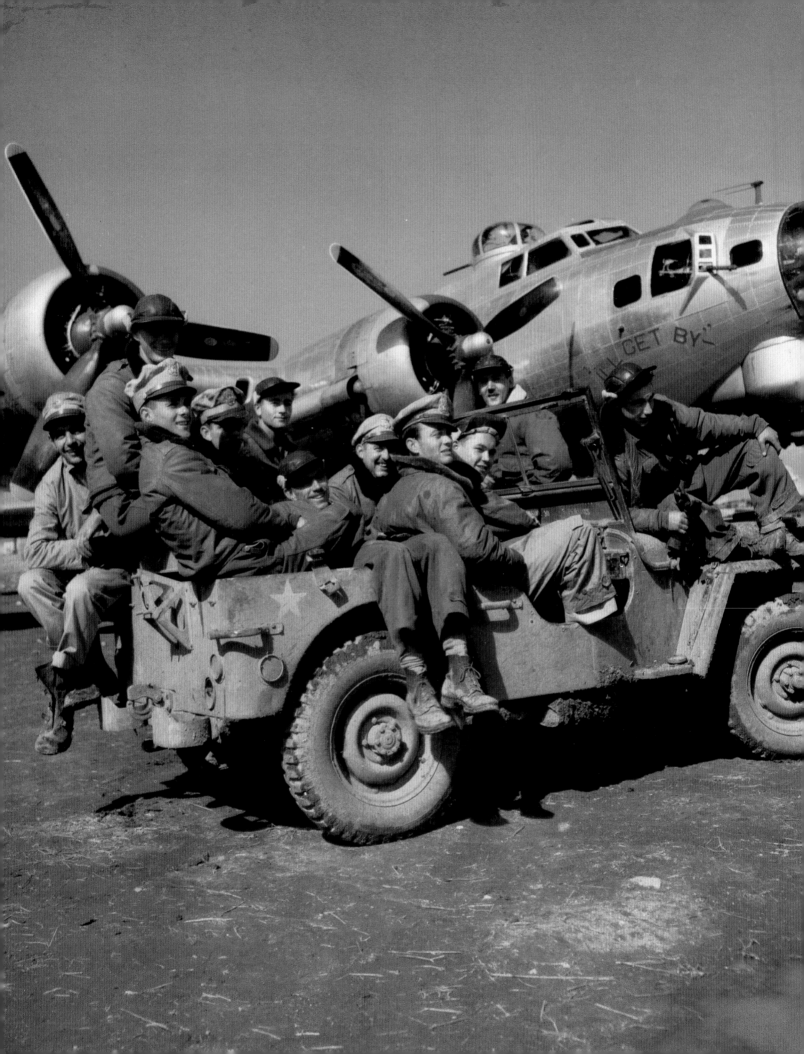

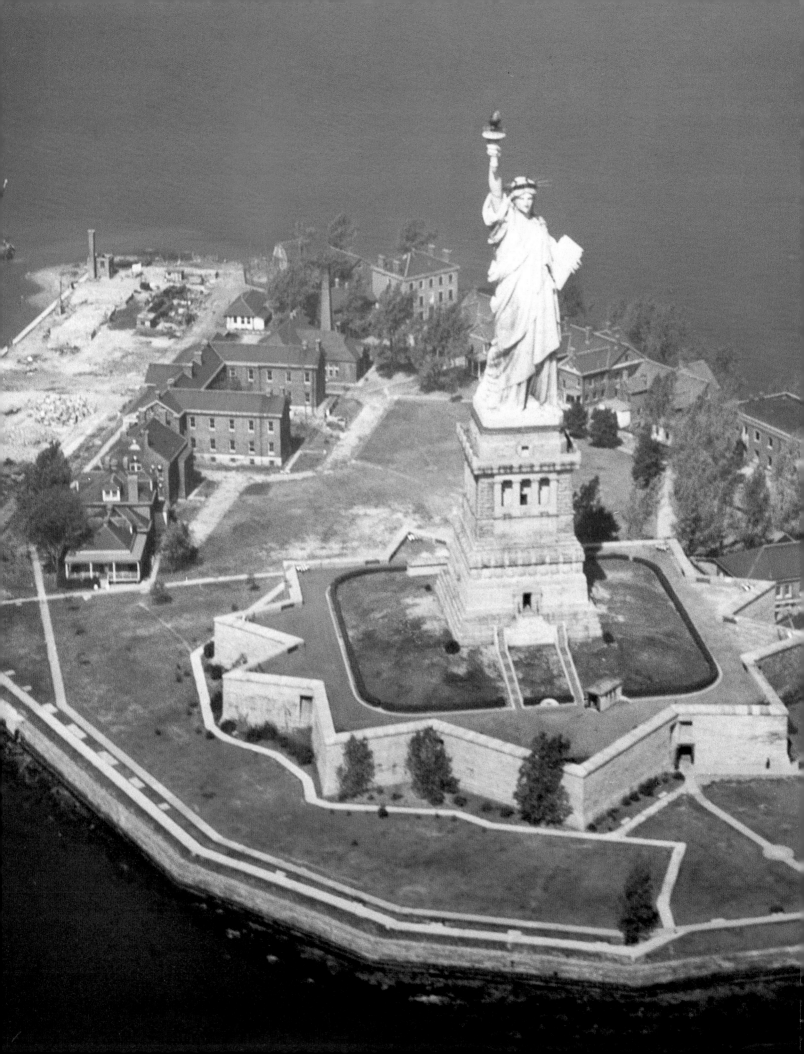

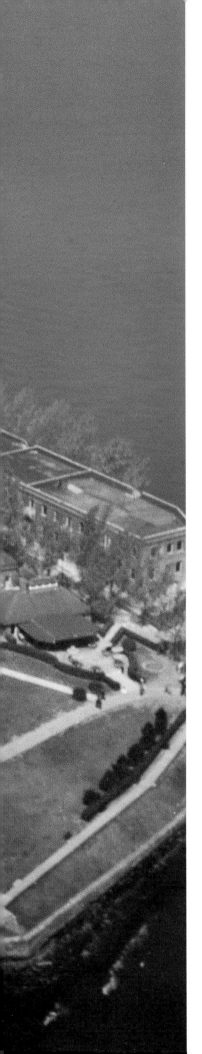

1929-41

THE INEVITABLE WAR

WITH HINDSIGHT IT SEEMS OBVIOUS THAT EVENTS IN EUROPE AND ASIA DURING THE 1930S WOULD INEVITABLY LEAD TO A CATACLYSMIC GLOBAL WAR. JAPAN'S OVERT MILITARISM AND AVOWED EXPANSIONISM, ADOLF HITLER'S AND BENITO MUSSOLINI'S STRIDENT FASCIST RHETORIC AND THEIR DREAMS OF NEW GERMAN AND ITALIAN EMPIRES, AND THE MACABRE DRESS REHEARSAL OF THE SPANISH CIVIL WAR, WERE THE THUNDER CLAPS HERALDING THE STORM.

But, at the time, the vision of the free world's leaders was, with a few exceptions, clouded. In most cases this was not because of latent fascist sympathies or ignorance and naivety but because of a desire for continued peace and a hope that other nations' bitter ideological differences need not spread worldwide. For the leaders of Britain, France, and the United States, the defining experience of their lives had been World War I: the anguish had been so great that it was thought that another such war must be avoided at virtually any cost.

Such views were particularly strong in the U.S. America was not concerned with ideology—the great monolith of the constitution took care of that—nor with security—two great oceans and national pride took care of that. The government had grave domestic issues to deal with; it was not inclined to worry about strife abroad.

Even America's mighty self-confidence had been shaken by the Wall Street Crash of 1929 and the ensuing Great Depression. The 1920s boom had produced record profits. Goods were available in ever-increasing quantities, but not enough people could afford them. Output had rocketed, fueled by over-confident speculators and increasing upper- and middle-class affluence. Between 1925 and 1929, the value of all stocks listed on the New York Stock Exchange leaped from $27 billion to $67 billion.

But the bubble had been blown too large by the hot air of overconfidence. The shock waves caused when the bubble burst were to reverberate for ten years; the aftershocks for decades. On "Black Thursday," October 24, 1929, Wall Street was hit by blind panic. Share prices plummeted, as people, shorn of all confidence, sold as rapidly as possible. Attempts to stem the tide failed and the downward spiral continued until, by November, prices had fallen to 1927 levels.

The catastrophe spread across the country and the world. By 1932, U.S. production output had fallen by 40 percent, wages by 60 percent. Few escaped: many of the rich became impoverished; many of the poor became destitute. Homes and farms were repossessed, the unemployed (at least 12 million of them) roamed the streets, or scoured the

LEFT

The Statue of Liberty in 1940: a symbol of peace in a world where war was raging in Europe and Japan was on the march in Asia.

country looking for work. Soup kitchens, vagrants, hobos, and beggars became ubiquitous symbols of the new poverty.

Amid hardship and despair, however, America found a savior. Franklin Delano Roosevelt was an unlikely popular hero. A rich and successful son of the New York aristocracy, he had all the advantages of privilege and learning. But fate had given him an unwanted additional "asset." In 1921, he had been struck down by polio, which left him unable to walk unaided. This had both humbled him and made him appealing to the humble. He was seen as a man who had attained high office by having the courage to overcome adversity.

In his speech on winning the Democratic Party's nomination for the 1932 presidential election, Roosevelt promised a "new deal for the American people." At the election, thirty years of Republican domination were swept away as he won 472 electoral-college votes to Herbert Hoover's 59.

Roosevelt changed the political complexion of the U.S. for the next fifty years. The "rugged individualism" of Republican politics had been unable to meet the challenge of the Depression. Roosevelt began a program of federal intervention to rebuild the American economy. In his inaugural address on March 4, 1932, he promised "action, and action now" in this "dark hour of national life."

During a remarkable "Hundred Days," Congress enacted fifteen significant pieces of legislation, laying the foundations of long-term economic reform. Recovery did not happen overnight, and many areas of Roosevelt's strategy were flawed, but together they represented a positive plan and led to a new and vitally important optimism.

As Roosevelt's presidency matured, he was challenged by more progressive Democrats not only to plan for economic recovery but also to plan for liberal social reform. His response, although cautious and pragmatic, led to significant improvements in social welfare and employment legislation.

These successes received massive popular endorsement in the 1936 presidential election—Roosevelt won all but eight electoral-college votes—but a sudden recession in 1937 produced both an economic downturn and a conservative backlash, which effectively ended his reformist New Deal policies. However, events on the world stage were about to take precedence in American life.

U.S. foreign policy in the decade after World War I could be summarized as "polite avoidance." Diplomats stood by their government's pledge to pursue peace and took a steadfastly non-interventionist line on international conflict. As the Depression bit deeper, American public opinion turned from polite avoidance to obdurate isolationism—ranging from idealistic pacifism to overt nationalism.

Three Neutrality Acts, in 1935, 1936, and 1937, reflected these sentiments. Whatever his private feelings, President Roosevelt famously declared, "I hate war," and promised to "pass unnumbered hours, thinking and planning how war may be kept from this nation."

American neutrality played into the hands of the expansionist plans of Germany, Italy, and Japan; the more so because France and Britain were pursuing similar, if less vociferous, avoidance policies.

Japan's aggression had begun long before, in 1904–5, with the Russo-Japanese War—which Japan won—and the occupation of Korea. In 1931–2 Japan seized Manchuria, then under Chinese control, and by 1937 it had sufficient confidence to invade mainland China.

In Europe, fascist dictators were on the march. In 1922, Benito Mussolini had come to power in Italy. By 1928 he had suspended parliamentary democracy and assumed the absolute power of a dictator. His invasion of Abyssinia (now Ethiopia) in 1935 revealed the Western democracies' unwillingness to resist aggression. This gave a clear signal to Mussolini's natural ally to the north, Adolf Hitler.

Hitler had been appointed Chancellor of Germany in 1933. With charismatic oratory and a shrewd exploitation of people's grievances, he had built up a notable populist momentum and support for his National Socialist Party. That support was fueled by national resentment of the draconian conditions imposed on Germany by the Versailles Treaty at the end of World War I; the resulting hardships had been greatly increased by the effects of the Depression.

The Führer (Leader) quickly assumed absolute power and systematically rebuilt Germany's economy and military infrastructure. German troops were soon flexing their muscles: in March 1936 they reoccupied the demilitarized Rhineland zone along the Franco-German border, and in spring 1938 they marched into Austria unopposed. Then, as tension mounted, and with the full support of President Roosevelt, the European policy of "appeasement" produced its greatest folly. Hitler demanded the annexation of the Sudetenland, the German-speaking province of Germany's neighbor Czechoslovakia. The British prime minister, Neville Chamberlain, and his French counterpart, Edouard Daladier, flew to Munich to meet with Hitler in September 1938. They struck a notorious deal whereby they agreed to this in exchange for Hitler's guarantee to respect Czechoslovakia's remaining borders. Just over six months later, on March 15, 1939, Hitler occupied the rest of Czechoslovakia.

In Madrid, on March 28, Spain's Republican government surrendered to the fascist rebels led by Francisco Franco, thus ending a civil war which had been a dress rehearsal for global conflict. Since the 1936 army mutiny led by Franco, Germany and Italy had lent major support to the fascist cause. Britain and France, adhering to an international non-intervention agreement, imposed a military embargo on both sides. The German Condor Legion's bombing of Spanish cities, most infamously Guernica, in April 1937, had been a portent of things to come.

Europe prepared for war, but Hitler was ahead of the deadly game. In August 1939 he signed a secret pact with Josef Stalin, premier of the Soviet Union. It opened the way for a German attack on Poland; the Soviets would strike from the east; and the country would be divided between them.

War came on September 1, 1939, one of the most fateful days in modern history. German troops poured into Poland in a ferocious blitzkrieg attack and, despite stiff Polish resistance, moved swiftly toward Warsaw. France and Britain, which had threatened Hitler with war if he invaded Poland, declared war two days later. The Soviet Union invaded Poland on September 17, and by the end of the month Polish resistance had effectively ended.

Although President Roosevelt responded with a proclamation of neutrality, he and all Americans were deeply shocked. The country was still determined to avoid involvement in another European war, but there was sufficient softening of isolationist thinking to allow Roosevelt to persuade Congress to pass a new Neutrality Act, which made provision for America's allies to buy arms on a cash-and-carry basis.

Strangely, there followed a period of relative calm which lasted until spring 1940. The panic of civilian evacuations, gas masks, and impending death and destruction from the skies gave way to tedium; the British called it a "phoney war."

But there was nothing phoney about Hitler's intentions. In April 1940 he unleashed his forces against Denmark and Norway, and on May 10 German troops invaded Belgium, Holland, and Luxembourg, while simultaneously outflanking the Maginot Line—France's formidable defensive fortifications along part of its border with

Germany—with a lightning armored advance through supposedly impassable terrain in the Ardennes. British troops, who had been rushed to France's aid, had to withdraw from the beaches of Dunkirk within three weeks, and on June 14 the German army entered Paris. Britain stood alone.

If Americans had been shocked by the fall of Poland, they were astonished by the rapidity of Hitler's new conquests. Their reaction gave Roosevelt some room for maneuver, and he was able to send Britain fifty much-needed naval destroyers to help in its defense. The U.S.A. was still not ready for war.

In November 1940 Roosevelt was re-elected for an unprecedented third term. Despite his campaign pledge not to involve the U.S. in a "foreign war"—fresh from victory, and with the heartfelt pleas of Britain's new prime minister, Winston Churchill, ringing in his ears, —he was able to get his Lend–Lease program enacted, allowing Britain to obtain vitally needed supplies.

Britain had survived the aerial Battle of Britain in the summer of 1940 and its cities had undergone a winter and spring of heavy bombing in the Blitz. But still the American public resisted war, even when German U-boats sank U.S. Navy ships in the North Atlantic. When war did come, it came not from Europe but from Asia.

The Roosevelt administration was aware of Japan's incursions into mainland Asia and its designs on strategic resources in the Pacific, but believed that economic sanctions would deter further overt aggression. When Japan occupied China and expanded further into Indo-China in July 1941, the U.S. tightened sanctions, particularly on oil supplies. To the Japanese this was intolerable; there was no honorable alternative to war with the United States.

On December 7, 1941, at Pearl Harbor, Hawaii, the U.S. Pacific Fleet was caught unawares and virtually destroyed by an attack by aircraft-carrier-launched planes; American bases in the Philippines and on the Pacific islands of Guam and Wake were also attacked. On December 8, President Roosevelt declared war. The United States had at last been shaken out of its complacency.

Inexplicably, the Axis powers then made a monumental mistake. Three days after Japan had awoken the "sleeping giant," Germany and Italy also declared war on America. Churchill rubbed his hands with glee. The free world was still on the edge of the abyss, but the U.S.A.'s economic and military power would alter the whole balance of the war.

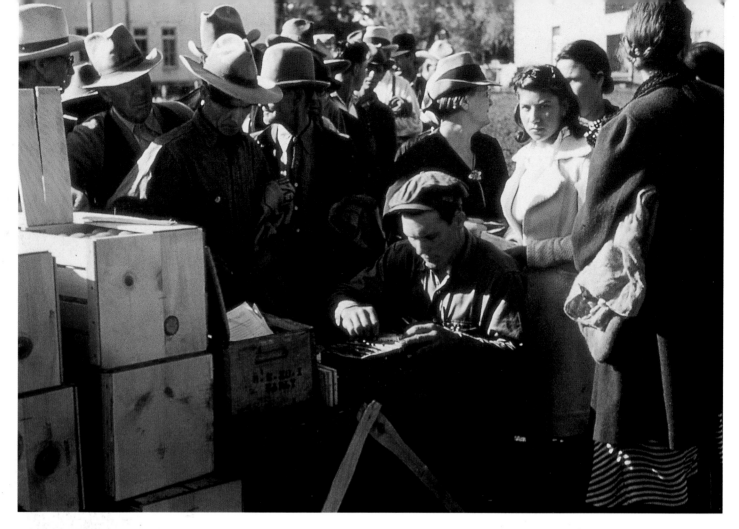

THE DEPRESSION

The Depression of the 1930s had hit America hard, giving its self-confidence a severe jolt. The suffering of those years, like the horrors of World War I, led the American people and their leaders to focus on domestic issues rather than the impending threats of fascism in Europe and Japanese expansion in Asia.

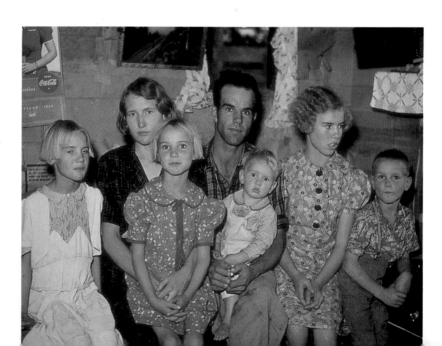

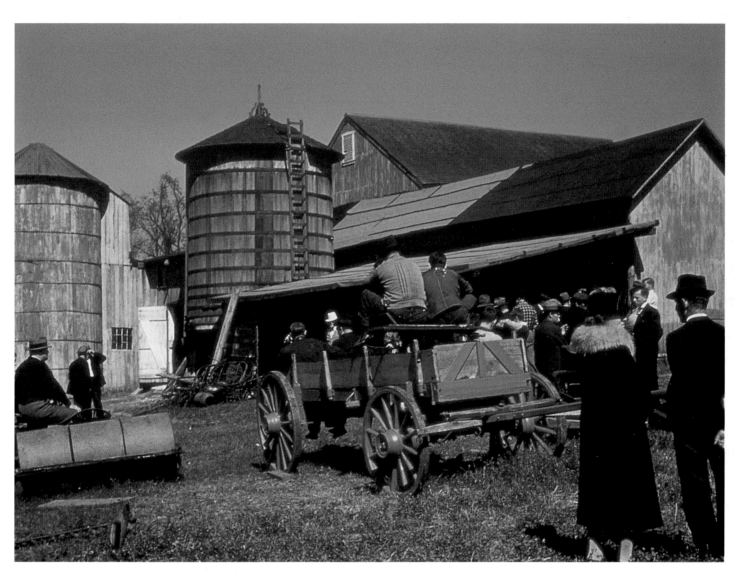

ABOVE

A farm auction in Derby, Connecticut, in
September 1940. Auctions like these had been
all too common during the Depression years.
Now farms were returning to production to
feed a nation and a world at war.

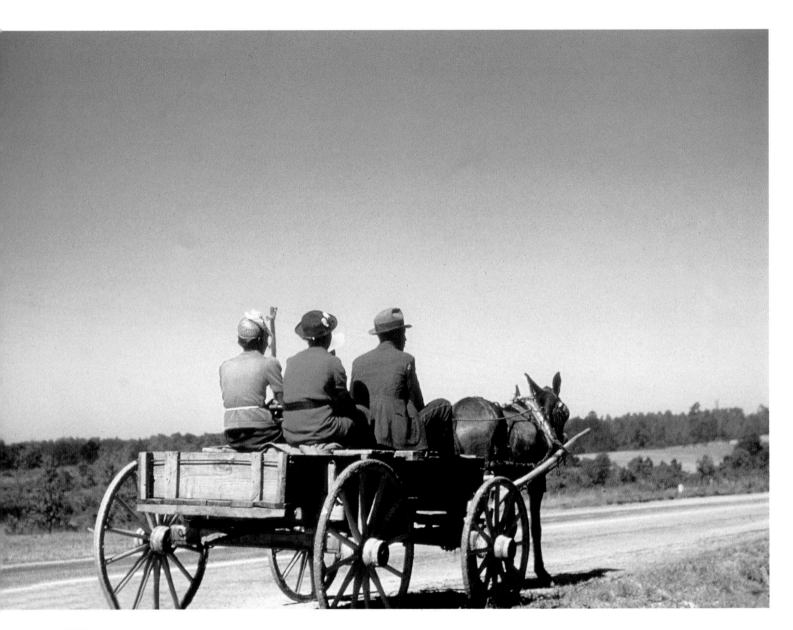

ABOVE

Going to town on Saturday afternoon, Greene
County, Georgia, May 1941. World War II
accelerated change in America. Scenes like
these soon became a thing of the past.

Negro migratory workers outside
their shack at Belle Glade, Florida,
in February 1941. War work
brought new hope to African
Americans, but many people's
hopes were dashed: the poverty of a
rural shack was merely exchanged
for the squalor of an urban ghetto.

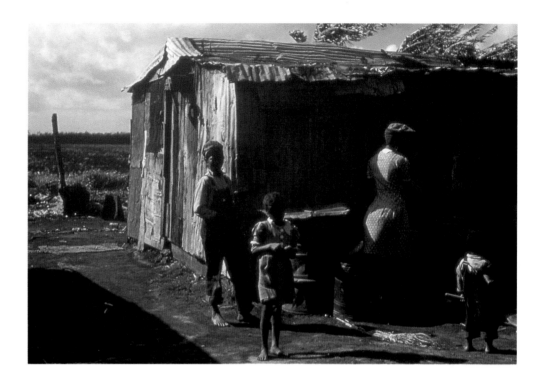

BELOW
This sad-faced young boy was photographed near
Cincinnati, Ohio, in about 1940. The war years
brought a significant movement of African Americans
from the South to the cities of the urban North.

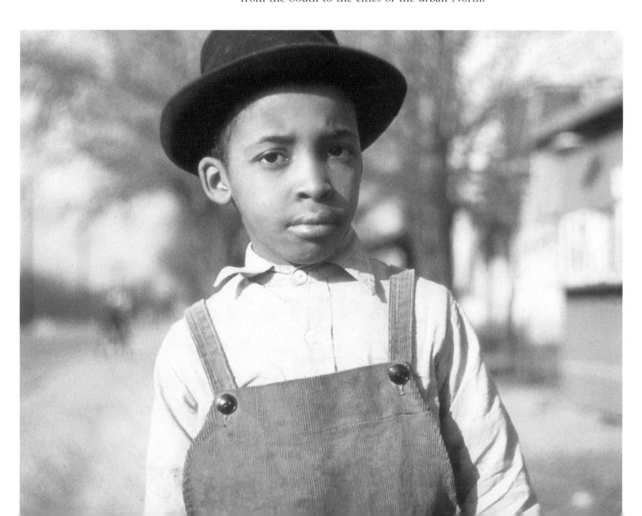

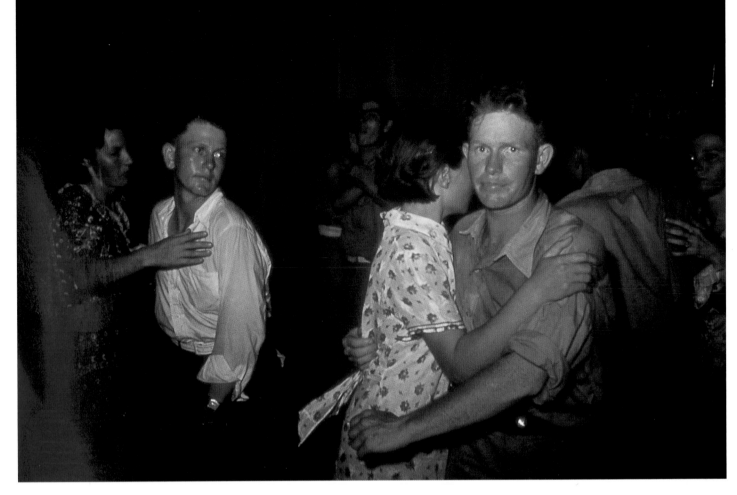

ABOVE

A square dance in McIntosh County, Oklahoma, in about 1940. Rural life in the U.S.A. was severely disrupted by the war. Many men went overseas to fight; many women and families found new work in war production. Nothing was ever the same again.

RIGHT

The war touched even small communities like Cascade, Idaho, whose main street is shown in July 1941. Faraway places like Iwo Jima, Guadalcanal and Saipan, which few had previously heard of, became household names throughout America.

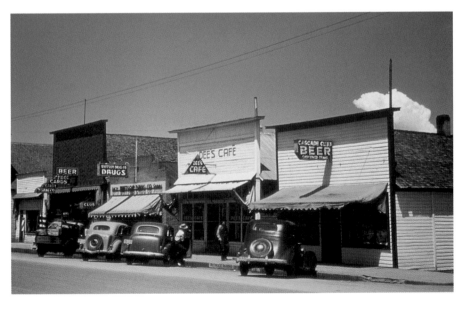

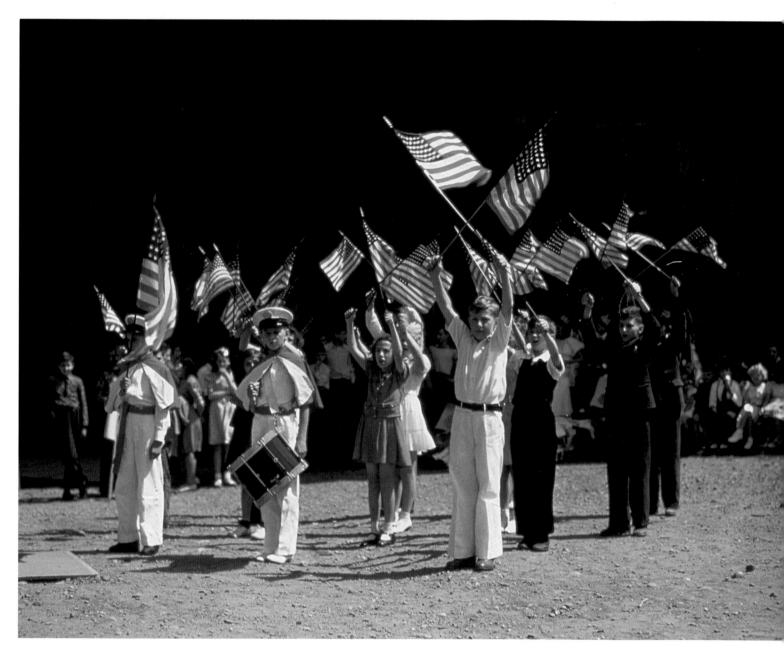

ABOVE

Children stage a patriotic demonstration in Southington, Connecticut. The events that had propelled the U.S.A. into the war stirred not only the nation's leaders, but also its population, out of their isolationism. The United States was to regard itself as the bastion of freedom for many decades to come.

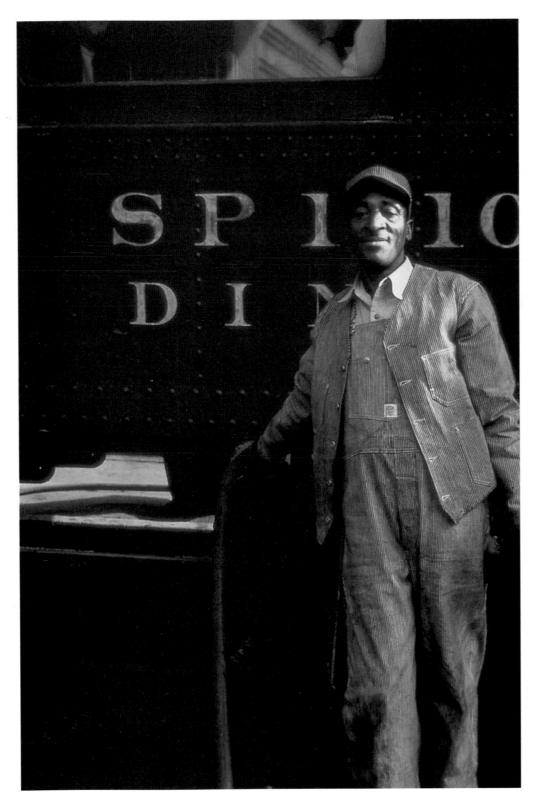

ABOVE

A railroad worker poses for a soldier's camera during a
troop-train's stop to take on water. The soldier would
almost certainly have been white: in summer 1941, when
this photo was taken, there were few African Americans in
active units, because the armed forces were still segregated.

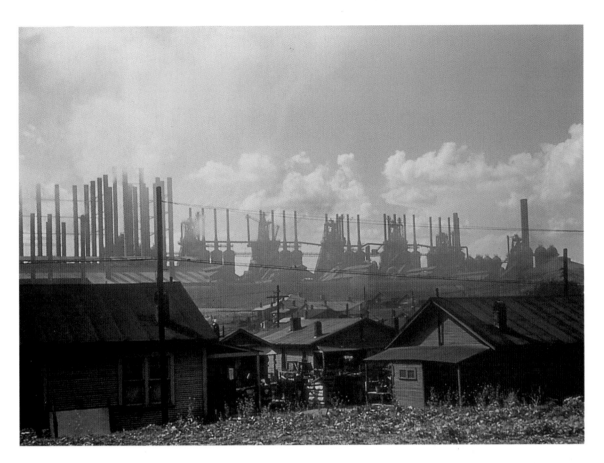

ABOVE

Houses and factories form a skyline typical of the U.S. industrial heartland in about 1940. This was the powerhouse that earned the United States the nickname of the "Arsenal of Democracy."

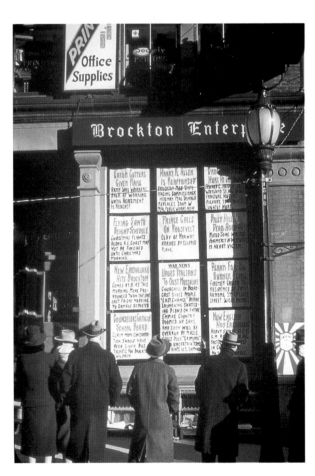

RIGHT

The latest headlines posted in the window of the *Brockton Enterprise* newspaper's offices in Brockton, Massachusetts. On December 27, 1940, disguised by flying a Japanese flag, the German raider "Komet" had shelled phosphate plants on the Australian protectorate of Nauru.

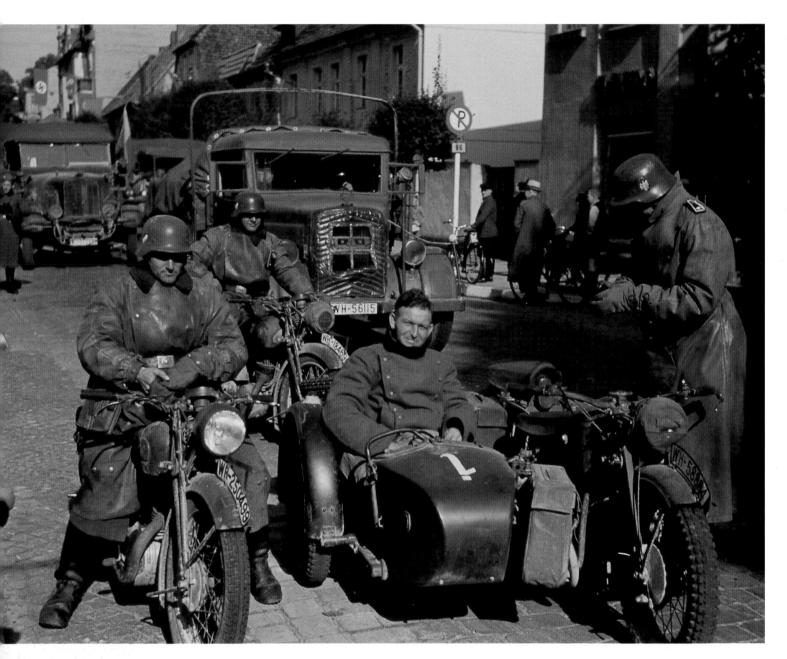

THE RISE OF HITLER

German resentment at the terms of the Versailles Treaty, which was drawn up at the end of World War I, economic crisis, nationalism, militarism and anti-Semitism all helped to bring the Nazis to power under the leadership of Adolf Hitler. Hitler was appointed Chancellor of Germany in January 1933. When President Hindenburg died, Hitler combined the offices of President and Chancellor to become the Führer, and Germany became a centralized state ruled by one party.

In March 1938, German troops "unified" Austria with Germany; Austria did not regain its independence until after the war. Members of a German army motorcycle unit, part of the Anschluss (unification) forces, are seen taking a break in April 1938.

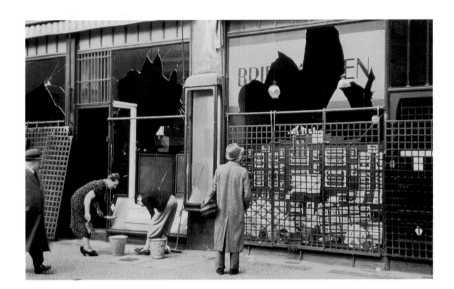

LEFT
The morning after Kristallnacht: on November 11, 1938, Jewish shopkeepers begin clearing up glass from broken windows in Berlin's Potsdamer Strasse after Nazi mobs attacked Jewish shops and businesses.

BELOW
Adolf Hitler in the uniform of the Sturmabteilungen (Storm detachment), better known as the S.A., takes the salute of marching columns in Adolf Hitler Platz during the Reich's Party Congress in Nuremberg, Germany, in September 1938.

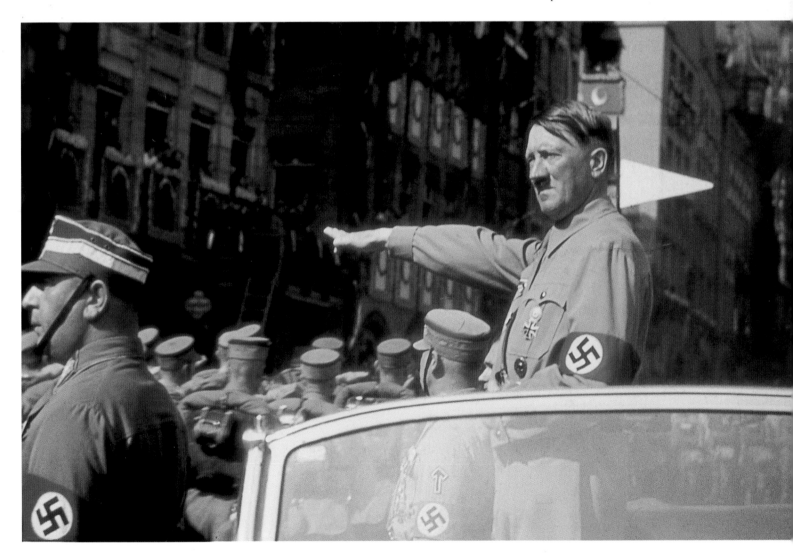

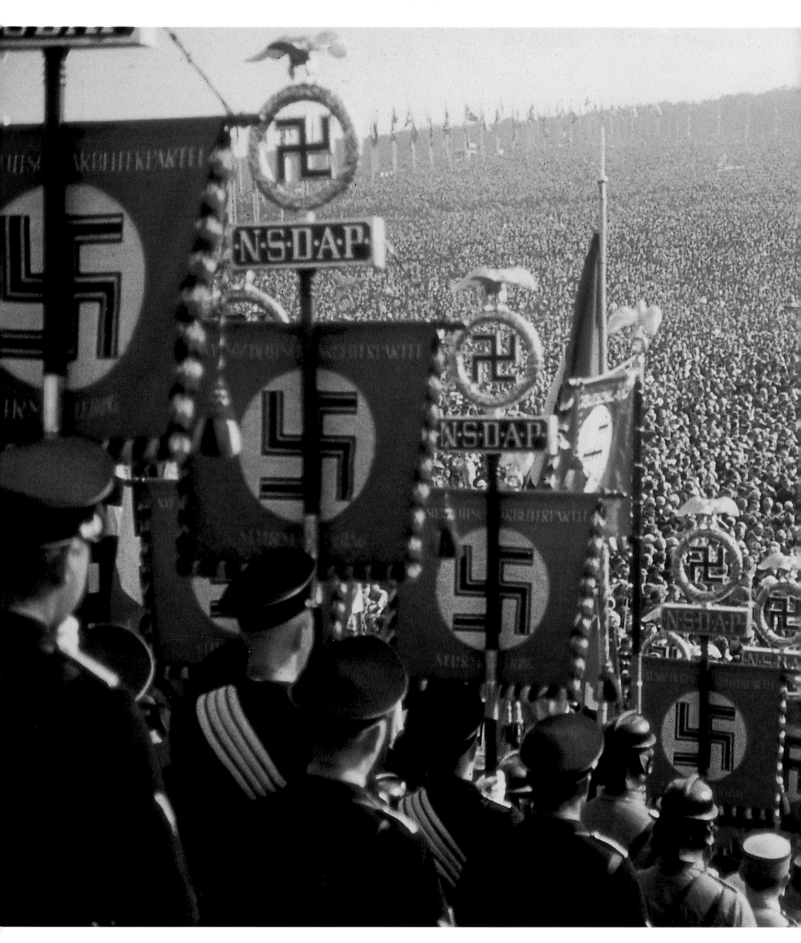

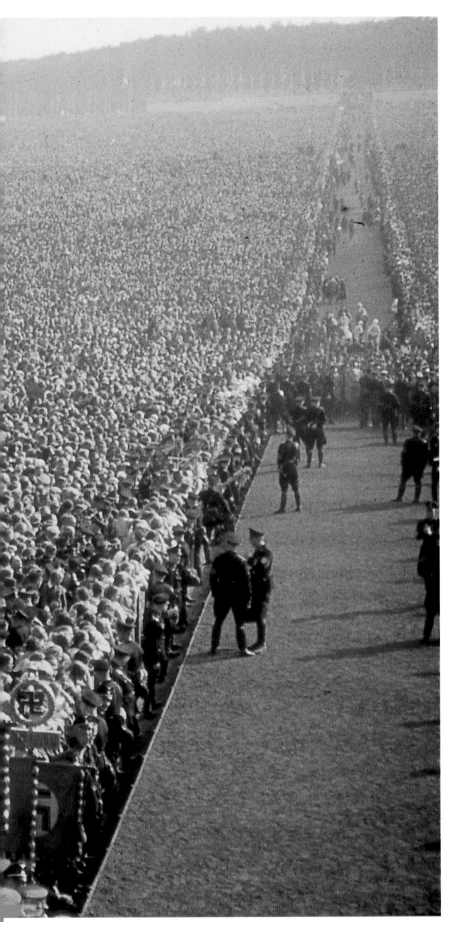

LEFT

"Buckeberg bei Hameln," Thanksgiving Day, 1937.
"The Street of People." The awesome massed ranks
at a Nazi rally illustrate the power that Hitler's
message exerted over the German people.

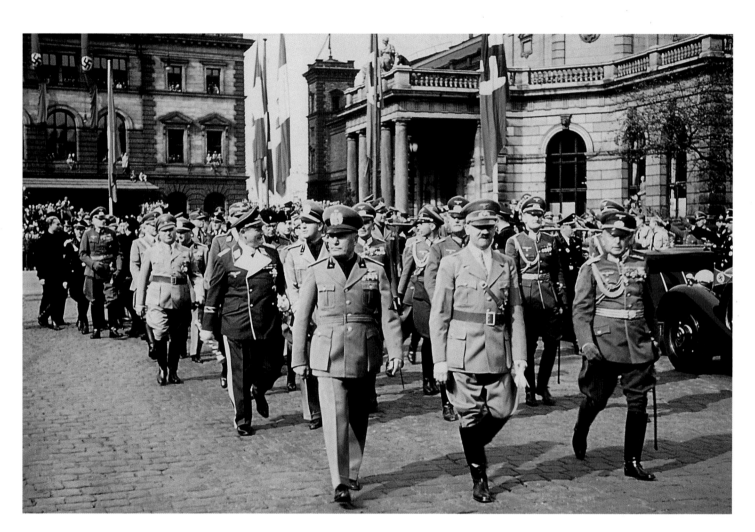

THE AXIS POWERS

Whilst Hitler consolidated his power within Germany, a number of international agreements provided him with a network of allies. The Rome–Berlin Axis formed by Hitler and Mussolini in October 1936 and the Anti-Comintern Pact, concluded between Germany and Japan the following month, paved the way for Hitler to pursue his expansionist aims.

ABOVE

In September 1938, the Italian dictator, Benito Mussolini (seen on Hitler's right), and Hitler met the prime ministers of Britain (Neville Chamberlain) and France (Edouard Daladier) in Munich, and the four leaders signed the infamous Munich Agreement. The pact led to the virtual dismemberment of Czechoslovakia, with Germany taking possession of the Sudetenland, Czechoslovakia's German-speaking region.

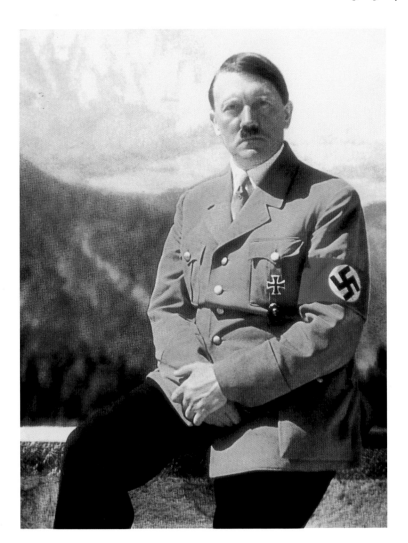

Hitler at the Berghof, Obersalzburg, Bavaria, in 1940. In his address to the German Reichstag on July 19 that year, Hitler revealed his hope for an alliance with Britain when he stated, "Mr Churchill ought perhaps, for once, to believe me when I prophecy that a great Empire will be destroyed which it was never my intention to destroy or even to harm."

The Japanese Ambassador to Germany in 1939. In November 1936, Germany and Japan had signed the anti-Comintern Pact. However, Japan was reluctant to become a signatory of Hitler and Mussolini's Berlin Pact of May 1939. It was not until September 1940 that Germany, Italy, and Japan formed the tripartite alliance referred to as the Axis.

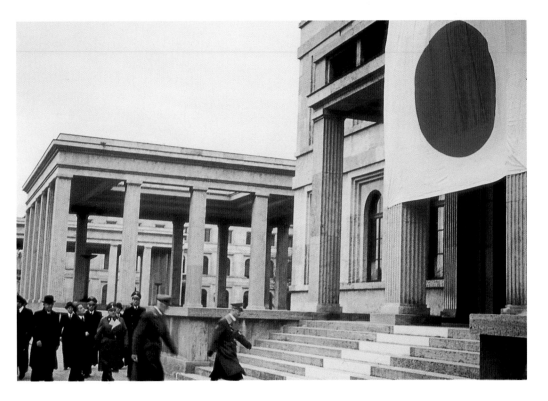

HITLER'S MASTER RACE

From the beginning, Germany's expansion was far more than a military campaign. Hitler's philosophy was viciously racist; his new world order attempted to contain, imprison and finally annihilate all opposition and anybody who did not conform to the racial criteria of the Aryan race outlined in his Nazi doctrines.

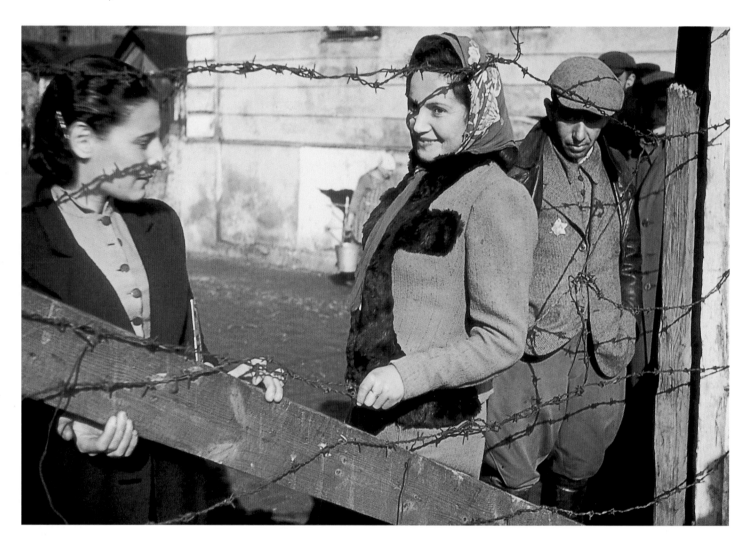

ABOVE

Jews in the Kutno ghetto, Poland, in October 1939. Immediately after the invasion and defeat of Poland, ghettos were established for the concentration of Jews. The methodology for this was laid down in an order from the deputy head of the Gestapo, Reinhard Heydrich, on September 21, 1939.

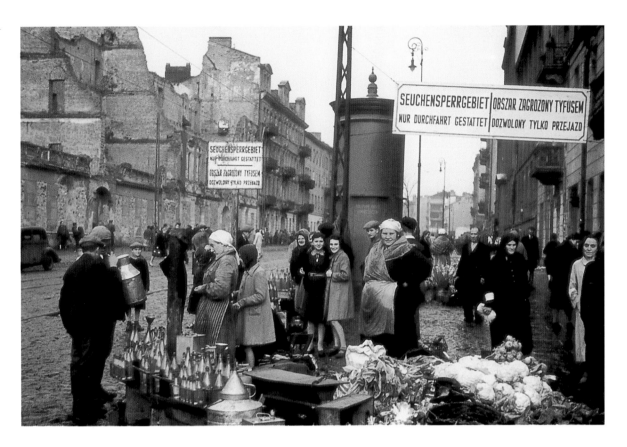

ABOVE

A street market in the Warsaw ghetto, Poland, in October 1939, after the German occupation. Destitution was only the first of the horrors that were to be inflicted on the Jews of Europe by Nazi Germany.

BELOW

Warsaw in October 1939, after the German bombardment. The city was the first of Europe's capitals to suffer the devastation of blitzkrieg (lightning war).

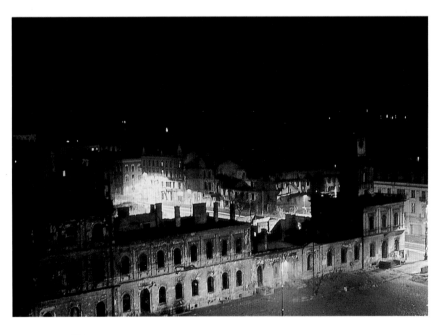

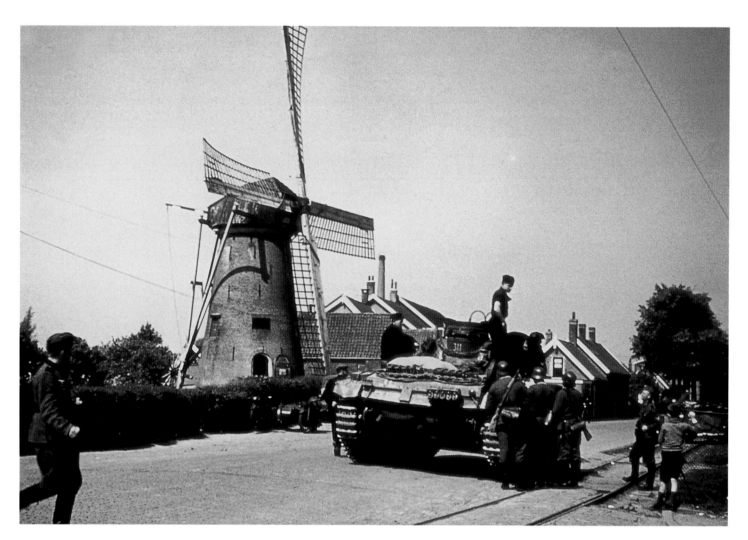

ABOVE

After the fall of Holland, in May 1940, a
German tank commander asks German
soldiers in Riysoord for directions to the
front. A young Dutch boy looks on. Hitler
launched his westward attack in early
May, and the whole of Western Europe
lay within his grasp in a matter of days.

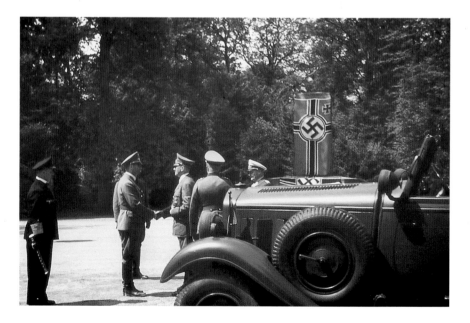

RIGHT

Adolf Hitler, pictured on June 21, 1940, after
the armistice negotiations with the French at
Compiègne in northern France. He had insisted
that the meeting be held in the same railway
carriage in which Germany's leaders had signed
the formal surrender at the end of World War I.

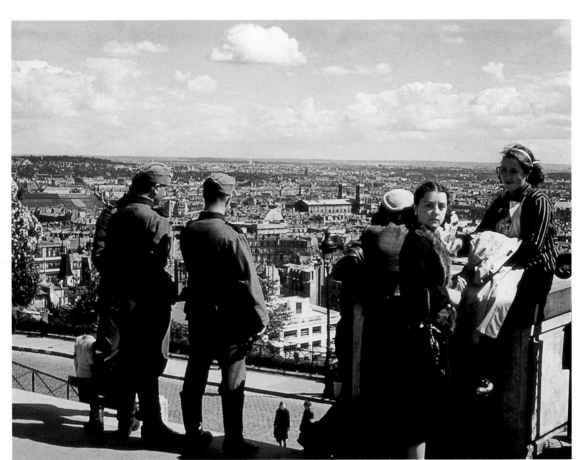

German troops sightseeing in Paris after the fall of the city to the German army on June 14, 1940. The French girls seem oblivious of the soldiers but interested in the camera (almost certainly held by another German soldier). The scale of French collaboration with the German occupation became a source of national shame for the French people.

La Panne near Dunkirk after the British retreat in June 1940; the British Expeditionary Force's attempt to shore up the defense of France had proved futile. The dramatic rescue of a significant proportion of British and other Allied troops by the Royal Navy and a flotilla of small craft was put into context by Winston Churchill when he said, "We must be careful not to assign to this deliverance the attributes of a victory. Wars are not won by evacuations."

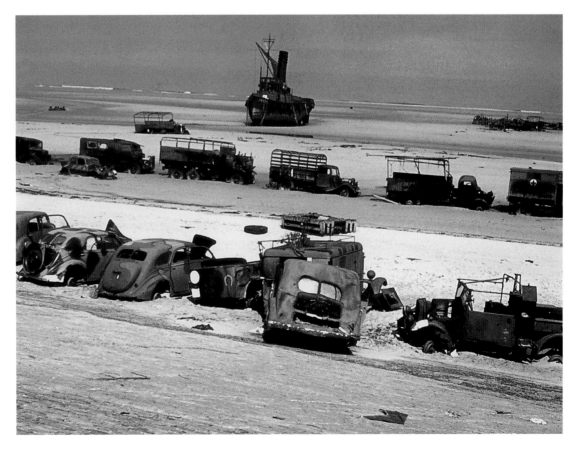

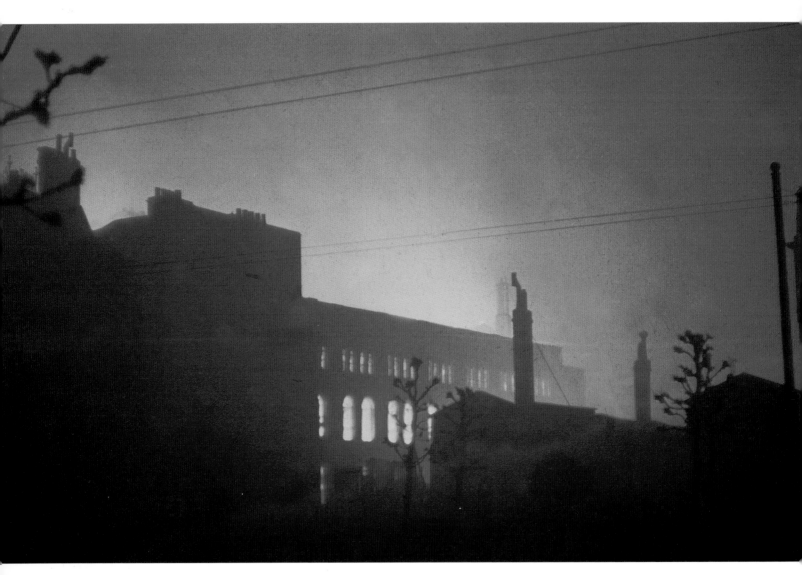

THE BLITZ

The collapse of Western Europe in 1940 under Germany's assault was frighteningly rapid. This left Britain alone as a bastion of European freedom. It was a major blunder on Hitler's part not to invade Britain in mid-1940, but instead to turn his attention to the Soviet Union. Britain breathed a sigh of relief, but had to endure years of hardship from rationing and shortages and the horror of aerial bombardment.

ABOVE

London's burning: the sky above the city is illuminated by the light from buildings set ablaze during a bombing raid by the Luftwaffe in summer 1940. The Blitz, as it came to be known, was at its worst from September 1940 to May 1941. Altogether, over 40,000 British people were killed in such raids.

RIGHT

The remains of the Temple, in the heart of London's legal district, after a bombing raid in fall 1940. The famous twelfth-century Temple Church survived this attack, but was grievously damaged in a later raid in May 1941.

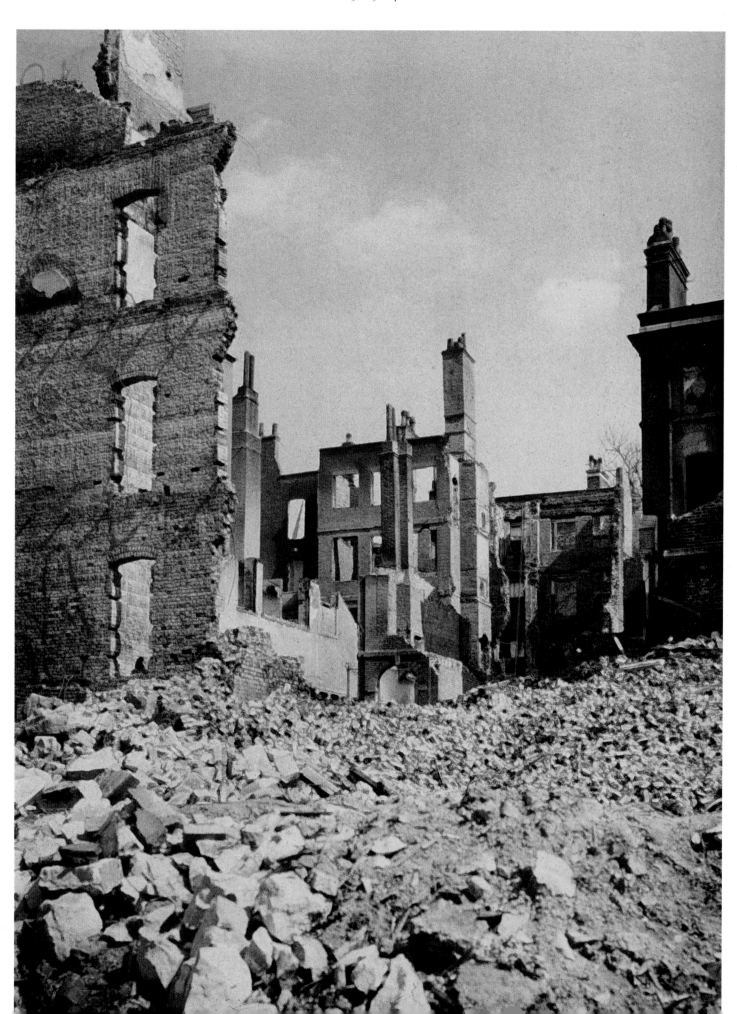

THE ARSENAL OF DEMOCRACY

America was not to enter the war for over a year. In the meantime, it tried to get on with life, whilst at the same time using its vast production potential to maintain a lifeline to Britain.

A New York City theater marquee for Charlie Chaplin's *The Great Dictator*, in September 1940. The film is a satire on Hitler's Germany in which a Jewish barber is mistaken for dictator Adenoid Hynkel.

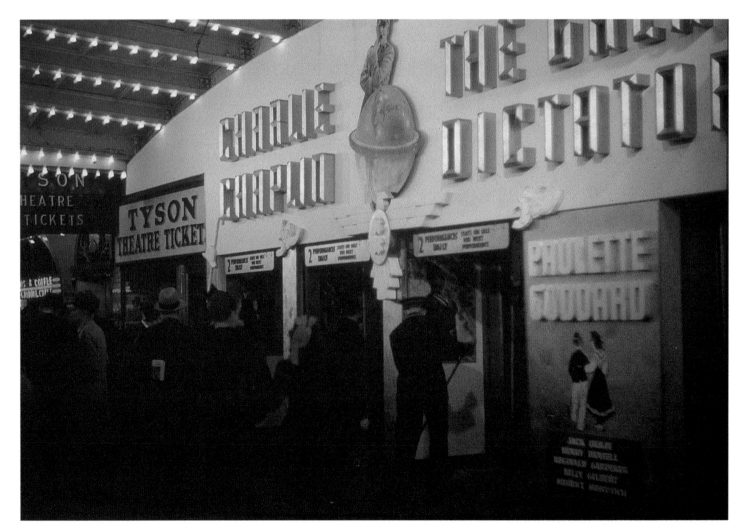

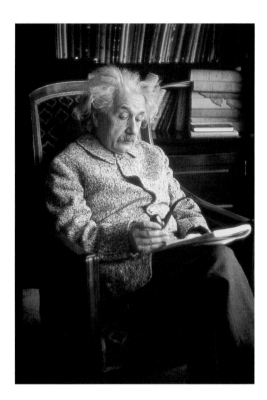

ABOVE

Physicist Albert Einstein reading in his study in 1939, while in exile. Born in 1879 of Jewish parents in Ulm, Bavaria, Einstein took Swiss nationality in 1901. When Hitler came to power in 1933, Einstein resigned his position in Berlin and left Germany to lecture in the U.S.A. In 1939 he wrote to President Roosevelt, warning that Germany would inevitably strive to create an atomic bomb. That letter helped initiate America's atomic weapons research program, code-named the "Manhattan Project."

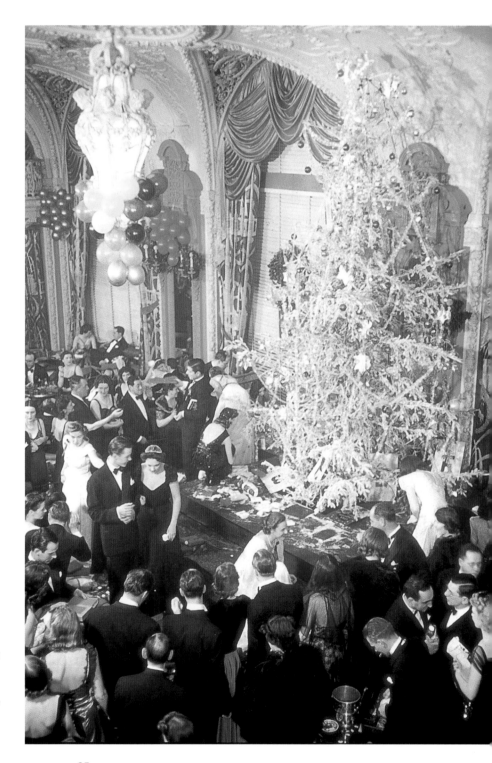

RIGHT

An elegantly dressed crowd hovering around a white Christmas tree at a society party, December 1940. In an address to the people on December 29, President Roosevelt suggested that "We must be the Arsenal of Democracy;" but the majority of Americans had not yet felt anything like the full impact of the war.

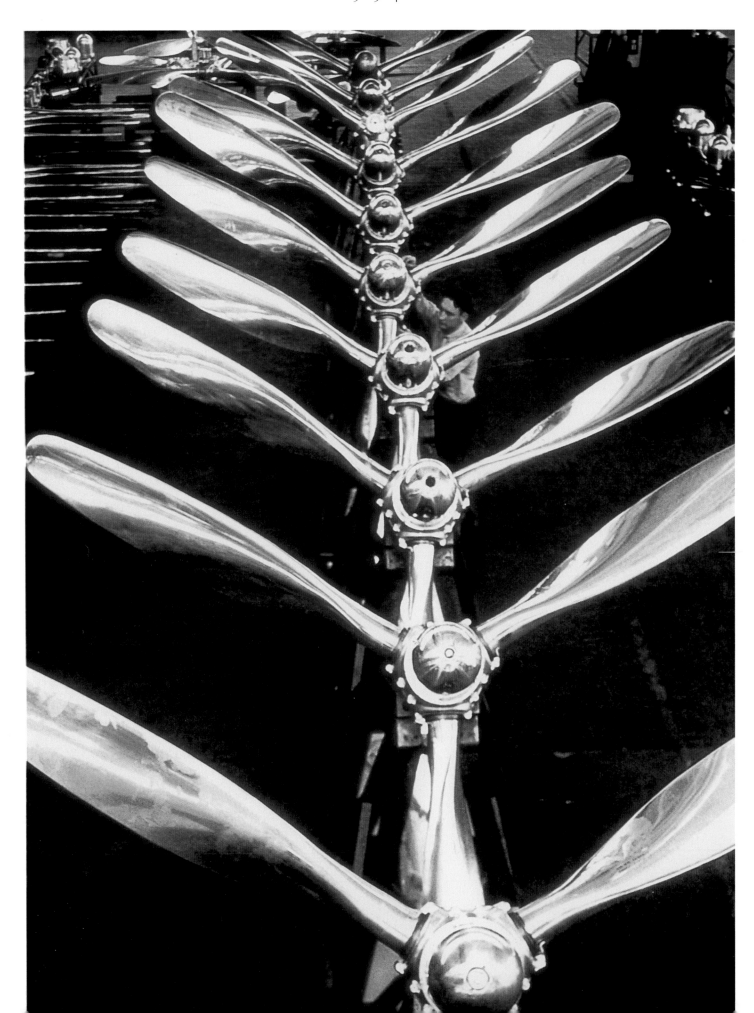

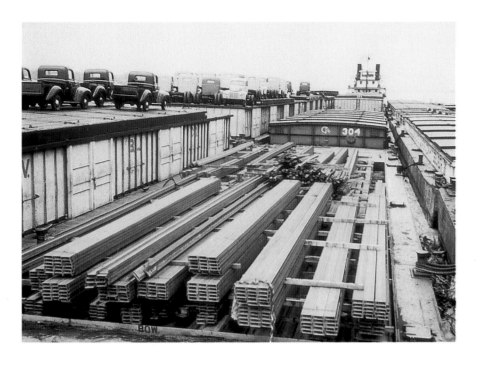

LEFT

Steel girders and Ford trucks being carried on a series of barges on the Mississippi River.

BELOW

The impressive prow of the *Oklahoma*, a Texaco oil tanker, photographed at Sun Shipbuilding & Dry Dock Co. shipyards (owned by the Sun Oil Co.), Chester, Pennsylvania in 1941.

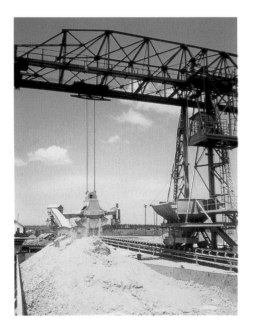

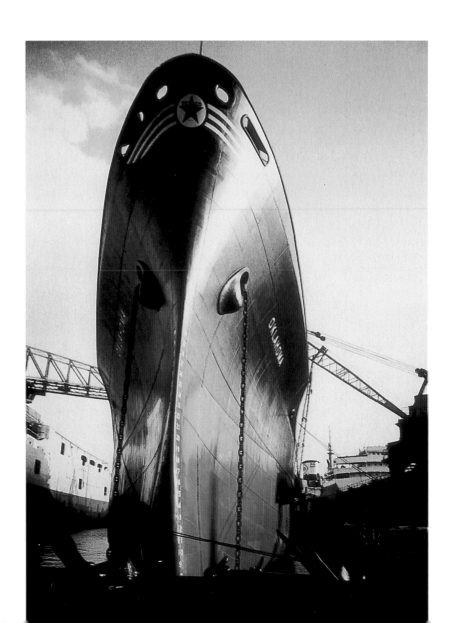

ABOVE

A crane dumps sulphur into open barges for transport up the Mississippi River to chemical plants in West Virginia and Pennsylvania, 1941.

LEFT

Once it got into gear, the "Arsenal of Democracy" proved formidable indeed. A worker checks a row of gleaming aircraft propellers at the Pratt & Whitney aircraft parts factory in Hartford, Connecticut, in 1941.

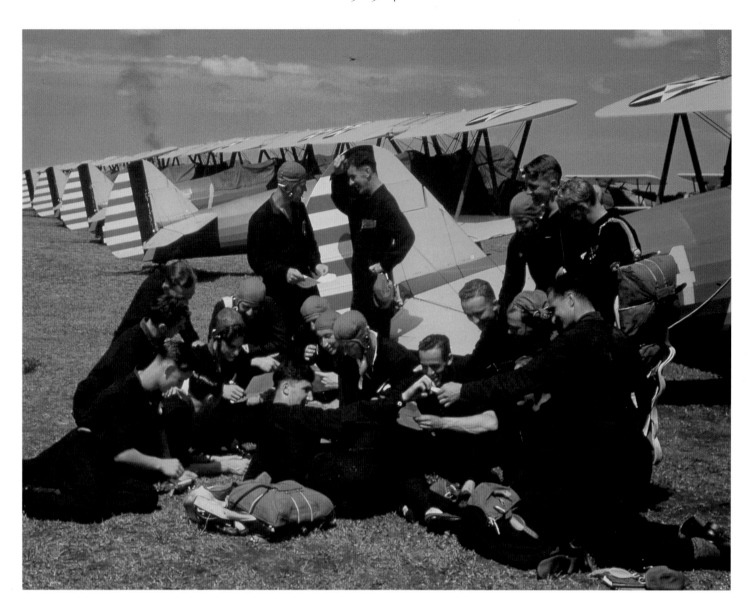

ABOVE

British R.A.F. cadets—on a training course in the United States in summer 1941—take a break from the heat of the Florida sun beside a Stearman PT-17 training aircraft of the U.S. Army Air Force. In December 1940, President Roosevelt had argued that, "The best defense of the United States is the success of Great Britain defending itself."

RIGHT

The crew of a Royal Air Force Short Stirling Mk I bomber in full flying kit, in spring 1942. The pilot, Flight Sergeant Leonard A. Johnson (2nd from left), is an American volunteer with the R.A.F.

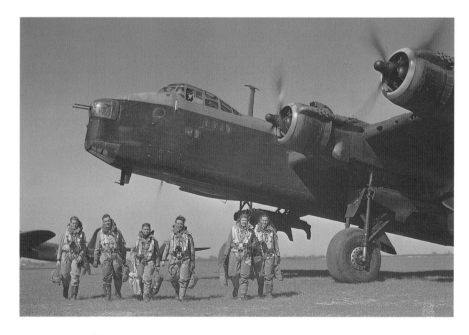

BELOW
British R.A.F. cadets take a break from training and demonstrate their fitness on a tennis court in Clewiston, Florida, summer 1941.

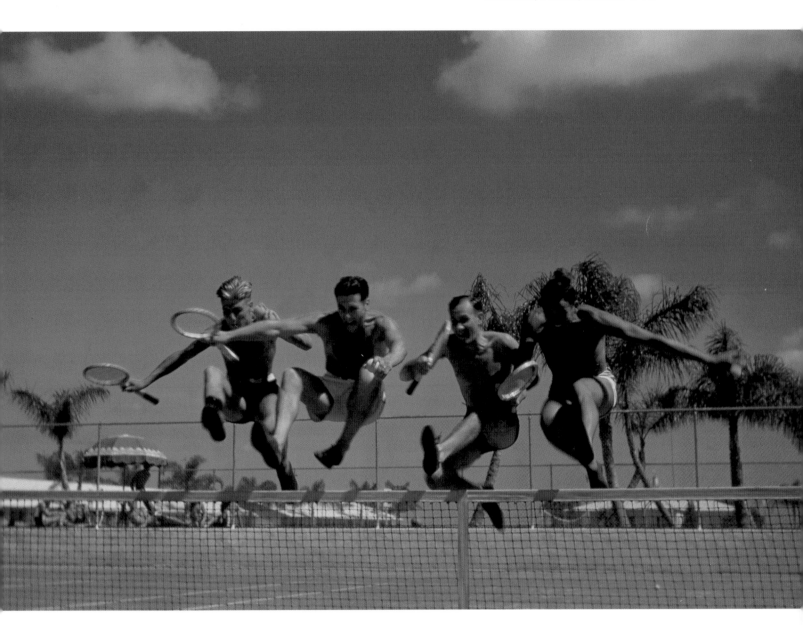

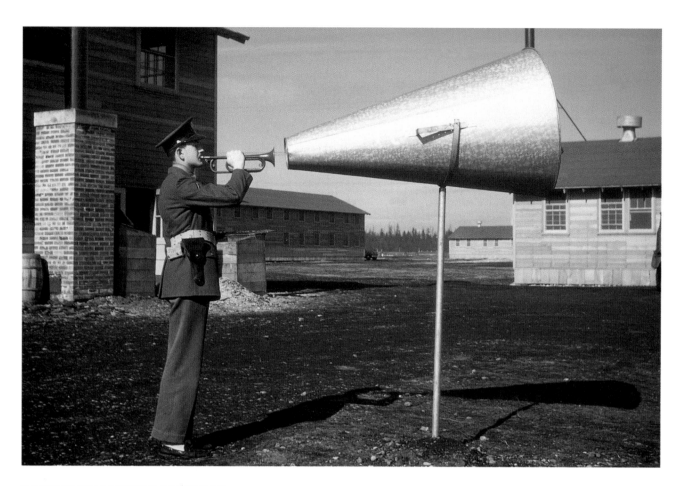

MOBILIZATION BEGINS

By the middle of 1941, there was little doubt in the minds of most Americans that war was imminent. The military was beginning to mobilize its resources on to a war footing. By the end of the war twelve million Americans would be in uniform.

ABOVE
Bugler Tim Metcalfe, pictured at Fort Lewis army training center in 1941, uses a simple horn device to amplify his calls at the 41st Cantonment Area.

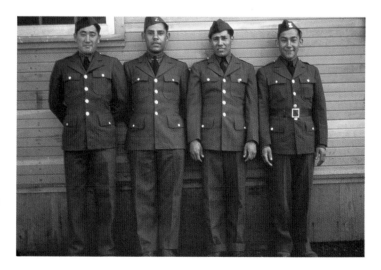

RIGHT
Fort Lewis, 1941: four draftees proudly pose in their newly issued first "Class A" uniforms. The quartet appears to comprise two African Americans, one draftee of Asian origin and one possibly of Native American background.

RIGHT
The intricacies of rifle handling are explained to new draftees assigned to the 186th and 162nd Infantry Regiments at Fort Lewis in 1941.

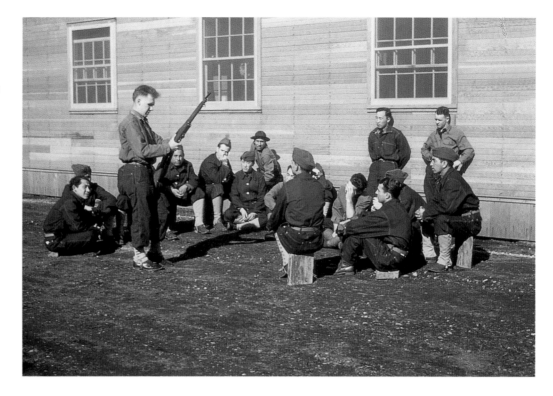

BELOW
Men in barracks during basic training at Fort Hayes, Columbus, Ohio, in October 1941.

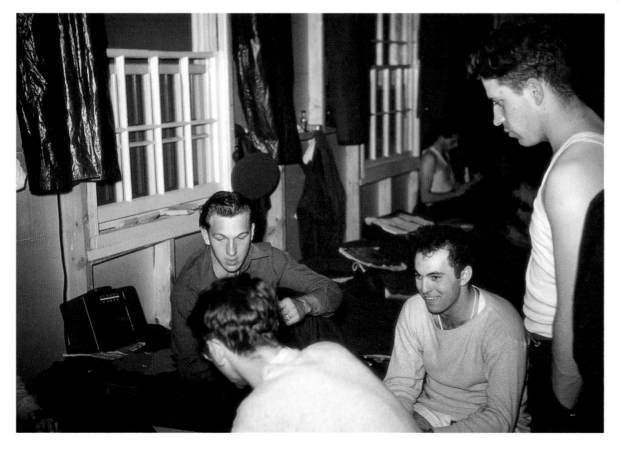

RIGHT
A gunner practices sighting
a 60mm mortar, 1941.

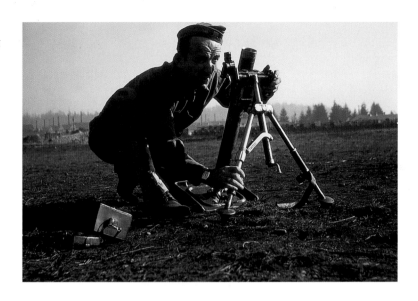

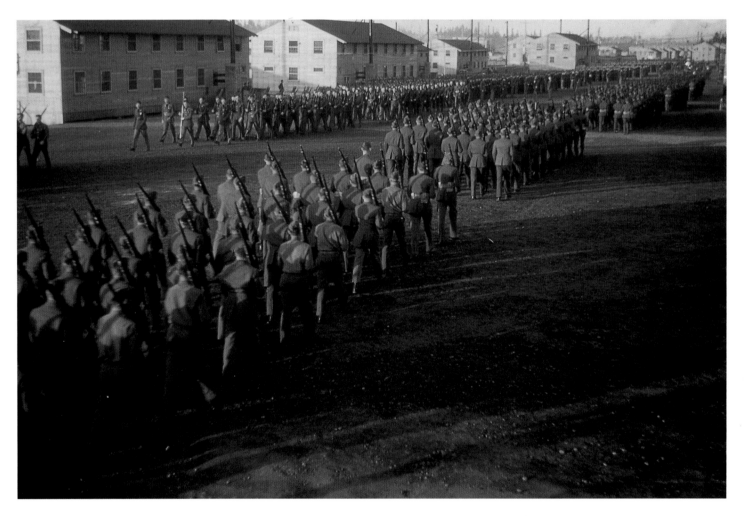

ABOVE
Draftees are drilled at Fort Lewis in 1941.

RIGHT
Infantrymen get to grips with their
gas masks during an exercise at
Wichita Falls, Kansas, in fall 1941.

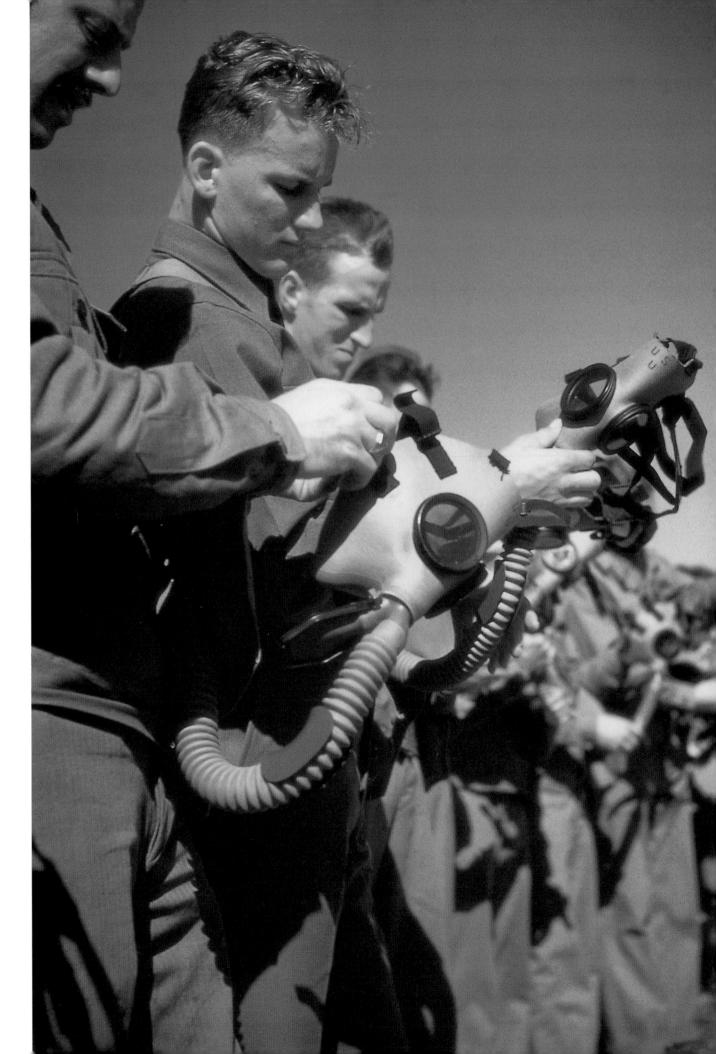

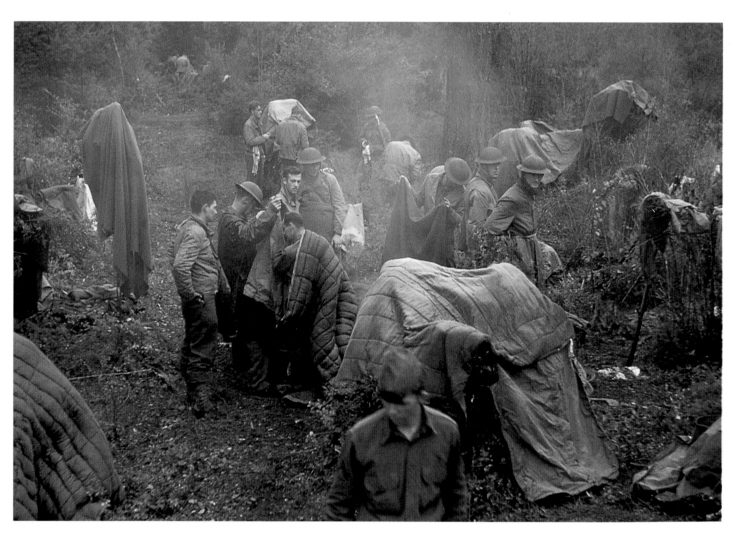

186th Infantry regiment pause during a field
exercise at Fort Lewis in summer 1941.

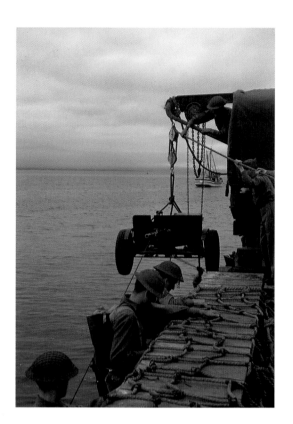

ABOVE

Infantry training at Monterey, California, on November 10, 1941: an exercise in lowering a 37mm anti-tank gun into a waiting lighter as troops clamber down cargo netting. The infantrymen have been issued with new MI rifles but are still using old-style helmets.

RIGHT

Men of the 53rd Infantry Regiment, 7th Infantry Division, train on an obstacle course at Fort Ord, California, in March 1941.

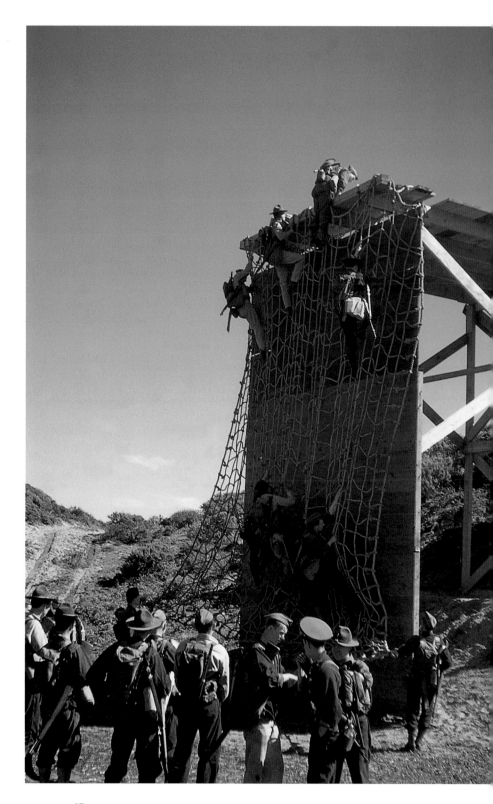

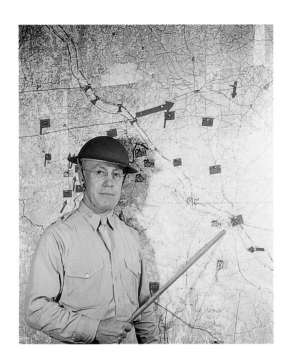

LEFT

A U.S. army training officer lectures on strategy in fall 1941, shortly before America entered the war.

BELOW

Flying cadets march "down the line" at Randolph Field, Texas, in 1941. That year aviator Charles Lindbergh said, in a speech in New York, "I ask you to look at the map of Europe today and see if you can suggest any way in which we could win this war if we entered it."

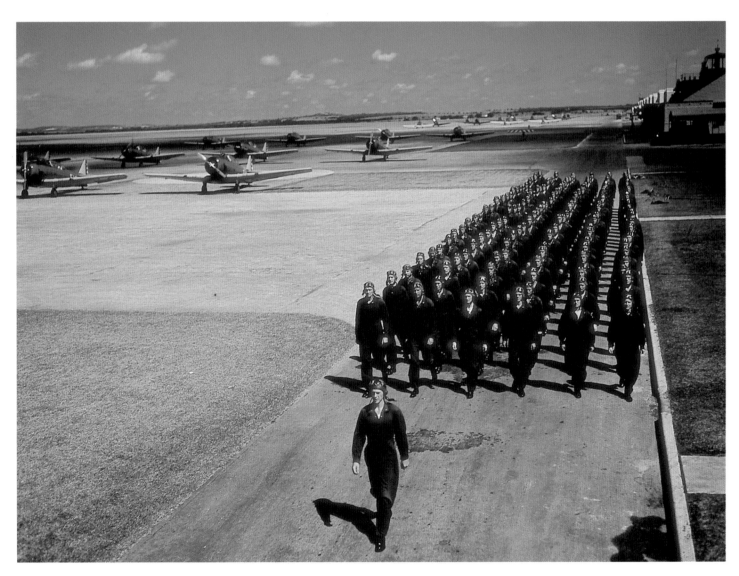

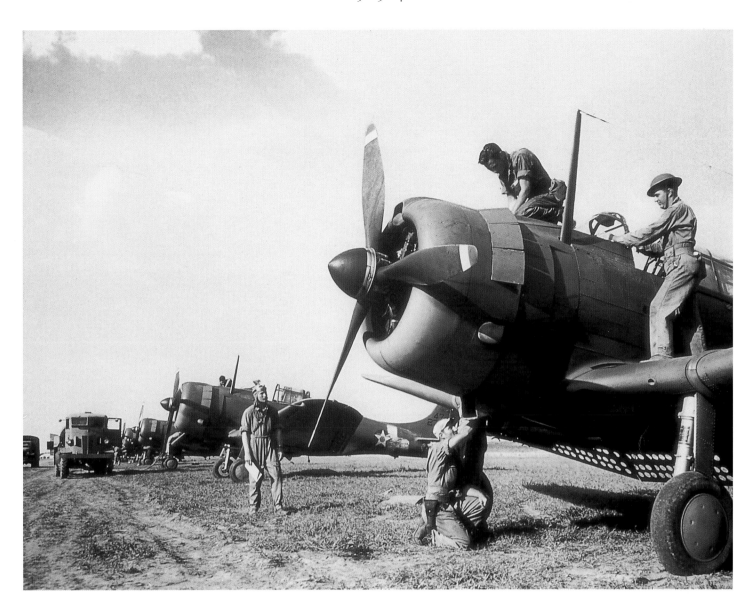

ABOVE
Aircraft maintenance, seen here being carried out in fall 1941, was to prove as important as construction and combat in determining the outcome of the war in Europe and the Pacific.

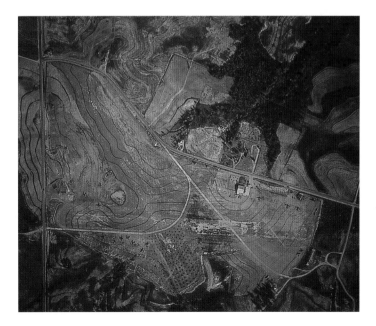

RIGHT
An aerial reconnaissance photo taken at 15:00hrs, on November 27, 1941, from a height of 12,000 feet, to assess camouflage effectiveness at Barksdale Field, Laurens, South Carolina.

PEARL HARBOR

The December 7, 1941 bombing of Pearl Harbor, in which more than 2,300 lives were lost, took the U.S. Navy completely by surprise. The whole nation was badly shaken, for few had thought a small country like Japan would have the capacity or the audacity to attack a power as significant as the United States. Denounced by Roosevelt as a "date which will live in infamy," it was a chastening experience, as well as one that filled the American people with anger.

RIGHT

Sailors being evacuated from the U.S.S. *California* before she sank. The U.S. Pacific Fleet was severely damaged in the attack, but not fatally so.

BELOW

The horror and confusion of the attack on Pearl Harbor are vividly conveyed in this well-known photograph of the U.S.S. *West Virginia*. The Department of Defense did not declassify this photo until March 1950.

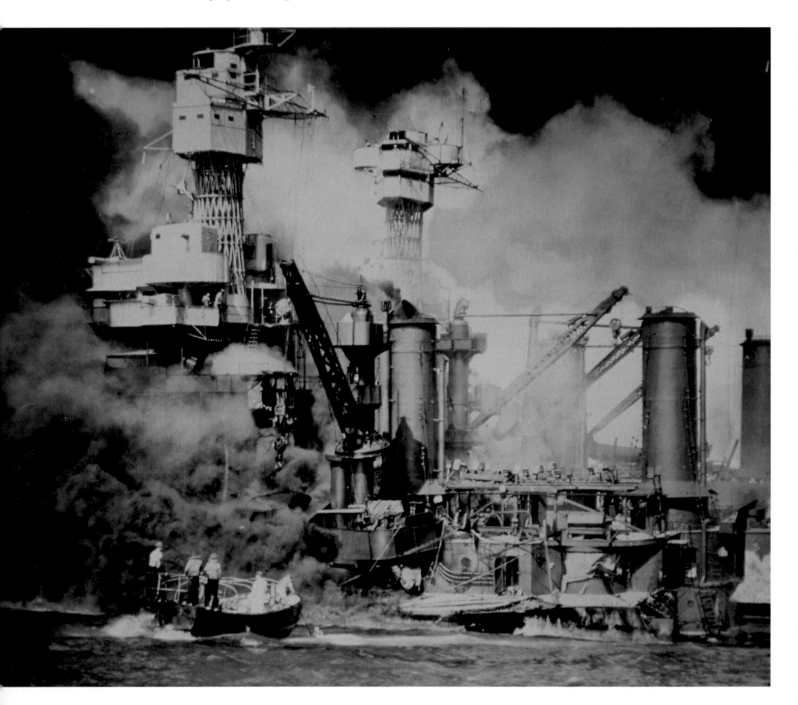

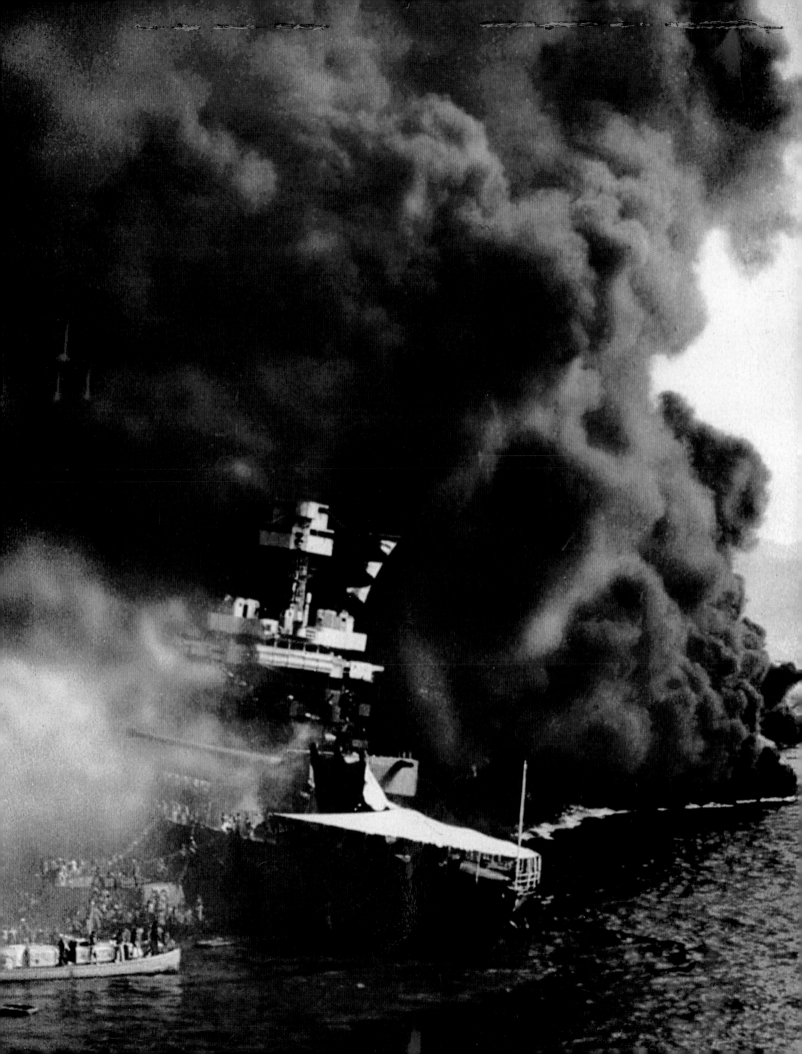

RIGHT

The U.S.S. *Arizona* was one of the battleships destroyed at Pearl Harbor; destroyers, cruisers, and other vessels were also lost or damaged. On December 9, two days after the raid, President Roosevelt said, "The United States can accept no result save victory, final and complete."

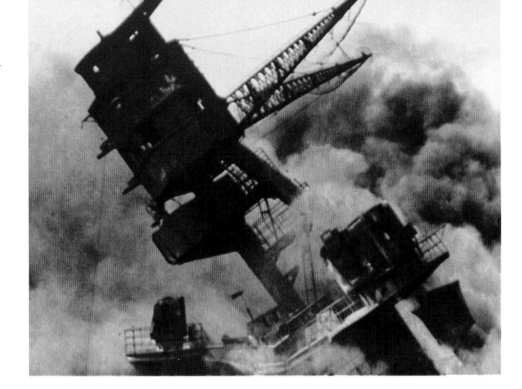

BELOW

Military airfields near Pearl Harbor also came under heavy attack. In a radio broadcast that day, President Roosevelt told the nation, "We are all in it—all the way."

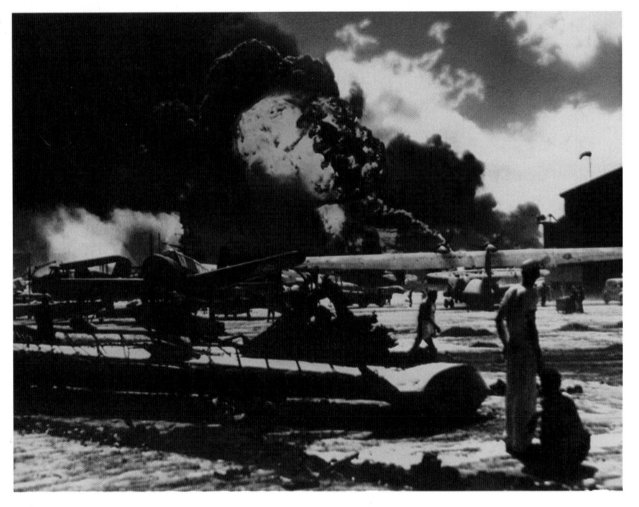

BELOW
A young boy stares into a store window prepared for Christmas 1941, America's first Christmas at war. His thoughts then were probably of gifts, but it is likely that after the war his most vivid memories would be of very different things.

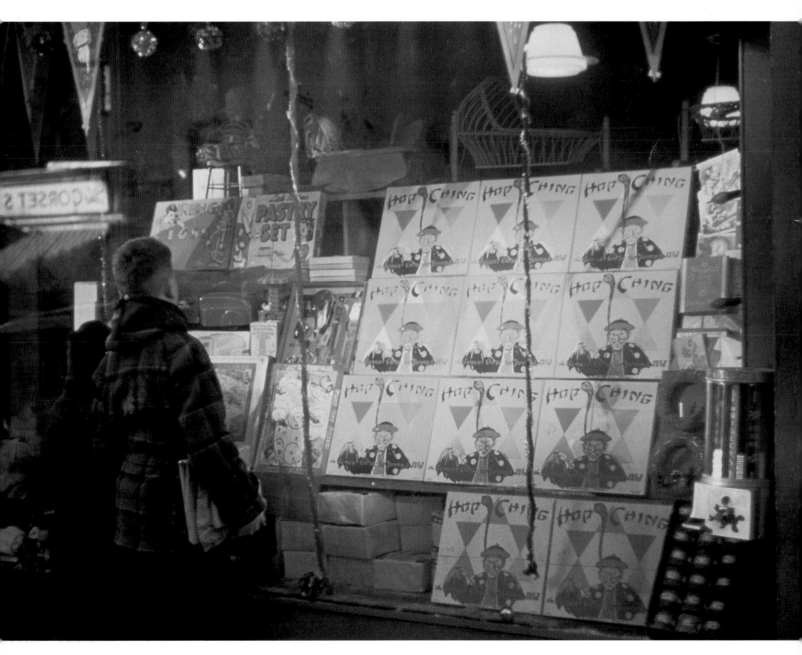

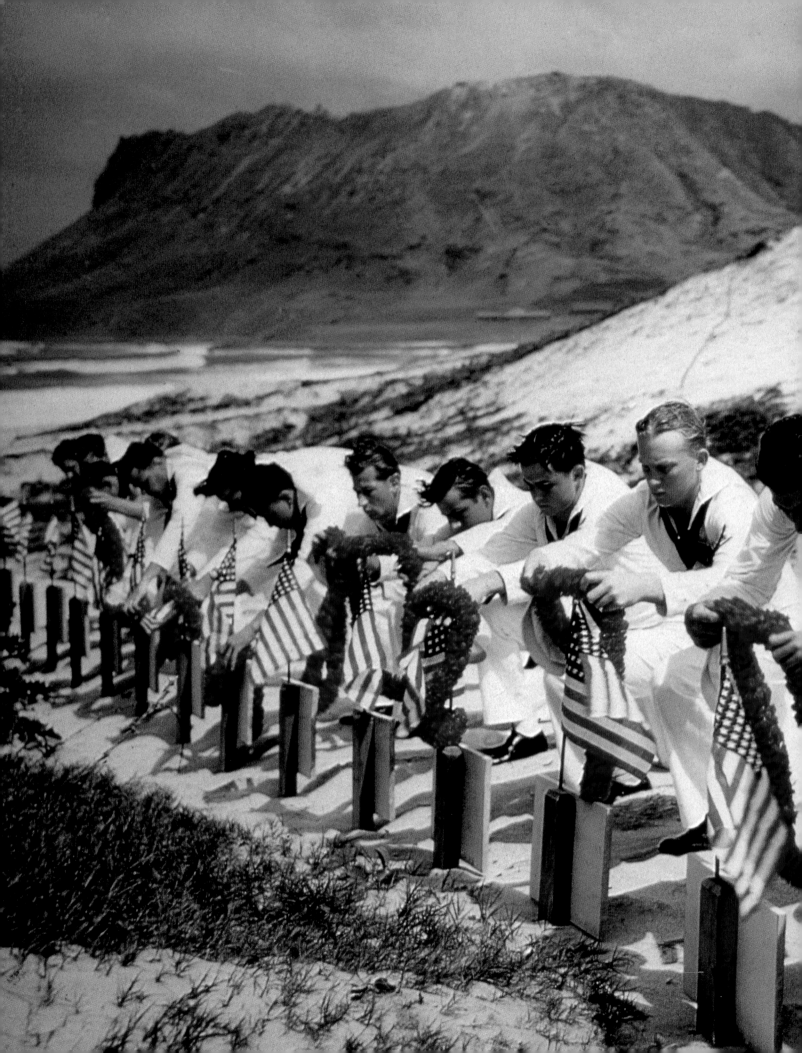

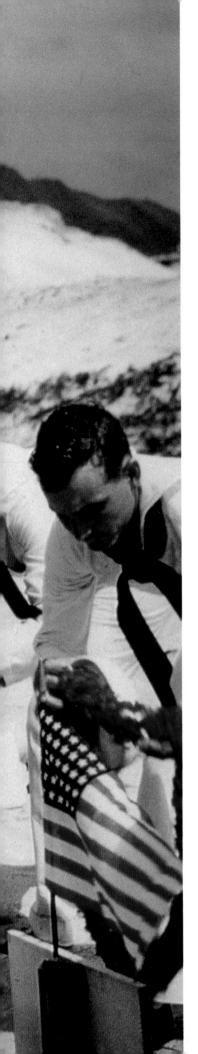

1942

STARING INTO THE ABYSS

To the Allies, the winter of 1941–2 must have seemed bleak indeed. Hitler controlled almost the whole of continental Europe. The British were isolated and reeling from the effects of aerial bombardment. In the North Atlantic, German U-boats were sinking huge numbers of ships and the vital supplies and matériel they carried.

On the Eastern Front, although the Red Army and its strongest ally, the Russian winter, held the Wehrmacht at bay, the Germans still had sufficient resources to mount a new offensive, as soon as the spring thaw softened the frozen ground. In North Africa, the Afrika Korps, under the dashing leadership of Erwin Rommel, was pushing the Allied forces closer and closer to the strategic lifeline of the Suez Canal.

In Asia, the situation was even worse. With the U.S. Fleet temporarily emasculated, there was almost nothing and no one to prevent the Japanese from devouring large stretches of territory at will. The Malayan peninsula fell within six weeks, leaving Singapore at the mercy of the invaders. The 60,000-strong British garrison, with no water and inadequate supplies, surrendered with barely a whimper; Churchill called it Britain's greatest military disaster. Thailand and Burma fell almost as rapidly, leaving India exposed to Japanese attack.

The Allies had seriously underestimated the Japanese Navy and the accuracy of the pilots flying from its aircraft carriers. In February, during the Battle of the Java Sea, an entire Allied fleet of Australian, U.S., and Dutch ships was destroyed. The Dutch East Indies fell and Japanese forces pushed across New Guinea, leaving Australia vulnerable; there were air raids on the northern city of Darwin. U.S. forces could do nothing to help, because their supply lines had been cut and they were fighting a rearguard action in the Philippines.

General Douglas MacArthur's defenders were trapped on the Bataan peninsula, unable to hold a tenacious and skillful attacker. President Roosevelt ordered MacArthur to Australia, where he made his promise that "I shall return," but his men continued their defense in increasingly atrocious conditions. In May 1942 the Philippines fell, but not before the defenders had created their own chapters in military history with the Bataan Death

LEFT

Shipmates of the sailors killed in the Japanese attack on Pearl Harbor lay wreaths on their comrades' graves in spring 1942.

March and actions like the heroic defense of "the Rock" on Corregidor island.

We shall never know exactly how close the world came to a modern Dark Age, nor how clearly the megalomaniacs in Berlin, Rome, and Tokyo could smell victory in the early months of 1942, but there is little doubt that the free world was staring into the abyss.

That summer Allied prospects looked even worse. On the Eastern Front, the German army, revitalized by the warmth of the sun, was advancing again. The redoubtable Winston Churchill was under pressure in Britain after the fall of the strategic stronghold of Tobruk in North Africa. And in the Pacific the Japanese were consolidating their conquests, which, in terms of surface area, represented the biggest empire the world had ever seen.

But, crucially, the three major Allies held firm. Moscow hadn't fallen, Britain was still the key bridgehead into Europe and bulwark of Western freedom, and, perhaps most critically of all, the mightiest weapon of the war was in high gear: U.S. industry. Every day that American factories and farms produced weapons and food, the balance of the war tilted in the Allies' favor.

Early in 1942, President Roosevelt had set unimaginably high production targets for the war effort. He asked for 125,000 planes, 75,000 tanks and 8,000,000 tons of shipping by 1943. The factories met the targets. By the end of the war, over a quarter of a million planes had been constructed. In 1940 Henry Kaiser's California shipyards took 355 days to build and deliver a ship; by early 1942 that time had been cut to just 69 days.

Industrial output on this scale had a significant impact on society. People had to move in vast numbers to man the factories. And, significantly, much of that "manning" was done by women for the first time. Twelve million Americans served overseas during the war, while 15 million of their fellow citizens moved home during the same period. For many civilians, spared the horrors of active duty or the threat of aerial bombardment or occupation, it was a time for change, even adventure, as the world offered new challenges and opportunities. Although the war years didn't bring immediate emancipation for American women, for many they did bring new responsibilities and a chance to assert their independence. However, for many American minorities, the war was a time of hostility and continuing denial.

In one of America's most regrettable actions, 127,000 Japanese Americans, living in California, were rounded up, moved to the interior and interned as a security precaution. It took forty years for Congress to acknowledge that this had been a mistake and the policy a product of "war hysteria" and "prejudice."

African Americans fared little better. Even when their country needed them, and when they were more than willing to serve, they were largely sidelined into segregated support roles within the armed forces and employment. In one of history's (and America's) tragic ironies, it seems barely credible that, while the U.S.A. was fighting for democracy and freedom around the world, its major towns and cities, including Washington, maintained strict rules on segregation in public buildings, transport, and entertainment, and wholesale discrimination in employment, education, and social attitudes. But there were some breakthroughs. Where African Americans did win the right to fight, they did so with distinction and won the admiration of many of their white comrades.

In domestic life, the war did provide employment opportunities, especially in the northern cities, which hadn't existed before. As a consequence, black claims for better treatment evoked some sympathy. In 1941, black labor leader A. Philip Randolph planned a march on Washington to protest at discrimination in employment and the armed forces. President Roosevelt proposed a compromise whereby the march would be called off in exchange for the establishment of a Fair Employment Practices Committee to fight discrimination in war industries. Randolph accepted. Subsequently, black employment in government work rose from 60,000 in 1941, to over 200,000 by the end of the war.

The second half of 1942 brought three significant turning points in the war, each of which was of enormous strategic and psychological importance.

The first was the Battle of Midway, on June 4–7, 1942. The commander-in-chief of the Japanese fleet, Admiral Yamamoto, knew that this would be the crucial naval battle of the Pacific war. He assembled an invasion fleet of over 140 ships to capture Midway Island, the most westerly U.S. possession in the Pacific. He planned to engage significant numbers of U.S. warships and destroy them, to invade the island and thus create a stepping stone for the subsequent conquest of Hawaii. Yamamoto's plans were extremely complicated and he made several tactical errors, but, most significantly, his U.S. counterpart had a secret "ace-in-the-hole." Admiral Chester Nimitz was a shrewd tactician and had at his disposal ULTRA intelligence information, which—unknown to the Japanese—revealed Yamamoto's plans for Midway. When the Japanese attacked, Nimitz was ready for them.

Crucially, U.S. Navy dive-bombers caught the Japanese aircraft carriers while their planes were refueling and rearming on deck and, in an audaciously brave and costly attack, sank three of them; a fourth went down the next day. The Americans lost the carrier *Yorktown*, but Yamamoto had seen enough and turned away. In that moment, Japan's almost unblemished naval record suffered its first defeat and the tide began to turn against Japanese military expansion in Asia.

The second turning point was not of equal strategic significance, but for the beleaguered British it was the psychological fulcrum of the war. Britain had been isolated for over two years. Its armed forces had suffered a series of embarrassing defeats. Its towns and cities had suffered the terror of constant aerial attack, and the deprivations of rationing, blackouts and shortages had sapped the morale of the civilian population. To a disillusioned few, even Churchill's great oratory was beginning to sound hollow, his bravura more like bluster than bravery. He needed a victory.

It came in the North African desert and was provided for him by "Britain's George Patton:" General Bernard Montgomery, known to all as "Monty." Erwin Rommel's Afrika Korps, only fifty miles west of Alexandria, was on the brink of overrunning Egypt. But Monty always picked his ground and, after holding the line, launched a counter-attack on October 23, 1942, at El Alamein. Rommel was in Germany for medical treatment; the Afrika Korps was overwhelmed and began retreating across the Libyan desert. Rommel's return could not halt the withdrawal and then, on November 8, in Operation Torch, a major Allied force landed in Morocco and Algeria.

In September 1939, church bells had been silenced in Britain, to be rung only to warn of an invasion. Now, over three years later, they were rung again, not to warn of an invasion, but to celebrate a long-awaited victory.

The third, and perhaps most significant, turning point came in what many regard as the war's most momentous battle, Stalingrad.

Throughout the middle years of the war, Hitler had been over-stretching the resources of the Wehrmacht against the advice of his generals. He made impossible demands of their bravery and courage. Ultimately, it was his undoing.

When he launched his summer offensive, in June 1942, he committed yet another tactical blunder. He split his forces in the south, sending one group deep into the Caucasus, the other along the Volga to capture Stalingrad. Initially all went well, the Soviet defenders yet again sacrificing men and territory in order to stretch the German lines of communication and supply. By mid-September, the German Sixth Army, under General Friedrich von Paulus, and the Soviet Red Army, under its legendary leaders Marshal Georgiy Zhukov and General Vasiliy Chuikov, were engaged in bitter hand-to-hand fighting on the streets and in the cellars of the city itself.

There are countless stories of heroism on both sides. But, if the Eastern Front was the rack on which the will of the German army was broken, Stalingrad became the ultimate cry of pain that symbolized its submission. But it was a near-run thing: fascist ideology against communist ideology; the Fatherland against Mother Russia. At one point, towards the end of September, German units were within a few streets of Chuikov's command position, but the Soviets held the last few acres of ground in the city center, west of the Volga. Moreover, in the east Zhukov was preparing a classic counter-punch.

In mid-November, he launched a pincer movement to the north-west and south of the city and trapped the entire German army in an encircling movement. Hitler refused to let them fight their way out, insisting that they hold their ground. A German relief force, under Field Marshal Erich von Manstein, got within thirty miles of Paulus's men, but then winter began to exact its terrible toll. Men starved or froze to death, or were picked off by the Soviets as the noose tightened around them. Eventually, at the end of January 1943, Paulus defied Hitler and surrendered his remaining 90,000 troops into Soviet hands. Of over 300,000 men who made the initial assault on the city, only about 5,000 ever returned to Germany.

1942 ended with yet more significant Allied success. After victory in the Battle of Midway, U.S. strategy turned towards the recapture of territory. The first crucial engagement was at Guadalcanal in the Solomon Islands, where, after two major naval encounters and a land battle that lasted into February 1943, the Japanese were defeated and the Allies' journey to Tokyo began. It was to be a long and tortuous road, washed with the blood of thousands of casualties on both sides.

THE U.S. ENTERS THE WAR

1942 was a long and exhausting year for the United States. Still reeling from the impact of Pearl Harbor, it had to move rapidly to mobilize its armed forces to prepare to wage war in Europe and the Pacific, while still maintaining the industrial and agricultural output necessary to support its allies, Britain and the Soviet Union.

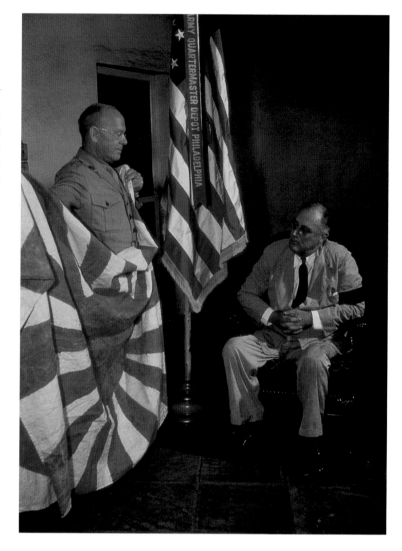

RIGHT

At the White House in 1942, General Thomas Holcomb of the U.S. Marine Corps shows President Roosevelt a captured Japanese flag. The flag may be from Guadalcanal, in the Solomon Islands, scene of the Allies' first northward invasion in the Pacific. The president is wearing a black armband in mourning for American casualties.

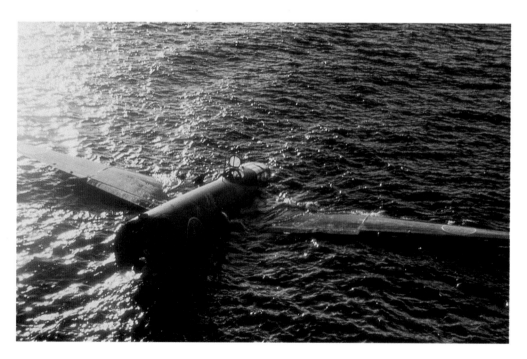

LEFT

A Mitsubishi Type 1 heavy bomber, shot down by Air Force fighters. It was photographed on August 7, 1942, off Tulagi Island in the Philippines, from the deck of the destroyer U.S.S. *Ellet*.

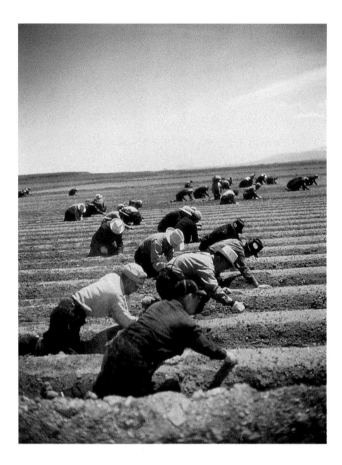

RIGHT

Interned because of the reaction to Japan's attack on Pearl Harbor, Japanese-American citizens were transported to internment camps across America. They were obliged to produce their own food; the internees pictured here are transplanting celery in 1942.

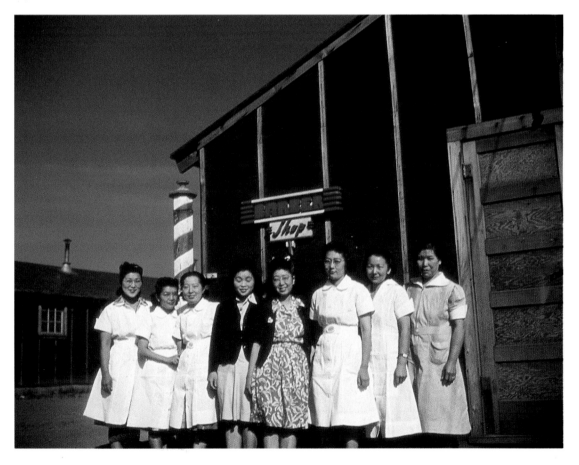

LEFT

A Japanese-American internment camp possibly in Malheur County, Oregon, in about 1942. Eight Nisei-American women pose in front of the camp barbershop.

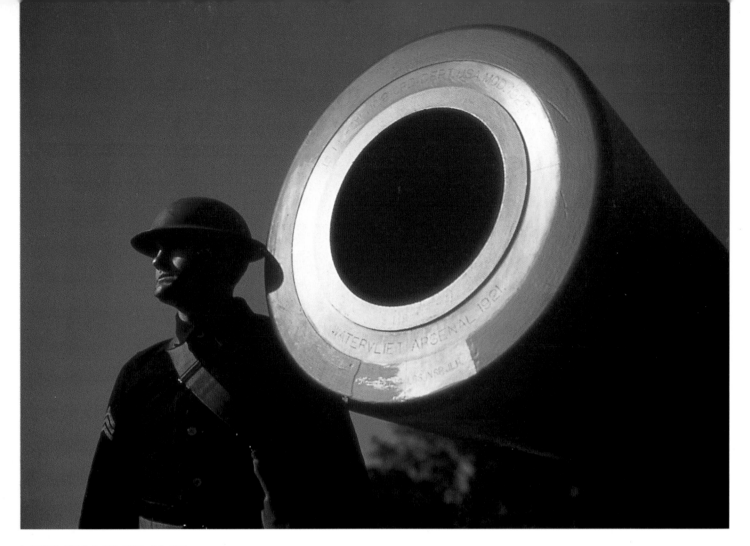

THE HOME FRONT

Although no fighting took place on U.S. soil, the war had a massive impact on American life. Twelve million service personnel were mobilized, millions of civilians moved house to work in war production and on farms, and the country's economy was transformed by the war effort.

ABOVE
This 16-inch coastal artillery gun, produced at the Watervliet Arsenal in 1921, was positioned at Fort Story, Virginia, in case of invasion or naval attack on the U.S. mainland. The photograph was taken in March 1942.

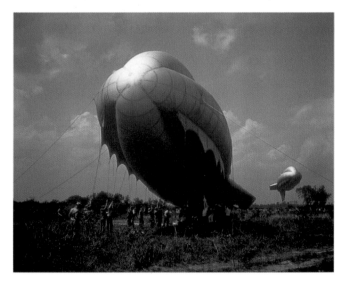

RIGHT
Defensive barrage balloons at Parris Island, South Carolina, in May 1942.

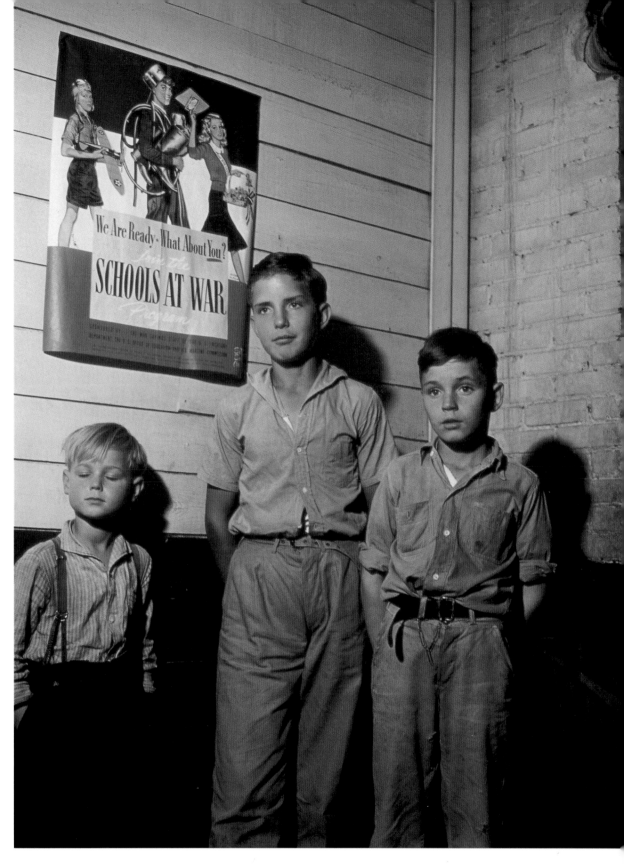

Schoolchildren photographed in San Augustine County, Texas. Children and young people throughout the country were encouraged to do their part to help the war effort.

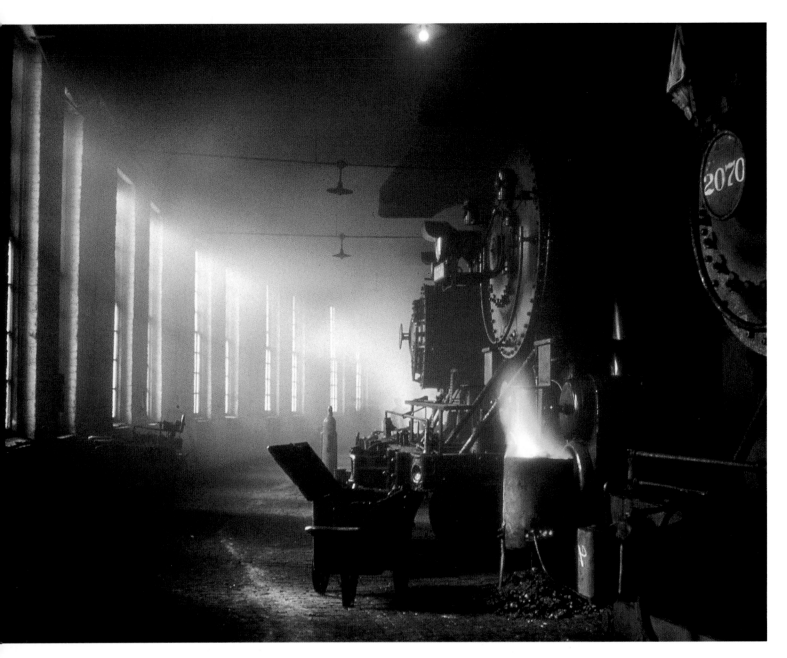

ABOVE
Inside the great engine roundhouse at a Chicago
and Northwestern Railroad yard, Chicago, in
December 1942. Railroads played a vital role in
the war economy.

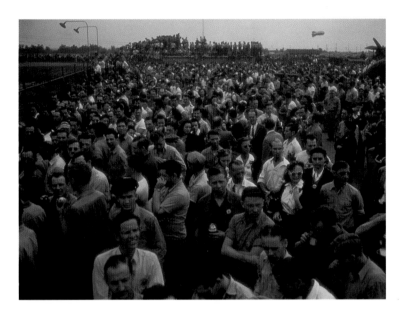

LEFT

Workers at the Consolidated Aircraft
Corporation, Fort Worth, Texas, in
October 1942. The Liberator bombers
built here eventually superseded the
famous B-17 "Flying Fortress" bombers.

BELOW

A worker in a large electric phosphate smelting
furnace in June 1942. This furnace, used to
make elemental phosphorus, was located in a
Terrence Valley Authority chemical plant
near Muscle Shoals, Alabama.

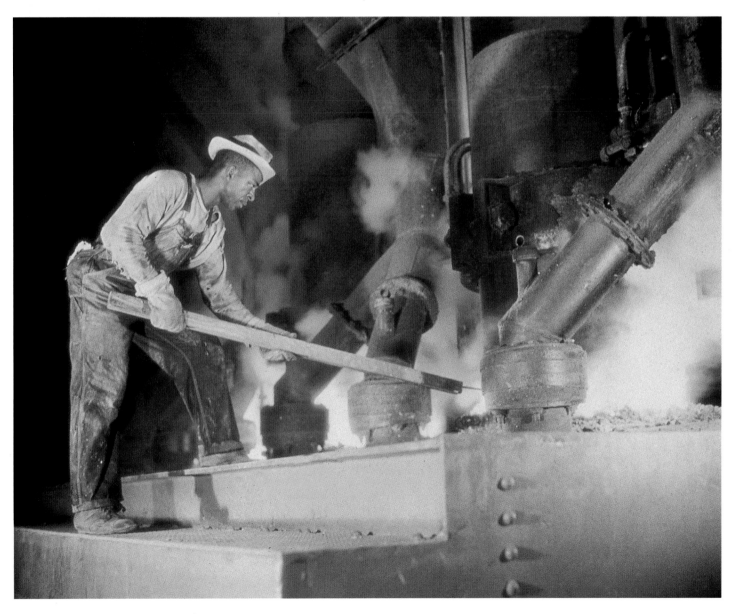

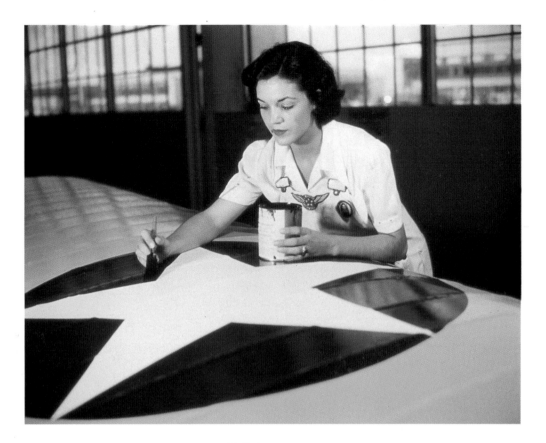

Mrs Irma Lee McElroy puts the finishing touches to a fighter plane in August 1942. In peacetime Mrs McElroy had been a civil service employee at the naval air base at Corpus Christi, Texas. Her husband was a flight instructor.

WOMEN IN WAR INDUSTRY

The war effort led to significant changes in the role of women in American society. Many of them served in the armed forces, even more entered areas of the workforce traditionally closed to them. In general, World War II enabled women to experience independence and undertake responsibilities previously denied them.

"Pearl Harbor widows have gone into war work to carry on the fight with a personal vengeance." Corpus Christi, Texas, August 1942: Mrs Virginia Young (right), whose husband was one of the first casualties of World War II, was a supervisor in the Assembly and Repairs Department of the Naval Air Base. Her job was to find convenient and comfortable living quarters for women workers from out of state, like Ethel Mann (left), who operated an electric drill.

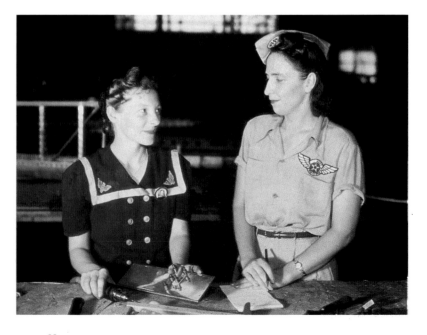

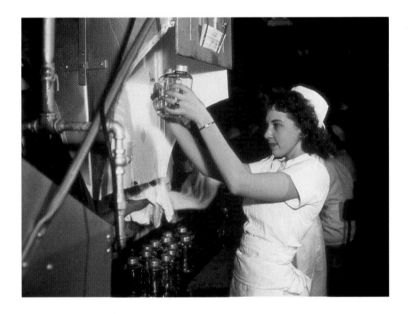

LEFT

Transfusion donor bottles, Baxter Laboratory, Glenview, Illinois, in October 1942.

BELOW

Mrs Annette del Sur publicizing a salvage campaign in a yard of Douglas Aircraft Company, Long Beach, California, in October 1942.

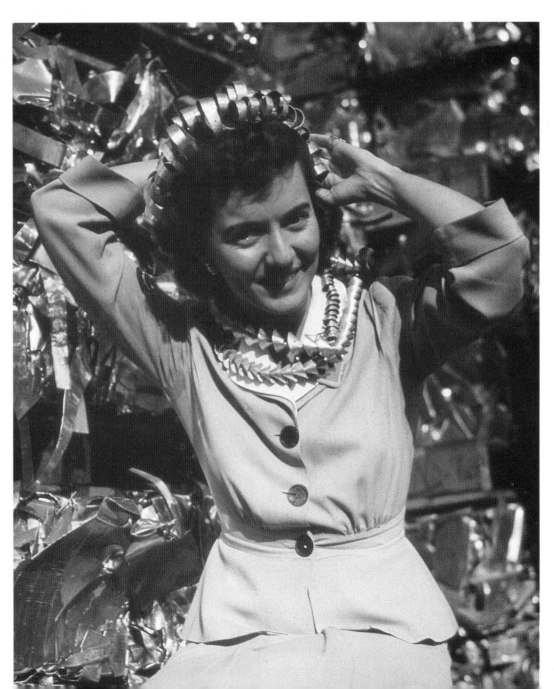

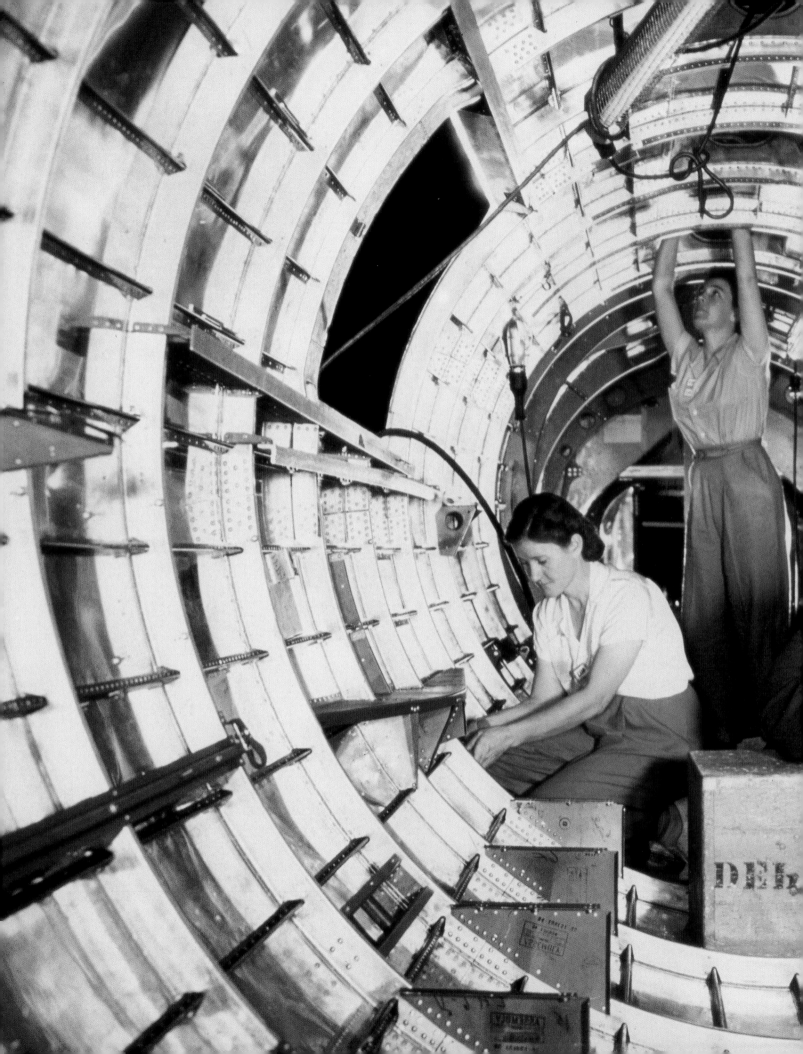

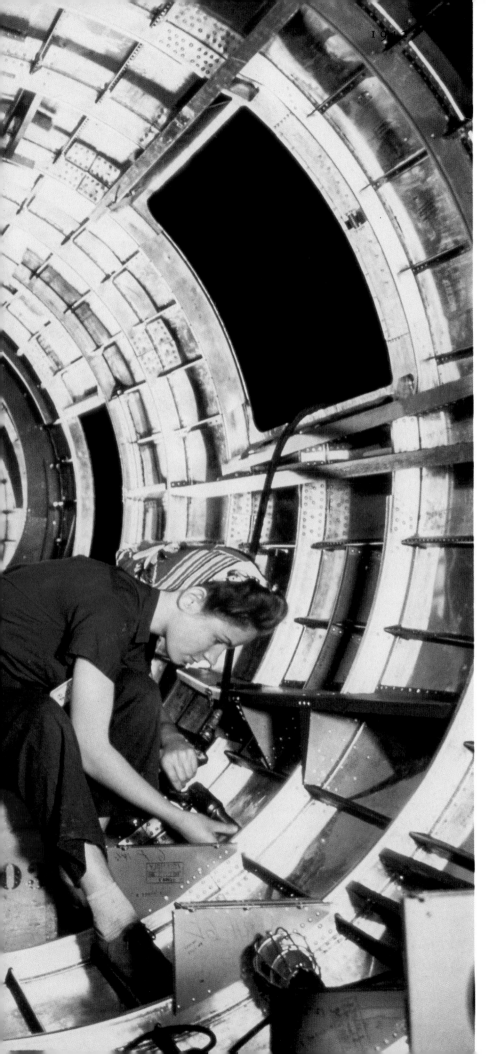

LEFT
Women workers install fixtures in the tail fuselage section of a B-17F bomber at the Douglas Aircraft Company, Long Beach, California, in October 1942. The B-17F was a later model of the B-17 Flying Fortress, and distinguished itself in action in the South Pacific, over Germany and elsewhere. It was a long-range, high-altitude heavy bomber, with a crew of between seven and nine men, and with sufficient armaments to defend itself on daylight missions.

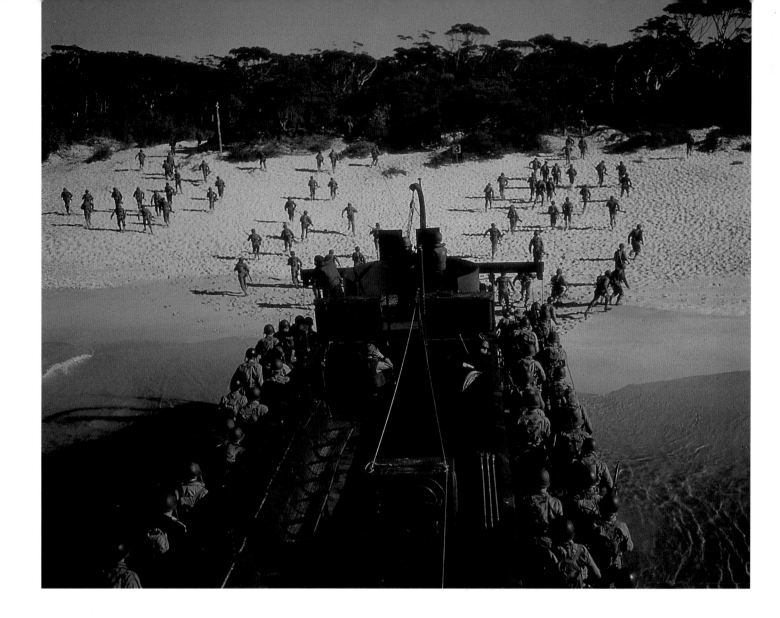

BATTLE TRAINING

Though 1942 began bleakly for the Allies, the latter part of the year brought significant successes. In North Africa the British defeated the Germans at El Alamein, and in the Pacific U.S. forces defeated the Japanese in the battles of Midway and Guadalcanal. The Allies' thoughts began to turn to invasion, for which amphibious landings on a vast scale would be needed; troops underwent intensive training in order to prepare.

The interior of a landing craft of the 41st Division, U.S. Army Infantry, at an Australian training school.

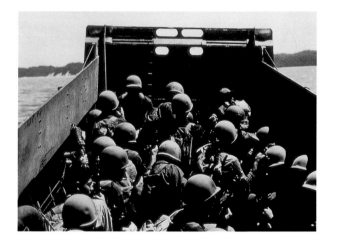

LEFT
Troops of the 32nd Division, U.S. Army Infantry, at Camp Gable, Queensland, Australia, undergo amphibious landing training at Nelson's Bay, New South Wales.

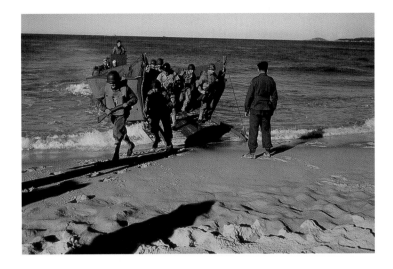

ABOVE
Men of the 32nd Division undertake amphibious assault training at the U.S. naval base at Nelson's Bay, New South Wales, Australia.

LEFT
Troops practicing boarding a rubber dinghy from their transport ship.

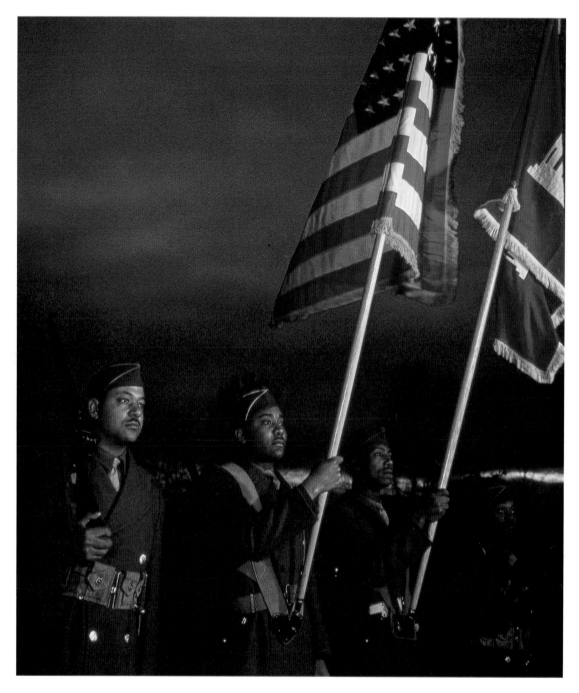

ABOVE

A ceremonial Color Guard of African American
engineers, possibly at Fort Belvoir, Virginia.

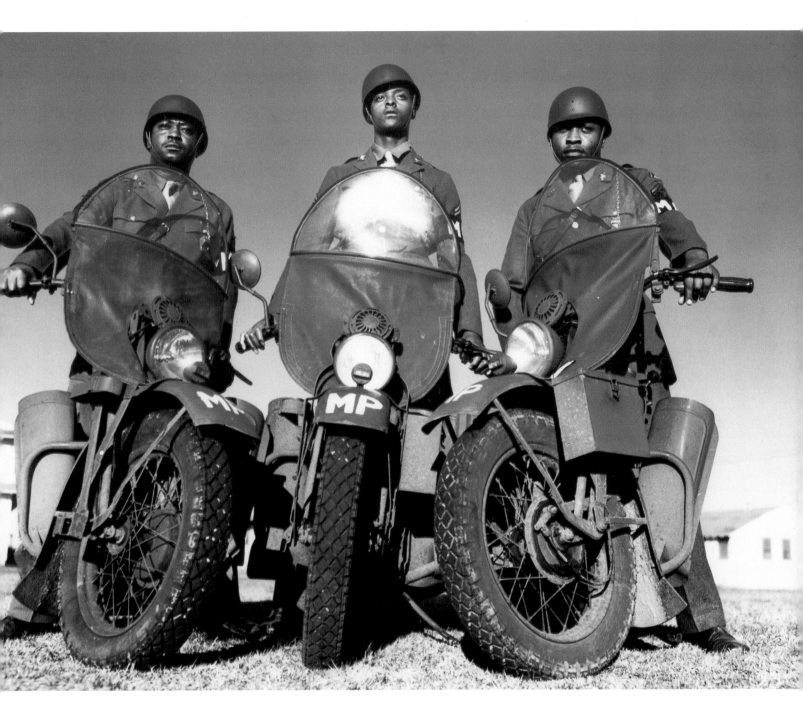

ABOVE

A segregated military necessitated both black and
white military police forces. Here three M.P.s of a
"colored" regiment pose during an exercise in the
United States in 1942.

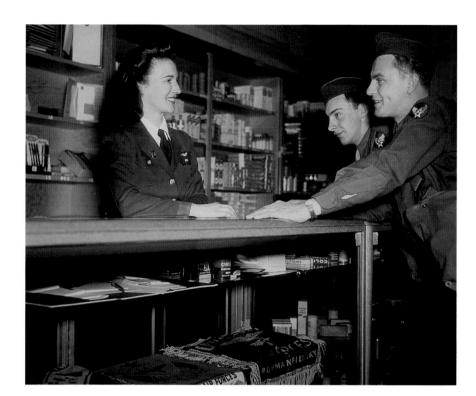

RIGHT

An air base exchange at Bowman Field, Kentucky, photographed by an unidentified member of the 1st Motion Picture Unit, A.A.F.

BELOW

Outdoor chow-time on the French island of Corsica, with flight chiefs Marlin Richardson (left) and Willie Sheehan (to his right). For once, the food was fresh, not "C" rations.

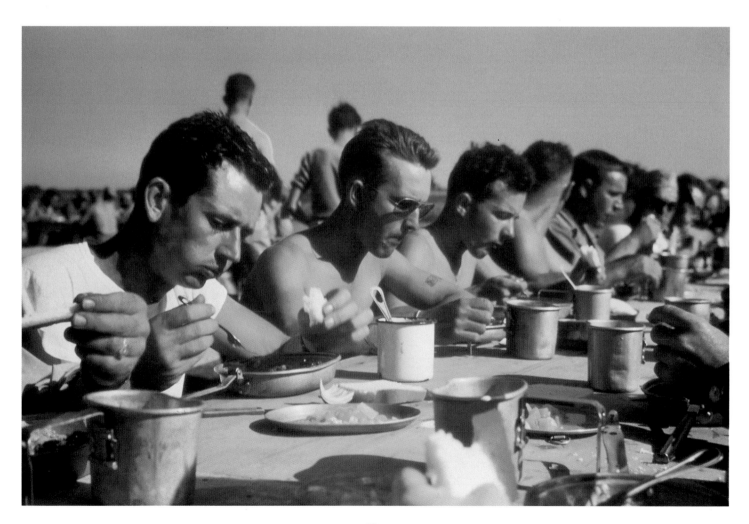

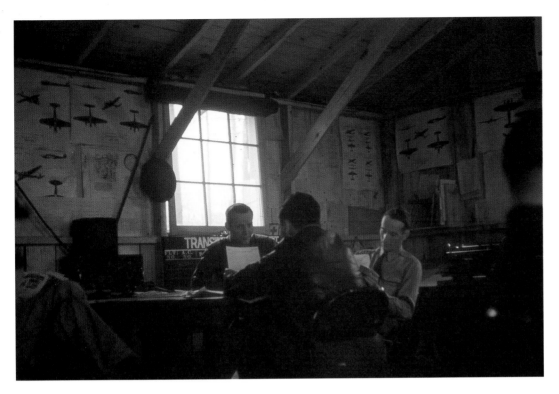

ABOVE

Operations office at Martin Field Baltimore, Maryland, shortly before the 33rd Fighter Group were shipped to North Africa with their P-40 fighters in March 1942.

BELOW

Airmen relax with a civilian guest during an open day in 1942.

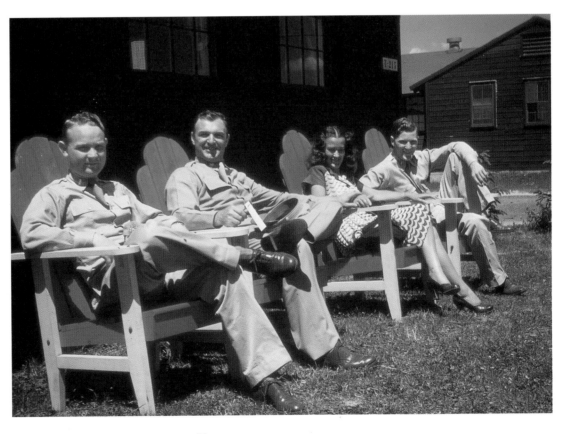

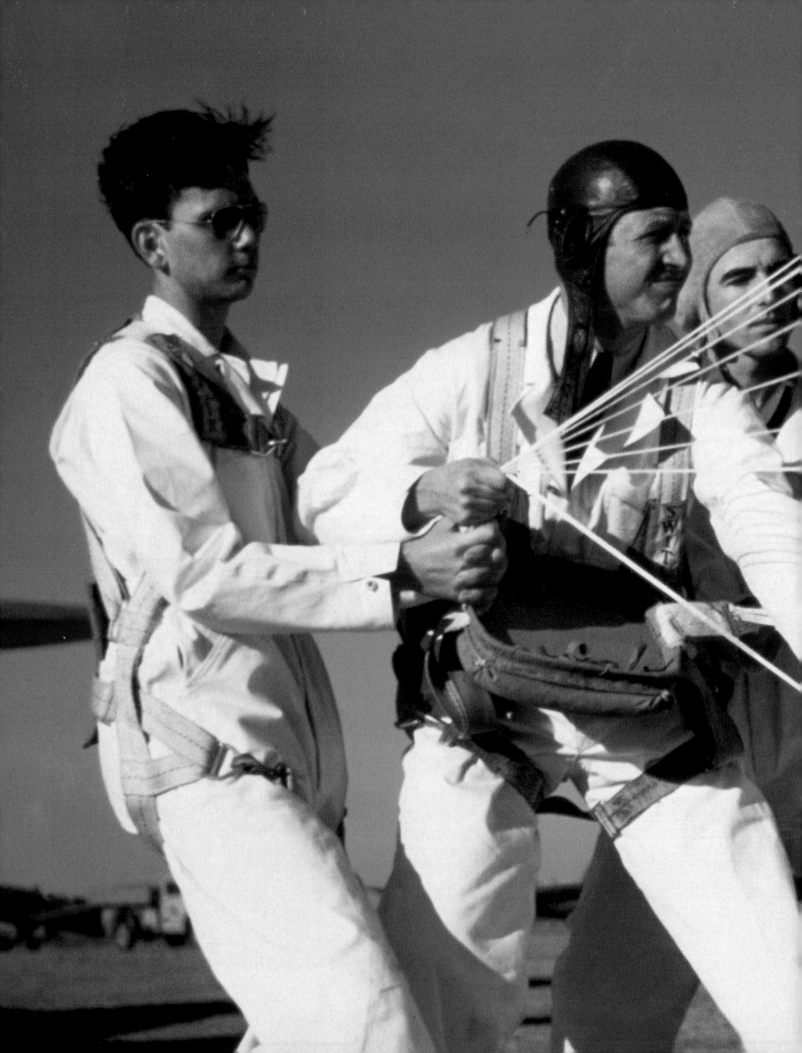

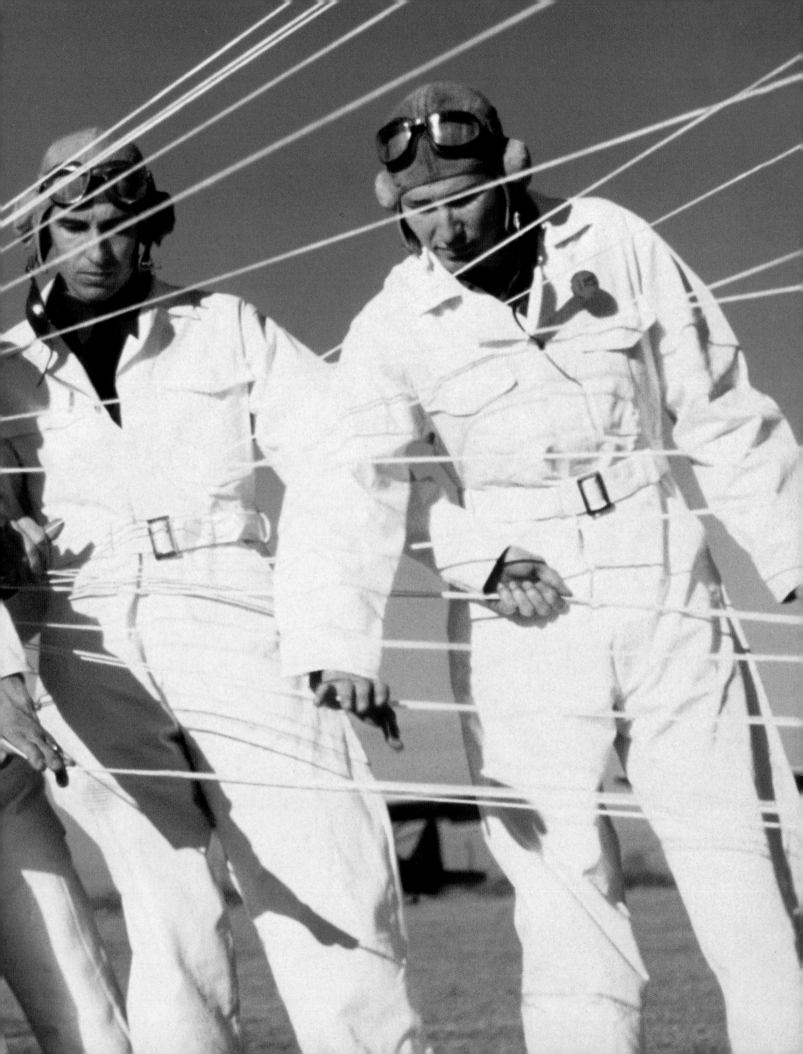

PREVIOUS PAGE
An instructor explaining the operation of a
parachute to student pilots at Meacham Field,
Fort Worth, Texas, in January 1942.

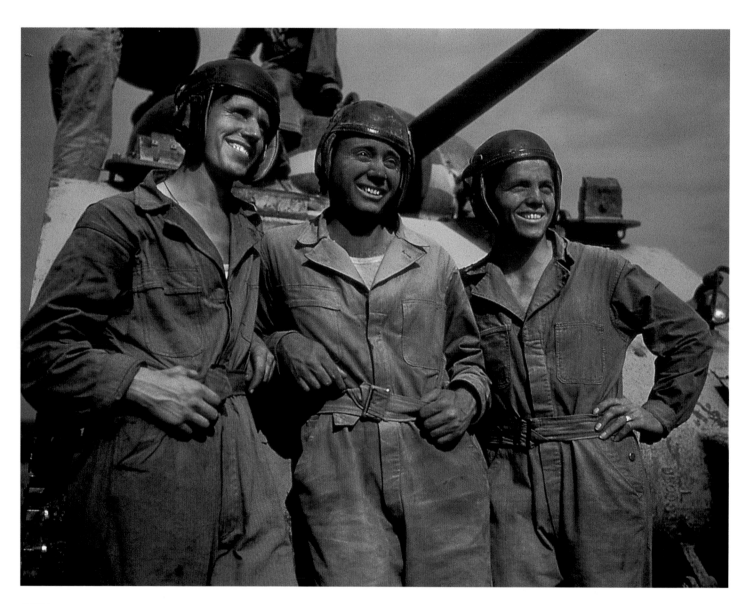

ABOVE
M-4 tank crews take a break during an exercise
at Fort Knox, Kentucky, in June 1942.

RIGHT
August 1942: A sailor at the Naval Air Base, Corpus
Christi, Texas, wearing the new protective clothing
and gas mask for use in chemical warfare. These
uniforms were lighter and less cumbersome than
the previous kind.

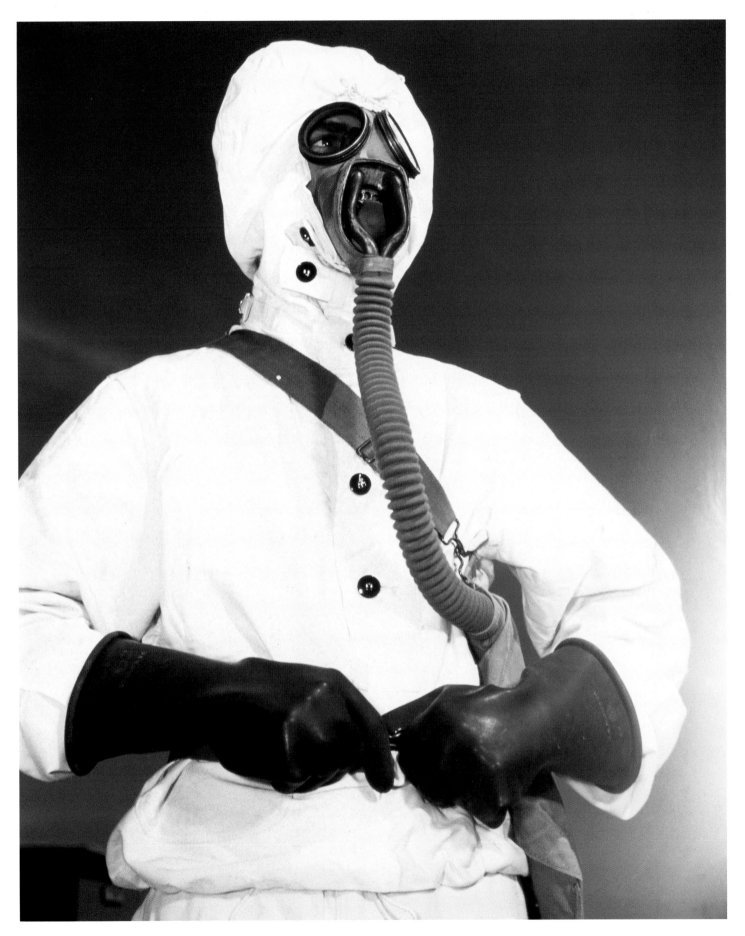

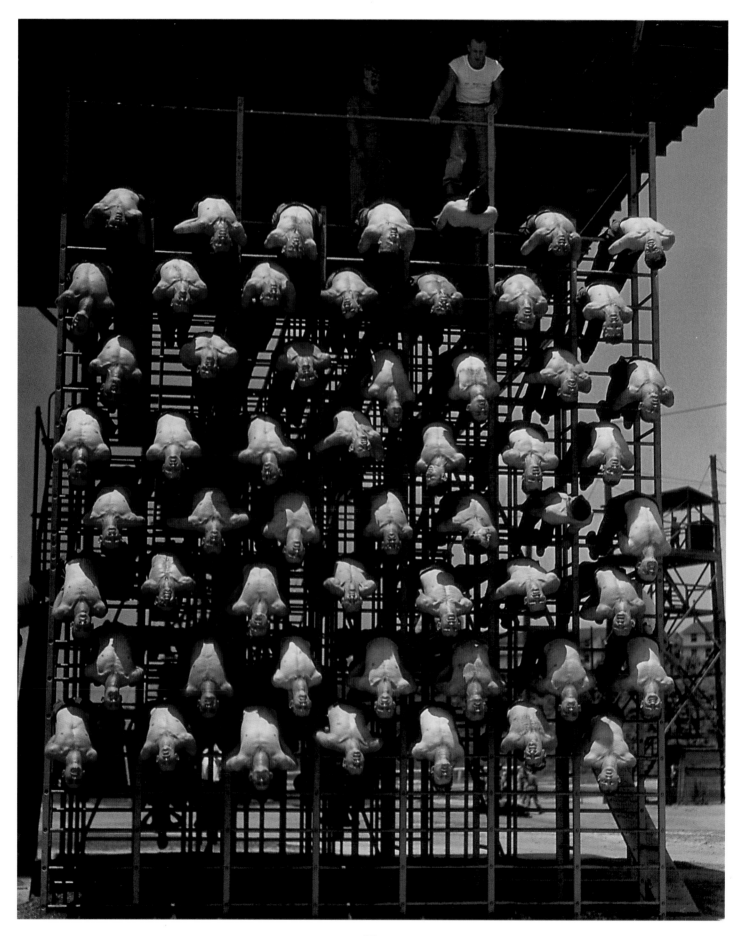

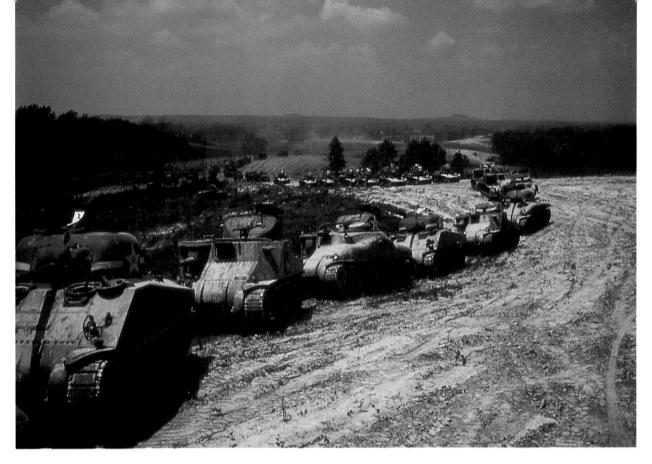

LEFT

Basic training the hard way
in 1942. New recruits perform
sit-ups on a scaffold.

ABOVE

A convoy of M-4 tanks stretching
almost to the horizon at Fort
Knox, Kentucky, in June 1942.

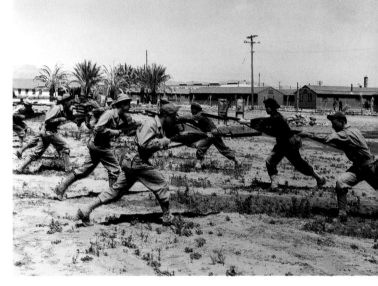

ABOVE

Despite recent advances
in military technology,
there was no substitute
for troops on the ground,
or for old methods of
combat: Infantry troops
at a boot camp practice
using their bayonets . . .

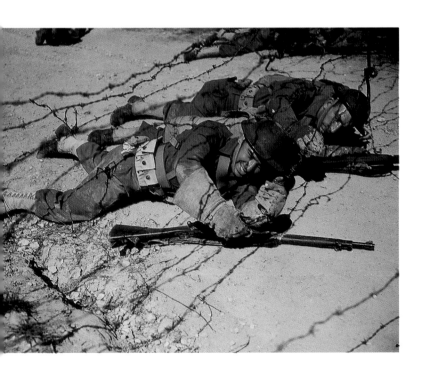

LEFT

. . . and penetrating
barbed wire during
an infiltration course,
circa 1942.

TROOPS SENT ABROAD

Besides mounting huge combined naval, Marine and infantry operations in the Pacific, U.S. forces were central to the liberation of Europe. There were over 3 million army personnel (including over 400,000 in the U.S. Army Air Force) serving in Europe by 1945, with a further 500,000 in the Mediterranean. This was close to 70 percent of army strength.

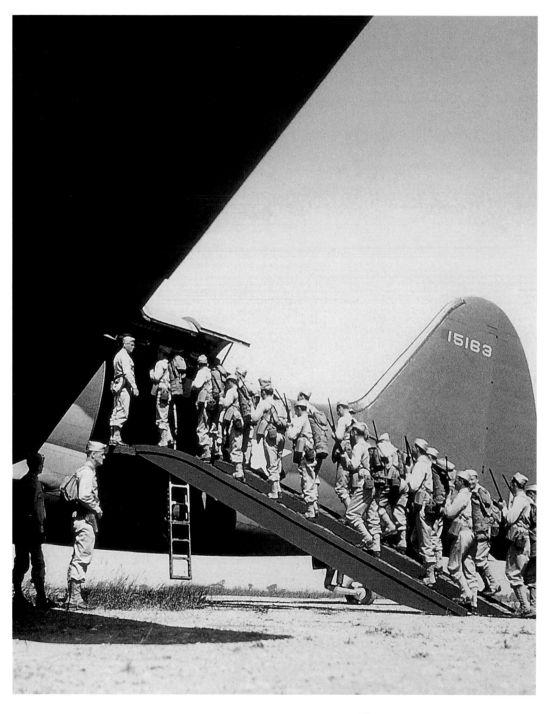

LEFT
Soldiers boarding a C-46 transport plane in Buffalo, New York, in August 1942.

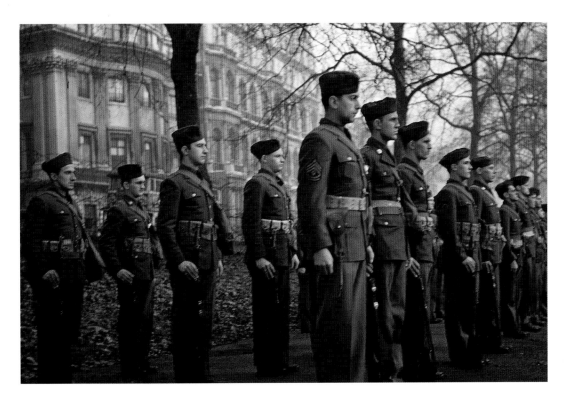

ABOVE

U.S. army soldiers stand to attention as they prepare
for inspection, in London in spring 1942.

BELOW

Infantry training on a beach in the U.K.—probably
in Northern Ireland where the first contingent of
U.S. troops was stationed in early 1942.

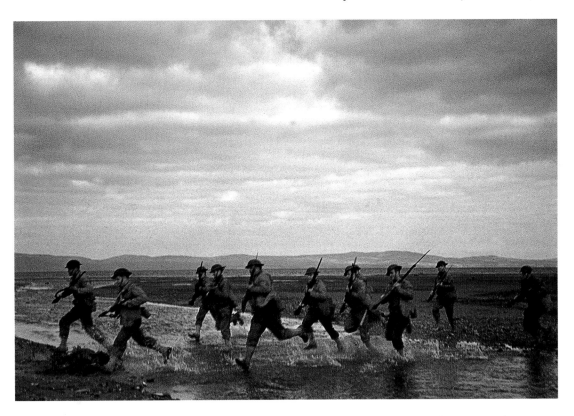

NORTH AFRICA

The Allies' first significant strikes against the Axis powers were in North Africa. Following the British victory at El Alamein, in November 1942 the Allies mounted Operation Torch, U.S.-led landings in French Morocco and Algeria. The troops met some resistance from Vichy French forces, but quickly established a vital bridgehead that enabled Churchill's Mediterranean strategy to unfold.

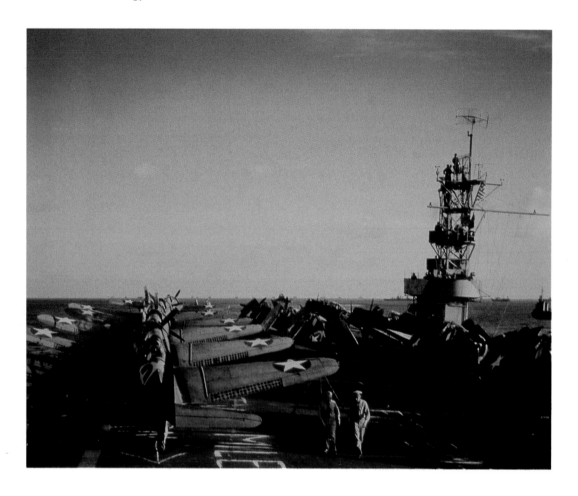

ABOVE

Operation Torch, the invasion of North Africa: landings commenced on November 10, 1942. Shipboard loudspeakers announced to the defending Vichy French troops, "Don't shoot, we are Americans."

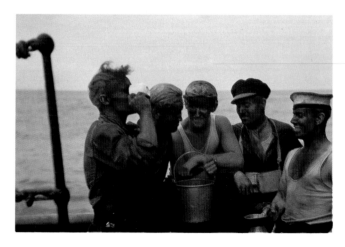

RIGHT

Sailors on deck get some respite from the grime of their ship's engine room. The threat of attack by German U-boats was ever present from the outbreak of war in September 1939.

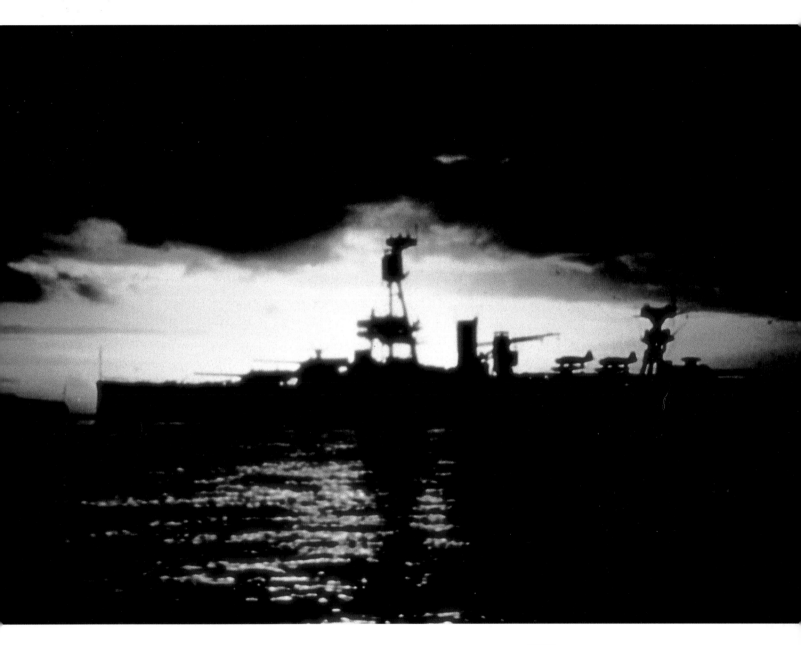

ABOVE

The U.S.S. *Texas* silhouetted against the
North Atlantic sunset, *circa* 1942.

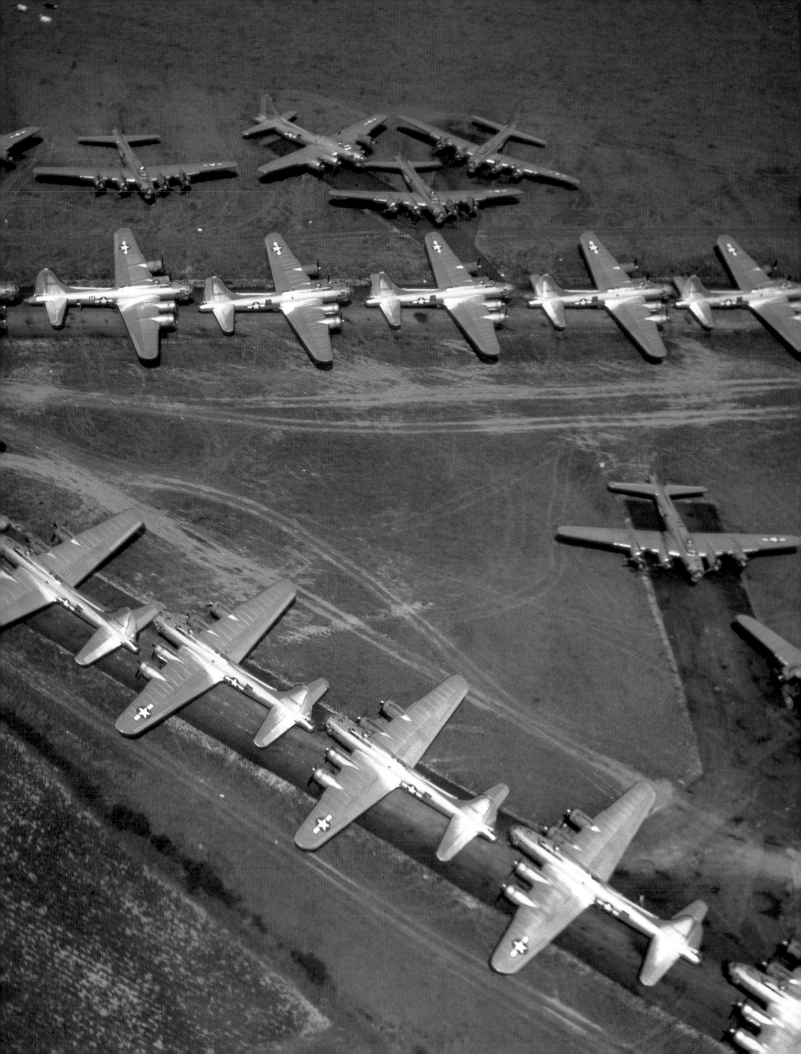

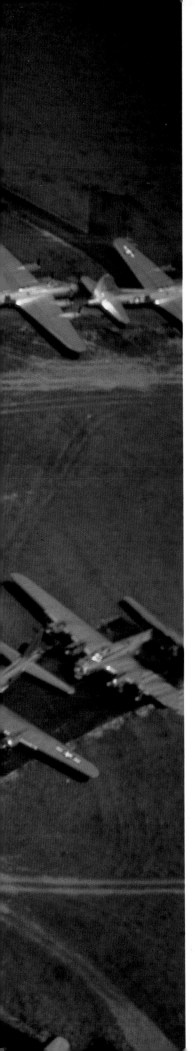

1943

THE LONG ROAD BACK

WARS ARE FOUGHT BY SOLDIERS, BUT SUFFERED BY CIVILIANS; THEY ARE PLANNED BY GENERALS, BUT PLOTTED BY POLITICIANS. ALLIED STRATEGY IN WORLD WAR II WAS CONCEIVED BY THREE REMARKABLE BUT VERY DIFFERENT POLITICIANS, REPRESENTING THREE ALMOST INCOMPATIBLE TRADITIONS. HOWEVER, THEIR DIFFERENCES WERE SUBSUMED BY THEIR OVERWHELMING DESIRE FOR VICTORY.

President Franklin D. Roosevelt was a democrat, firmly rooted in the meritocratic traditions of the United States. Prime Minister Winston Churchill was an aristocrat and a staunch defender of Britain's imperial heritage. General Secretary Josef Stalin was a despotic ruler of a strictly orthodox and viciously oppressive communist regime. However, despite countless differences, trials, and tribulations, these men forged a joint plan which was central to the Allied victory. What has been termed Roosevelt and Churchill's "special relationship" developed throughout the war, making the alliance between Britain and the U.S.A. stronger and deeper. And, at least on a populist level, "Uncle Joe" Stalin was admired; the deeds of his Red Army much more so. Even conservative politicians spoke glowingly of "our brave Soviet comrades."

A measure of the level of co-operation between the three Allies, or the "Grand Alliance," as Churchill called them, was Roosevelt and Stalin's reluctant agreement to Churchill's strategy for the European war. The British, seriously mauled by the German army in France in 1940, were reluctant to challenge the Wehrmacht until Hitler's panzer divisions had been seriously weakened by attritional tactics. The Americans, however, were eager to let their vast resources make the telling blow in northern Europe, and the Soviets felt that they were carrying by far the greater part of the burden in terms of men and machines on the Eastern Front (which they were) and that a second front should be opened immediately in France.

At the Casablanca Conference in January 1943, it was Churchill's view that prevailed. The Second Front would be launched in Italy, in what Churchill described as Hitler's "soft underbelly." It was the cautious option, and Churchill may well have been right, but the decision almost certainly extended the war by many months.

The "Mediterranean Strategy," as it was called, planned for a strike at Italy through Sicily in 1943,

LEFT

Replacement aircraft await dispersal to 8th U.S. Army Air Force squadrons, England *circa* 1943.

as soon as the Germans and Italians had been removed from North Africa, followed by an invasion in northern France in 1944.

Two other agreements at Casablanca were crucial to the outcome of the war. First, it was determined that the Allies would pursue the unconditional surrender of Germany and Japan as their ultimate military objective. This was significant, if only because it underlined the deep-seated ideological background of the war. Fascist states were engaged in a relentless war of terror against the Allies; for that, they were going to have to suffer total defeat. Second, it was agreed that a combined bomber offensive be launched against Germany. The British would bomb at night, the Americans by day. These raids would form part of the terrible price that Germany would pay for its part in the aggression of its fascist rulers and supporters.

In the Pacific, the "long road" to total victory was something of a misnomer. There were no roads, only vast expanses of ocean and jungle. Victory would come only after naval supremacy had brought control of the vast distances, and only after G.I.s and Marines had cleared the Japanese defenders from the jungles of the ocean's countless islands. Then roads—and, more importantly, airstrips—could be built by the indefatigable U.S. Navy construction battalions, the Seabees.

Following fierce fighting on Guadalcanal and New Guinea by U.S. and Australian forces, the Allied offensive in the Pacific began in June 1943, in the central Solomon Islands. It took many months of fighting, but slowly and surely headway was made. By November, New Georgia, Vella Lavella, Choiseul, and the Treasury Islands had been retaken. Over a thousand American troops died on New Georgia alone. The battle on Bougainville was a much more prolonged affair: not until August 1945 did the last Japanese garrison of 24,000 men surrender. U.S. forces in the Solomons campaign were very ably assisted by men from New Zealand and Australia. Island hopping—beach by beach, jungle by jungle, and naval encounter by naval encounter—would be the relentless pattern for the Pacific Campaign.

The Allies' strike at Hitler's "soft underbelly" began on the morning of July 10, 1943, on the Italian island of Sicily. Operation Husky was a combined force of over 180,000 men and over 2,500 ships. Generals Patton and Montgomery were the Allies' principal commanders, two men with formidable reputations and talents, but not known for their generosity towards their rival commanders.

Airborne support landings were hampered by strong winds, but the assaults on the beaches went much better. American forces landed between Licata and Cape Scaramia on Sicily's southwest coast. British and Commonwealth forces landed in the southeast, between Pozallo and Syracuse.

The ensuing battle involved some Allied bickering and stiff resistance from high-quality German units, and progress was slower than expected. But, significantly, Benito Mussolini fell from power on July 25, an indication of the lack of commitment to the Axis cause in the hearts of the Italian people. This led Hitler to rethink his strategy, and on August 11 the Germans began a tactical withdrawal from the island. As many as 40,000 German troops escaped, together with a large force of Italians; the Germans later formed the backbone of even stiffer resistance on the Italian mainland.

The Allies crossed the straits of Messina on September 3 and landed further up the coast at Salerno on September 9. By then the Italians had formally surrendered, but the campaign was far from over. Hitler was moving sixteen divisions into Italy. There was going to be nothing "soft" about his underbelly. His army would fight for every inch of ground. And most of the ground was mountainous and hard; any low ground available became difficult with the rains of winter. The attritional battle wore on into 1944, before significant breakthroughs were made north of Naples.

1943 also represented the turning point in the protracted struggle for the lines of supply between North America and Britain which, somewhat misleadingly, has been called the Battle of the Atlantic. A "battle" was never really fought; it was more a "war" for control of the high seas. 1943 was the critical year.

In order for Britain to be fortified in its defense against Hitler in Europe, the North Atlantic was crucial. Vast quantities of food, weapons, and equipment had to be transported in large convoys under naval protection. British and U.S. naval and aerial power meant that the most potent weapon available to Germany in attempting to cut Allied supplies was the German submarine, the U-boat. At the beginning of the war, and certainly until 1943, they were a terrifying menace, sinking millions of tons of shipping. They hunted in "wolfpacks," surfaced, and picked off their targets with ruthless efficiency.

But Admiral Karl Dönitz, who directed the U-boat fleet, had one major problem: he never had enough boats. Perhaps his greatest opportunities came in 1940 and 1941, but he had only twenty-seven vessels in 1940, and twenty-one in February 1941. With operational constraints, the number of boats at sea offering a real threat to shipping could dip into single figures. By the time the number of craft increased dramatically, in late 1942, it was probably too late, but only because of the horrible game of statistics called attritional war. Throughout 1942, Allied shipping losses had been appalling: over 8 million tons, mostly sunk by U-boats. But by early 1943 the U.S.A. could produce more merchant ships than the U-boats could sink. With cold calculation, the Allies determined that they could afford to lose two ships for every U-boat. The harsh statistics of war soon began to tell.

More sophisticated radar and a breakthrough by Allied intelligence in cracking the U-boats' communication cipher allowed the wolfpacks to be detected. This coincided with the deployment of better long-range air cover, to close the gap in air protection between North America and Europe. Whereas the U-boats had previously been able to operate unseen, and practically unchallenged, they themselves were now targets: nearly a hundred were lost in the first five months of 1943, forty-seven in May alone. At the end of the month, Dönitz withdrew his beleaguered boats and crews to port, their potency all but gone.

The aerial war against Germany also moved into a critical phase in 1943, with the beginning of the Allies' Combined Bomber Offensive. The objective had been set at the Casablanca Conference: "The progressive, destruction and dislocation of the German military, industrial, and economic system, and the undermining of the morale of the German people to a point where their capacity for armed resistance is fatally weakened." These were the plain, unemotional words of military planners, but their impact on the German population was to be catastrophic. They also required Allied aircrews to pay a heavy price in making them effective.

In March, R.A.F. Bomber Command launched a massive raid, involving over 440 bombers, on Essen in the Ruhr industrial area of Germany. Even bigger raids on Hamburg in late July, by the R.A.F. by night and the U.S.A.A.F. by day, caused colossal damage. Over 40,000 civilians were killed, many in a "firestorm" created on the night of July 27, when an area of over eight square miles was incinerated in a cauldron of fire. The intense heat created high winds as the air rushed to feed the flames. Many people hiding in cellars were suffocated through lack of oxygen.

In August and September, the R.A.F. raided Berlin and the eighth U.S.A.A.F. attacked Rosenburg and Schweinfurt. British losses over Berlin were substantial—126 bombers lost from a total of 1,647—but American losses were even worse: 147 of the 376 planes dispatched were lost. In a second raid by the U.S.A.A.F. in October, 60 planes out of 291 were lost and 142 damaged. Such losses were unacceptable, and bombing was suspended until early 1944. But the Allies had given Germany a taste of what was to come, especially when, in March 1944, the P-51 Mustang was deployed as a long-range fighter to protect the bombers.

More and more Axis conquests were liberated during 1943. The Red Army's tanks had triumphed in the mighty armored Battle of Kursk and, by the end of the year, the Soviets had retaken Orel and Kharkov (August), Smolensk (September), and Kiev (November).

Towards the end of the year the Pacific campaign moved into the Central Pacific region, beginning with assaults on Makin and Tarawa islands, in the Gilbert and Ellis Islands, on November 20. Heavy naval bombardment preceded the attack, followed by amphibious landings by U.S. Marines. Although fiercely defended, Makin fell in a few days. But the situation on Tarawa was altogether different. There the Japanese had 3,000 elite marines of their own, dug in in heavily reinforced positions, and thousands more Imperial Army troops. The naval bombardment did little to soften them up. When the U.S. Marines went ashore, they faced not only withering fire but also a shallow approach to the beach, which meant that many of their landing craft could not reach the shore. The men had to wade several hundred yards waist-deep in water, under a hail of enemy fire. Almost a thousand of them died, but they exacted a terrible price from the Japanese. Slowly and inexorably, the defenders were cleared from their bunkers with grenades and flame-throwers. Of the estimated 20,000 defenders, only a handful came out alive, many perishing in last-ditch banzai charges.

1943 was the beginning of the long road back to victory. But the Sicilian and Italian battles, the losses of aircrew over Germany (well over 50,000 American and 50,000 British by the end of the war), and the price paid by the Marines in capturing tiny islands in the Pacific, all brought home to the American public the reality of war. The stark casualty figures, coupled with the pressures of the domestic war economy—now in full swing—emphasized that the United States was the fulcrum on which the outcome of the war pivoted; and that it would be a fight to the finish.

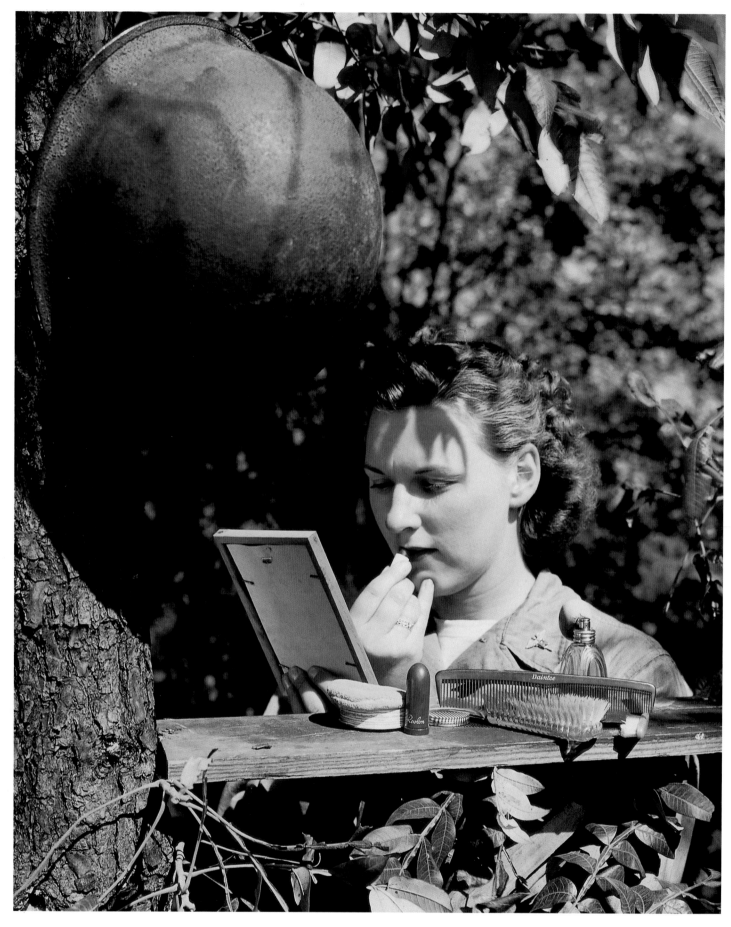

SEGREGATION

For African Americans, World War II represented a period of some limited opportunities, but, in large part, a time of frustration and resentment. There were some new areas of employment in domestic industry available, but generally only in lower-paid jobs. Discrimination was still rife throughout American society. The pattern was similar in the armed forces: a few steps forward in some areas, but generally, a segregated and even hostile military establishment.

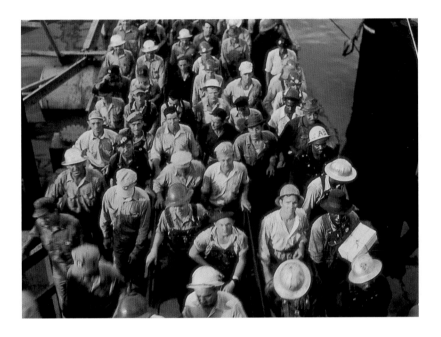

LEFT

Workers leaving the Pennsylvania Shipyards at Beaumont, Texas, in June 1943.

BELOW

Operating a hand drill at Vultee, Nashville, Tennessee, in February 1943. The aircraft under construction is a Vengeance dive bomber.

LEFT

A member of the W.A.A.C. (Women's Army Auxiliary Corps) finds a moment during training to apply a little lipstick.

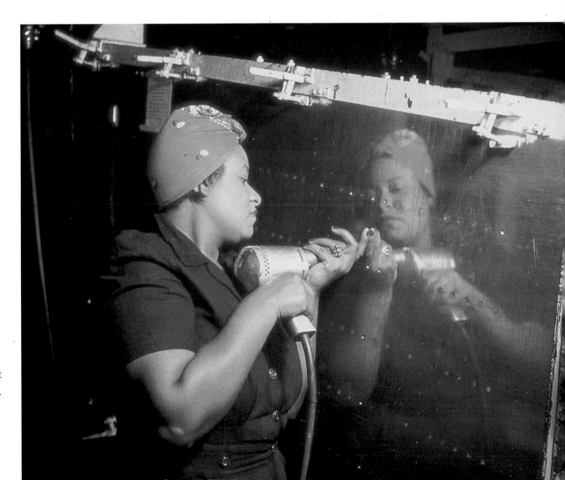

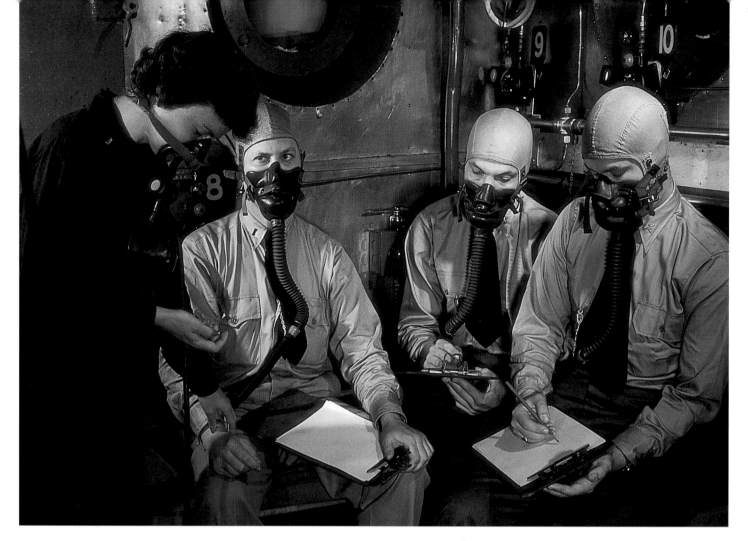

TRAINING AND PREPARATION

It became increasingly obvious to military planners and strategists during World War II that, for the conduct of warfare to be effective, increasing amounts of time and resources had to be spent on training, preparation and logistics. The scale of World War II and the technology levels attained by the mid-twentieth century made this vitally important. For the first time, nations went to war, not just armies.

A Navy nurse checks the pulse of an officer, while two warrant officers make notes, during pressure chamber experiments at the naval air station at Pensacola, Florida.

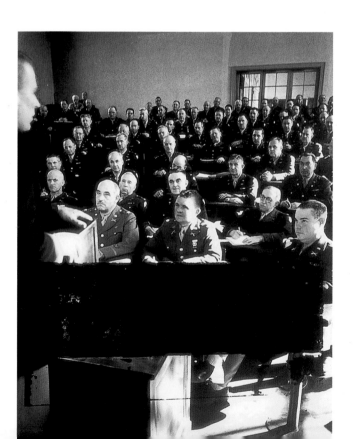

Charlottesville, North Carolina, 1943: U.S.A.A.F. officers listening to a lecture to instruct them in procedures for military government in areas of occupation.

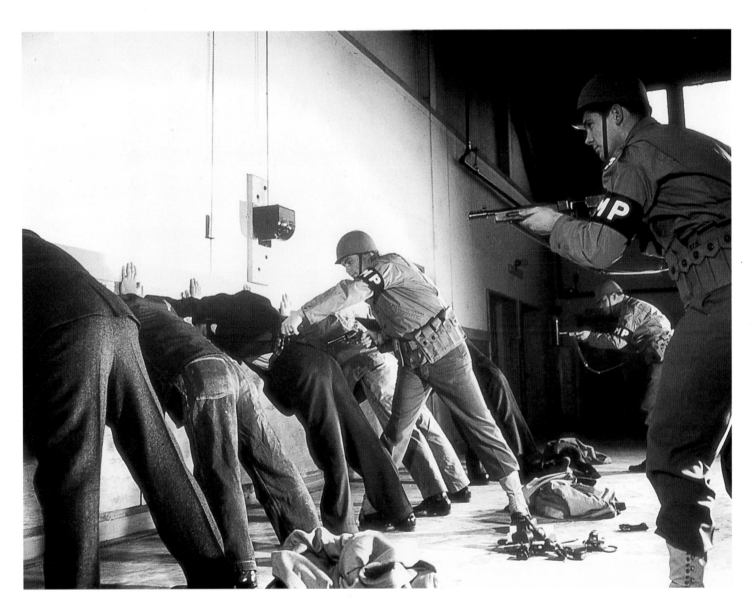

ABOVE

Fort Custer, Missouri, 1943: military policemen learn
how to search civilians.

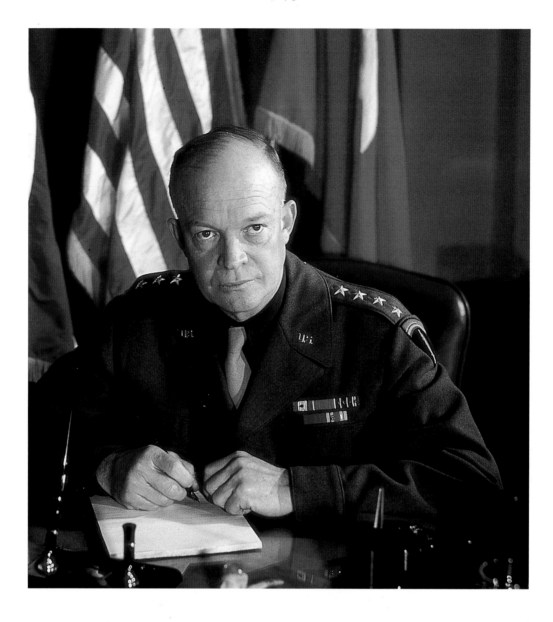

ABOVE
A formal portrait of General Dwight D. Eisenhower, taken in late 1943, at the time of his appointment as Supreme Commander of the Allied forces in Western Europe.

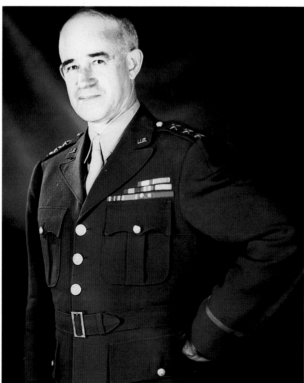

LEFT
General Omar Bradley, who had been a classmate of Eisenhower's at West Point, and who became his most trusted commander in North Africa and Europe.

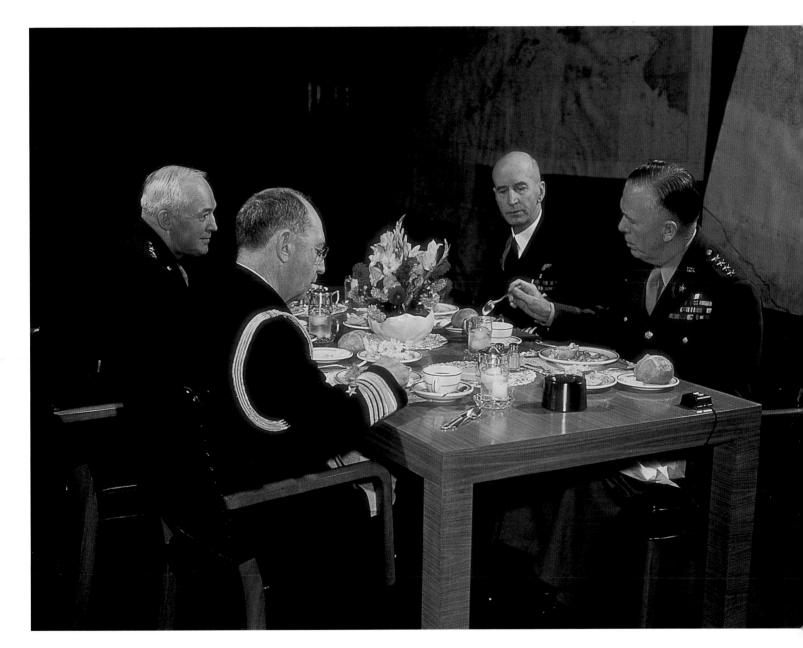

ABOVE

A meeting of the American Combined Chiefs of Staff continues over lunch, *circa* 1943. Left to right: Admiral William D. Leahy, U.S. Navy; General Henry "Hap" Arnold, U.S. Army; Admiral Ernest J. King, U.S. Navy and General George C. Marshall, U.S. Army.

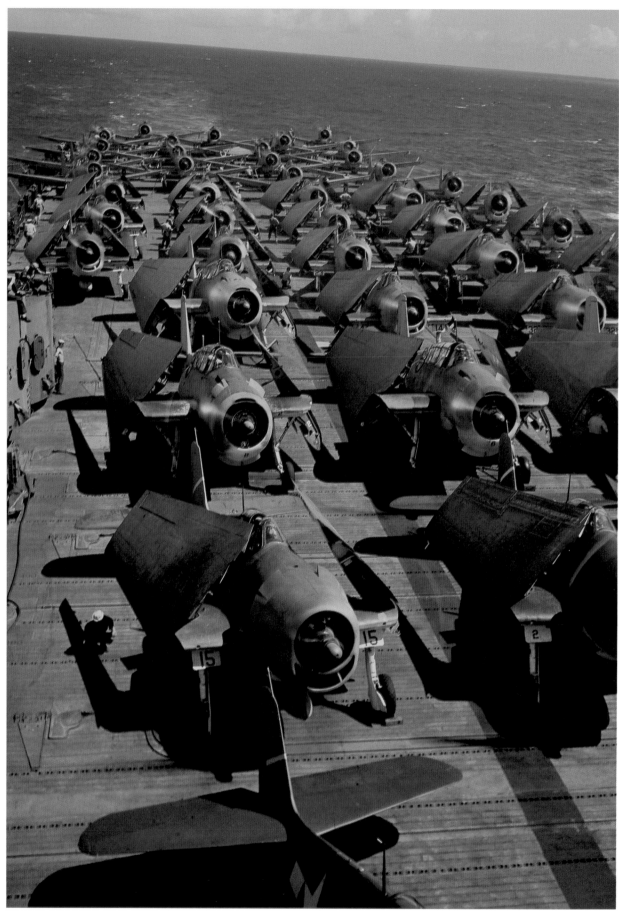

WAR IN THE PACIFIC

The fierce fighting on the Solomon Islands in the southwest Pacific lasted throughout most of 1943, with major battles on Guadalcanal, Vella Lavella, Choiseul and Bougainville. There were also five large naval engagements between July and November.

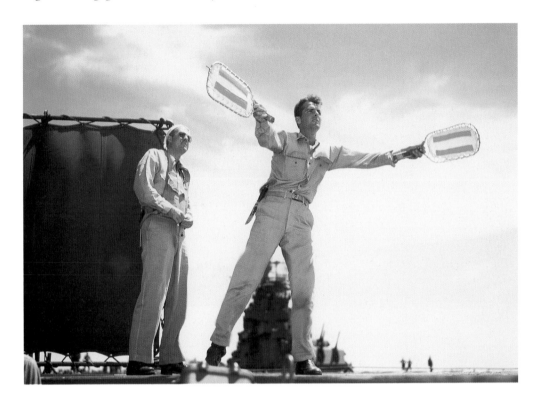

LEFT

Guiding aircraft home onto the deck of the U.S.S. *Lexington* after a raid on the Marshall Islands, *circa* December 1943. Lieutenant John Clark signals to a pilot to raise one wing as he makes his approach to the aircraft carrier deck.

LEFT

Aircraft warm up on the deck of the aircraft carrier U.S.S. *Yorktown*, during the campaign to recapture the Marshall Islands and Gilbert Islands. The picture was taken in November or December 1943 by a photographer of a U.S. Navy Photographic Unit.

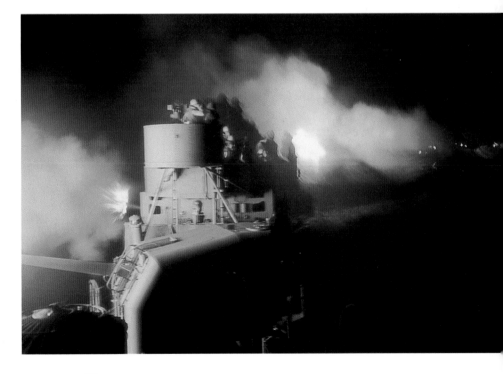

RIGHT

The naval artillery barrage on Kalombangara and New Georgia Islands in the Solomons by Task Force 18, on May 13, 1943. Photographed from the destroyer U.S.S. *Nicholas*.

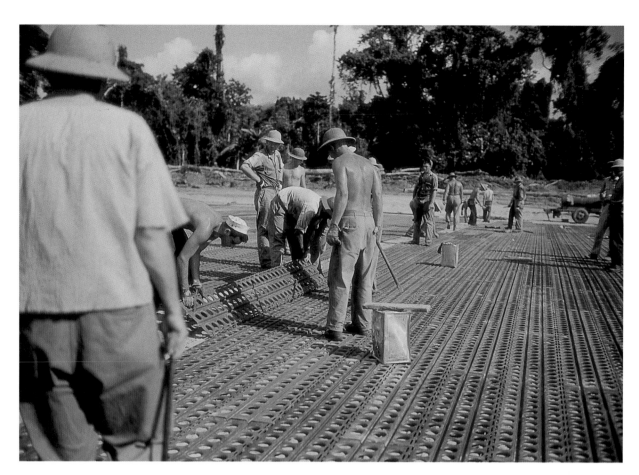

ABOVE

Shortly after the capture of
Bougainville, in the Solomon
Islands, from the Japanese in
December 1943, the U.S. Navy
Seabees set about the construction
of a hard surface at Torokina
Field. The rapid construction
of airstrips enabled fighter
protection to be provided, and
also extended the range of
operations against the Japanese.

LEFT

A Marines howitzer artillery
emplacement on Bougainville in
mid-December 1943.

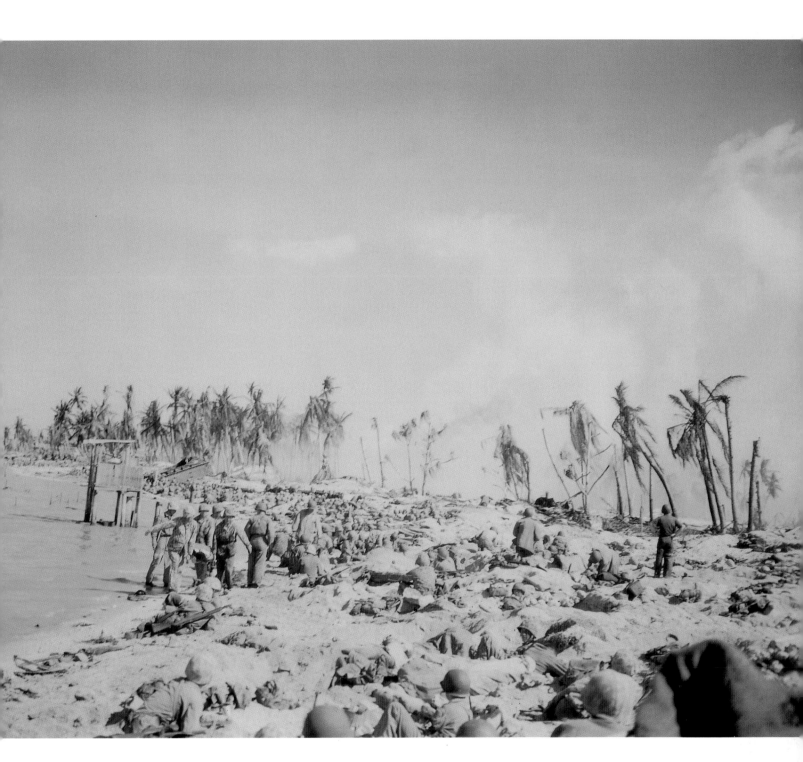

ABOVE

November 22, 1943: a view along the beach
on Tarawa, in the Gilbert Islands, following
a landing by the U.S. Marine Corps.

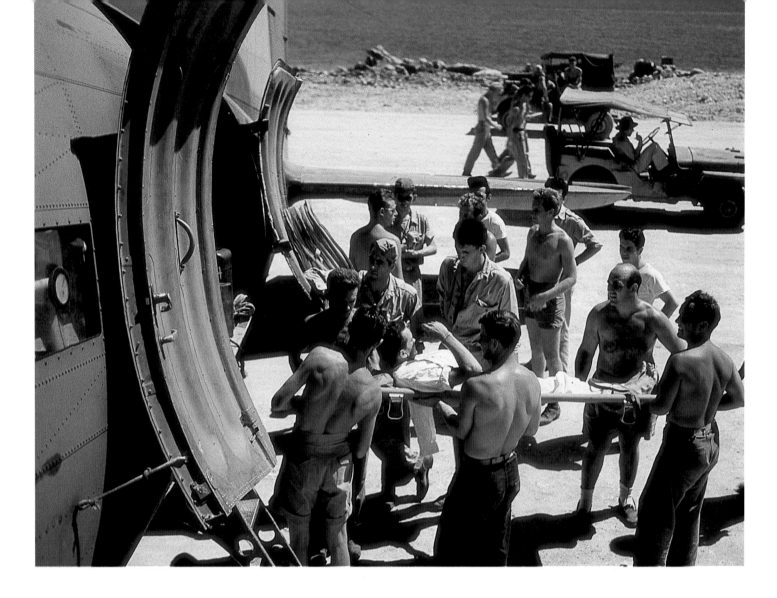

ABOVE
U.S. Marines wounded in the fighting to retake Bougainville are unloaded from a hospital evacuation plane at Vella Lavella in December 1943.

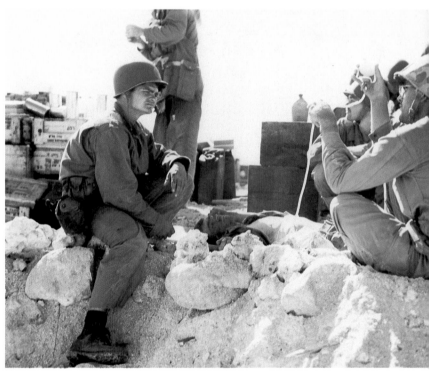

RIGHT
Plasma being administered to a wounded Marine awaiting evacuation from Tarawa, in the Gilbert Islands, on November 22, 1943.

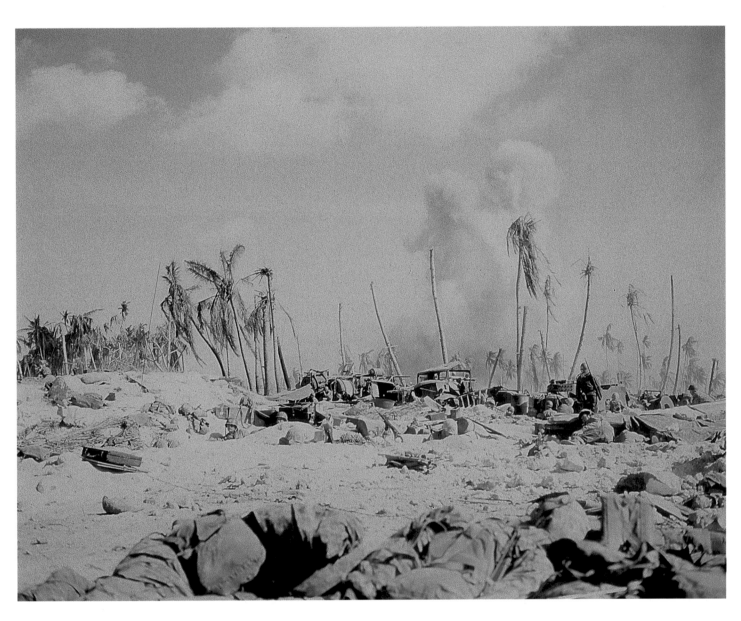

No-man's-land on Tarawa, seen from the head
of the pier on November 22, 1943.

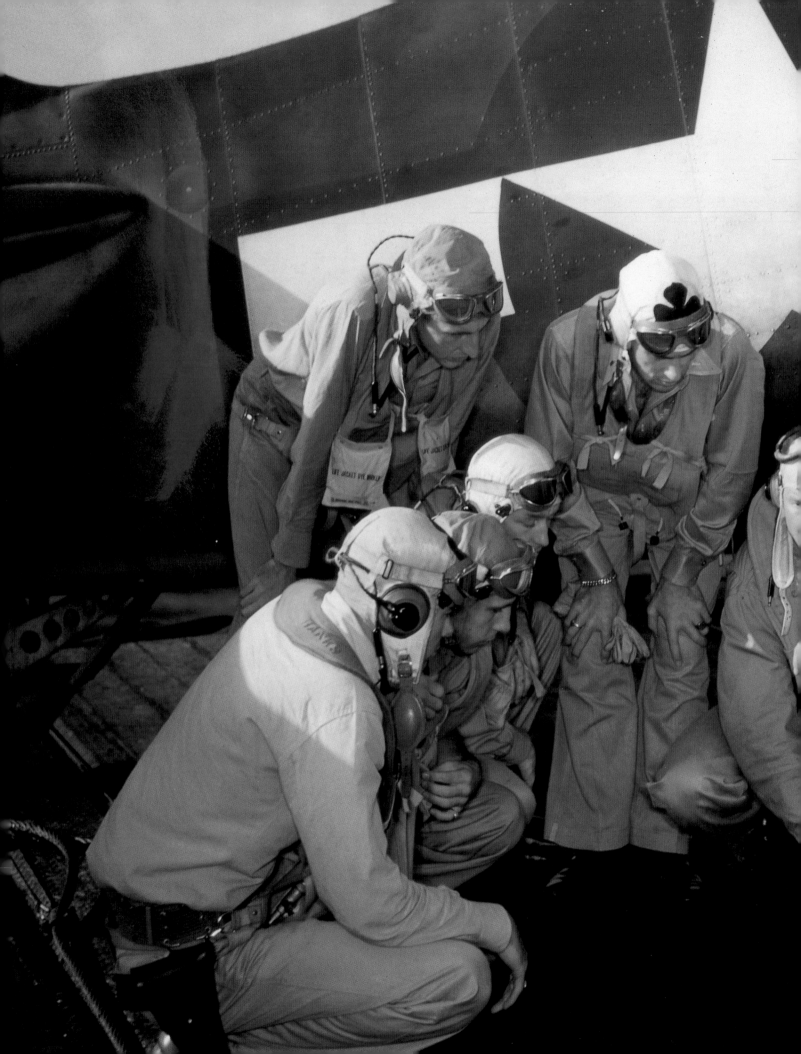

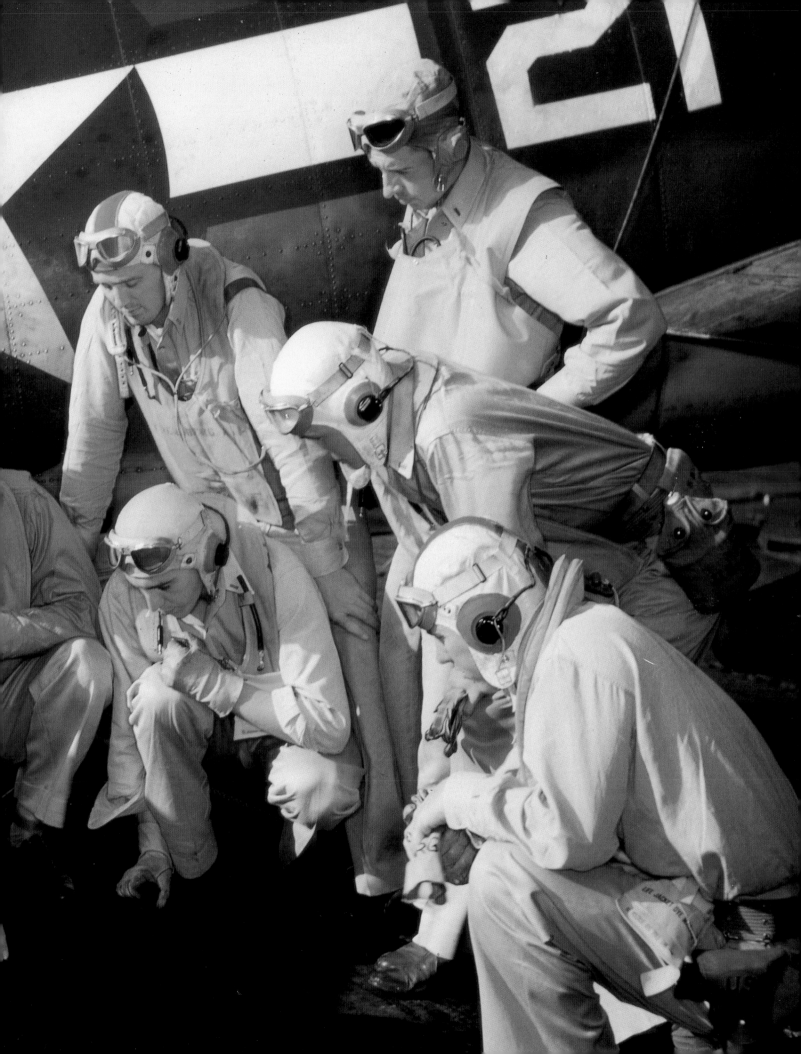

PREVIOUS PAGE
Lieutenant Commander Paul D. Bute, U.S. Navy, briefs pilots of his
fighter squadron aboard the U.S.S. *Lexington* off the Gilbert Islands in
late 1943. The aircraft in the background is a Grumman F-6F Hellcat,
a mainstay of the airborne effort against Japan's navy and air force.
In two years, naval Hellcats shot down over 5,000 Japanese aircraft.

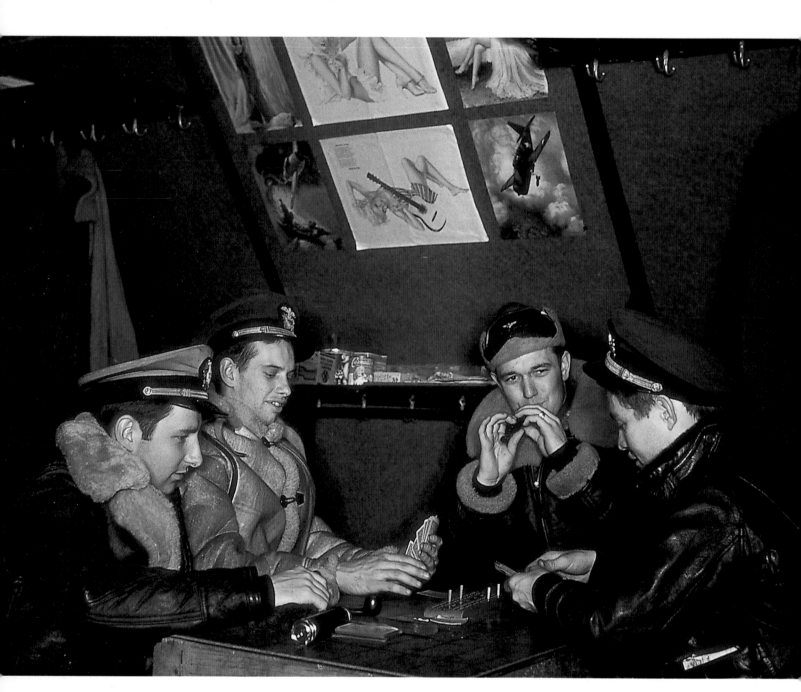

ABOVE
Navy pilots relax between missions with a game of
cribbage in their quarters at an advanced base in the
Aleutian Islands in the northern Pacific in mid-1943.

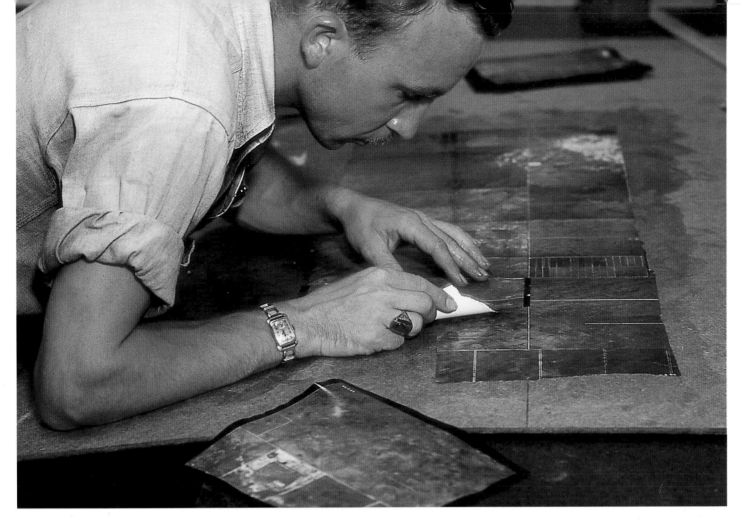

A navy photographer's "mate" assembles a
montage of aerial reconnaissance photos.

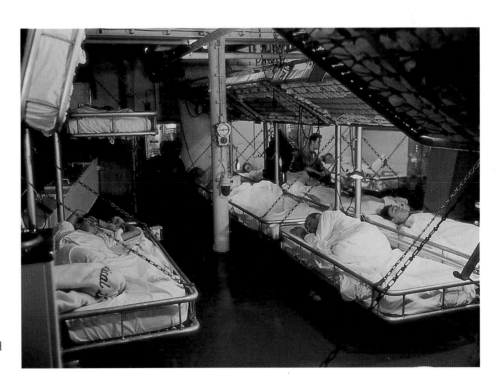

Part of the U.S.S. *Yorktown*'s
sick bay, photographed around
November 1943.

THE BATTLE OF THE ATLANTIC

The Battle of the Atlantic was a long, attritional campaign to keep the vital supply lines across the North Atlantic open to Allied shipping. By the middle of 1943, improved intelligence, better air cover and the sheer volume of shipping began to tip the balance in the Allies' favor. The threat from German U-boats began to diminish.

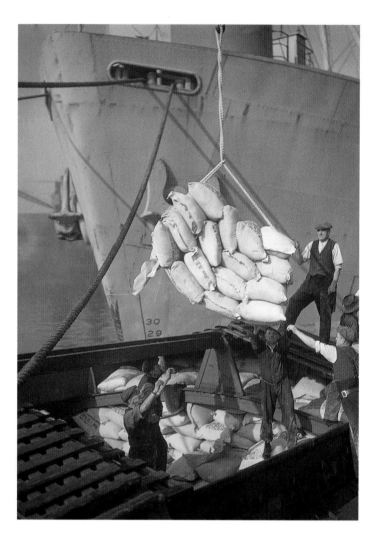

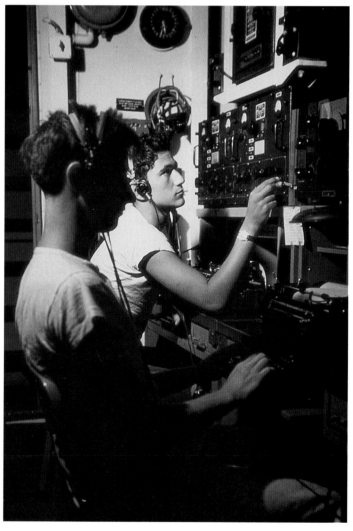

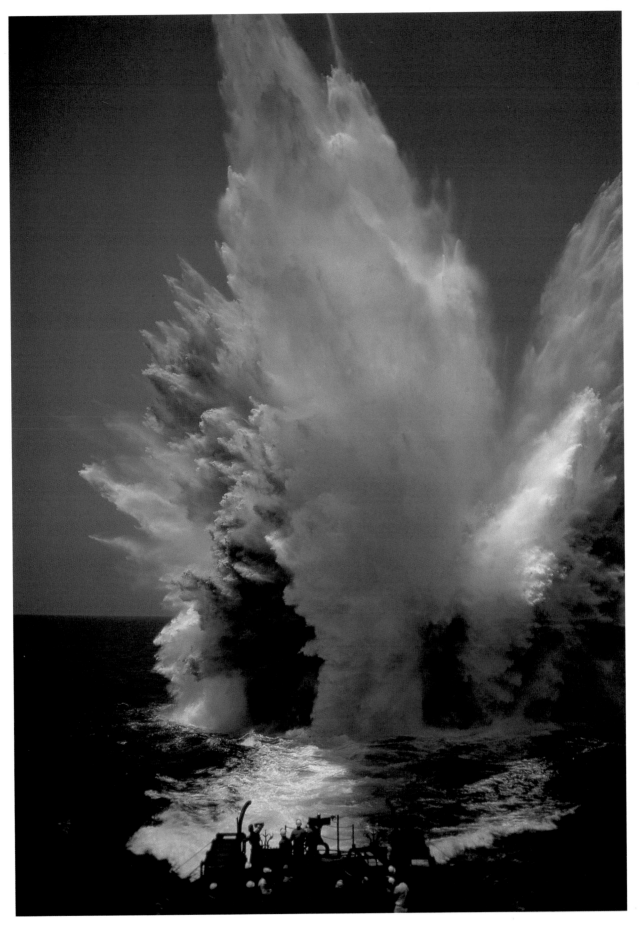

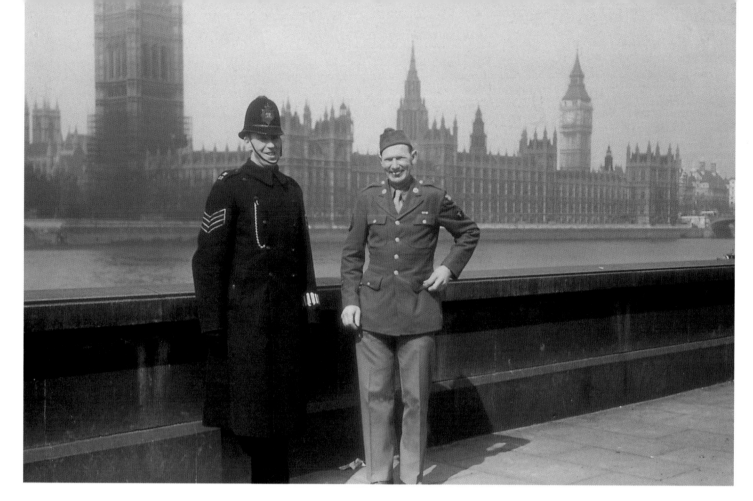

U.S. TROOPS IN BRITAIN

The British saw U.S. servicemen as a mixed blessing. It was widely accepted that their presence and military prowess were vital to the outcome of the war, but local male pride found the impact of their glamor, money, and demeanor on British women hard to stomach. There was respect and resentment in equal measure.

ABOVE
A British "Bobby," the Houses of Parliament and the River Thames make an ideal backdrop for the U.S. serviceman in this souvenir photo taken in London.

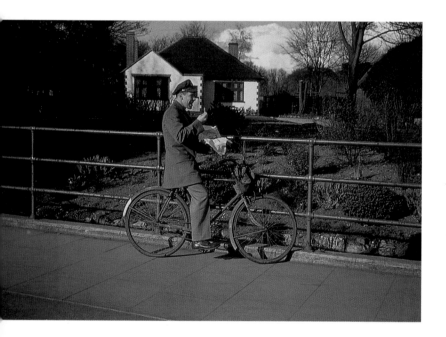

LEFT
An airman in the U.S.A.A.F. savors one of the joys of English life: fish and chips served in and eaten out of a newspaper.

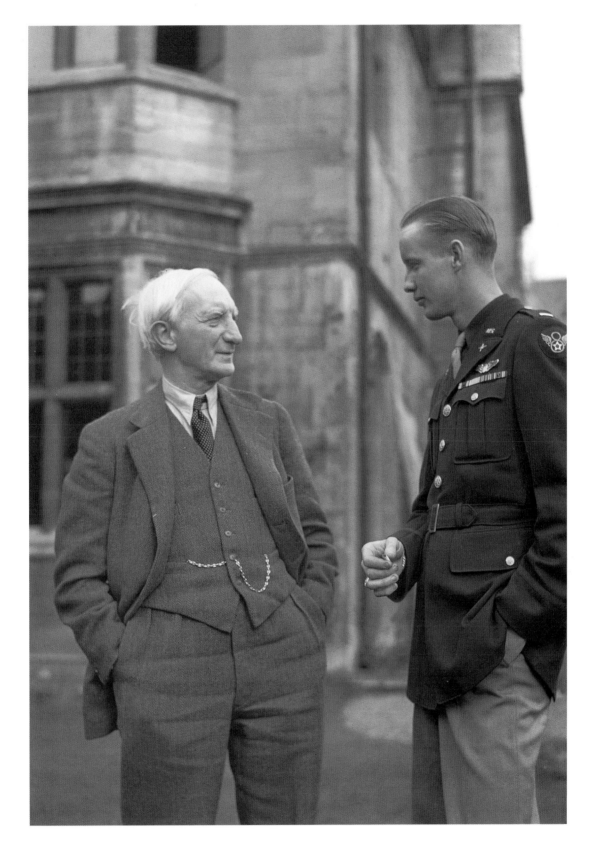

ABOVE

Lieutenant James F. Gaylor of the 8th U.S. Army, talking to the Master of University College, Oxford, Sir William Beveridge. Lieutenant Gaylor, a fighter pilot from Texas, was in hospital in Oxford after his eardrums were damaged in a dog fight, and was a guest at one of the regular tea parties given by Sir William and Lady Beveridge for American troops.

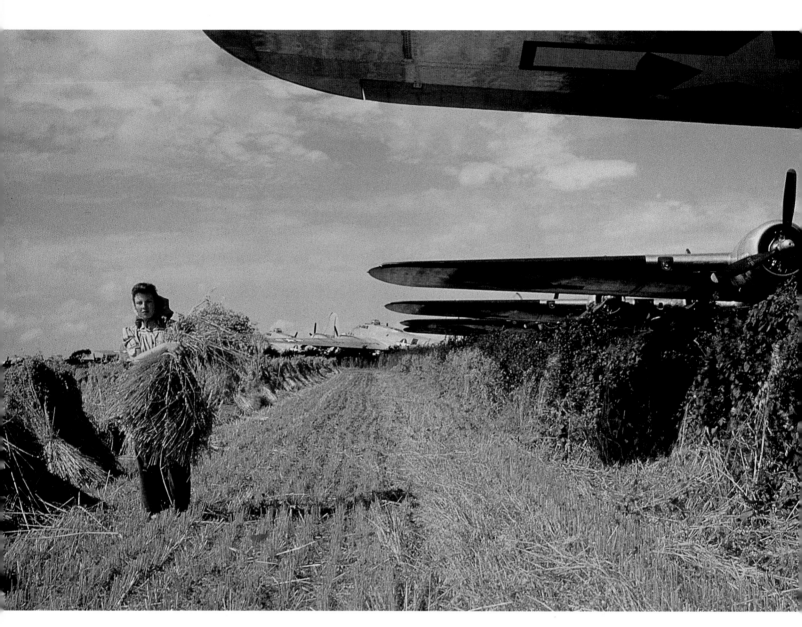

ABOVE

A young British woman of the Land Army gathers hay
under the wingtips of B-17s in the English countryside
at harvest time, probably in 1943.

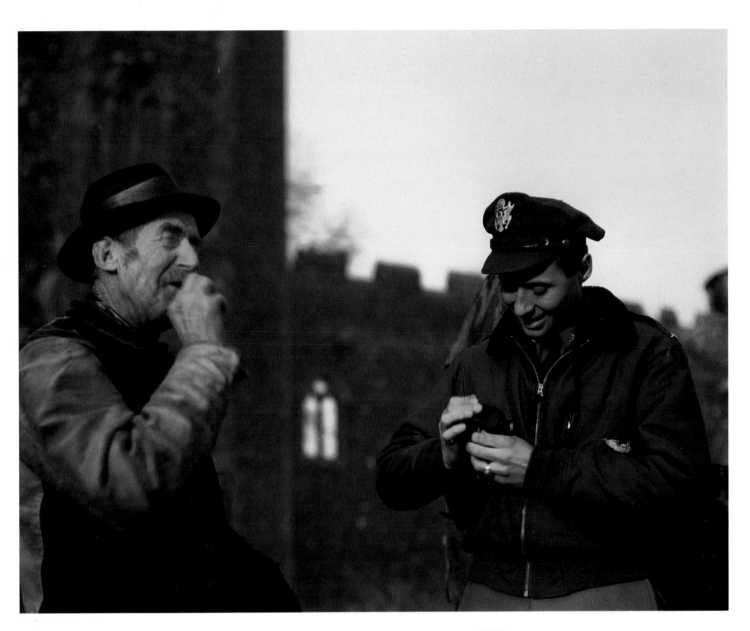

ABOVE

A resident of Eye, Cambridgeshire, shares an
end-of-day joke with a pilot from the U.S. 490th
Bomb Group, which was stationed nearby.

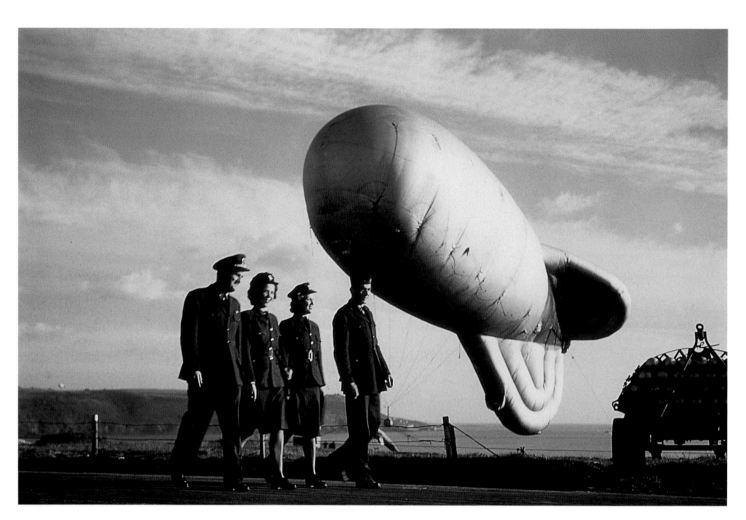

ABOVE

Taking a moment from anti-U-boat patrols over the Bay of Biscay, Lieutenant Commander R.D. Garland and Lieutenant John Ogden stroll around Plymouth, England, with two British W.R.A.F. (Women's Royal Air Force) companions. Barrage balloons offered some deterrent to low-flying German bombers and fighters attempting to bomb Plymouth, an important naval facility.

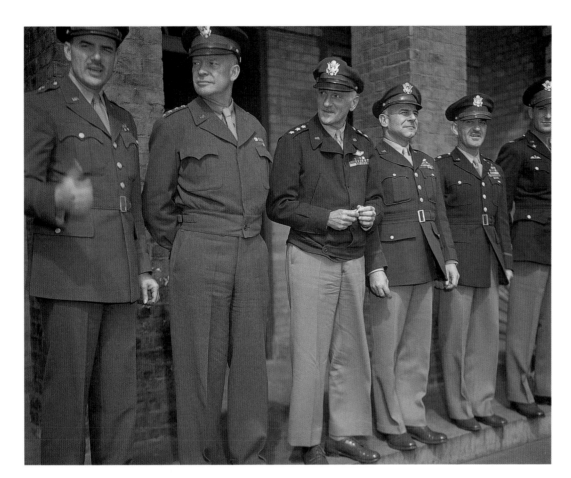

The top brass of the U.S. military pay a visit to the 4th Fighter Group's base at Debden, Essex, northeast of London. Standing outside the Officers' Club are (L–R) Brigadier General Jesse Auton (Commander of the 65th Fighter Wing), General Eisenhower, Lieutenant General Carl "Tooey" Spaatz (Commander of U.S. Strategic Air Forces Europe), Lieutenant General James H. Doolittle (Commander of the 8th Air Force), Major General William Kepner (Commander of 8th Fighter Command) and Colonel Don Blakeslee (Commander of the 4th Fighter Group).

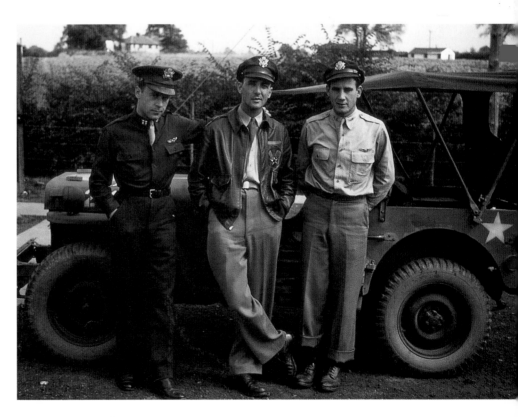

Captains Louis Sebille, Roland Scott and Howard Posson were among the first pilots to fly B-26 Marauders with 322nd Bomber Group. They were photographed near their base at Great Saling, England, in September 1943.

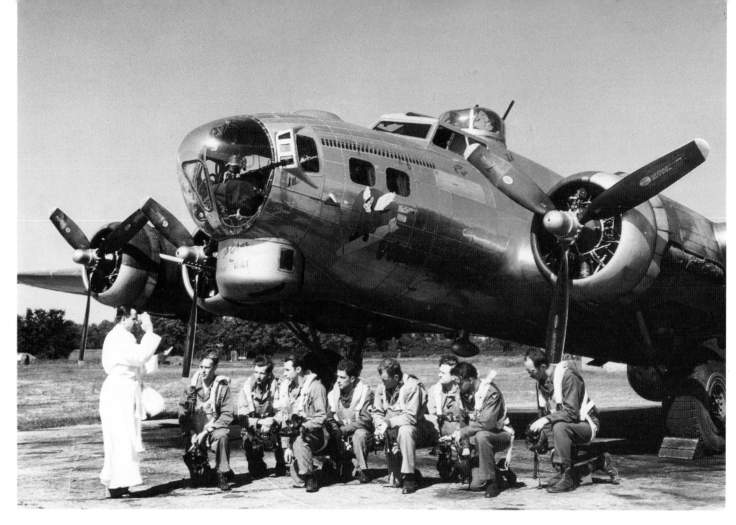

Roman Catholic padre Captain M.S. Ragan blesses a B-17 "Flying Fortress" crew before take-off. Before the war Captain Ragan, of Youngstown, Ohio, had been assistant pastor of St. Paul's Church, Cleveland, Ohio.

A briefing of P-47 pilots of the 56th Fighter Group at their base at Halesworth, England. Seated third from the left in the fourth row is fighter ace Bob Johnson, who by that time had shot down 27 enemy aircraft.

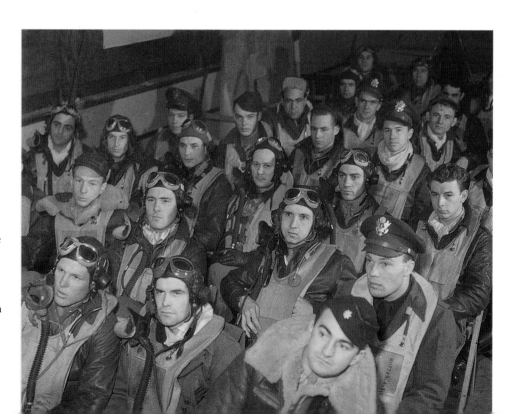

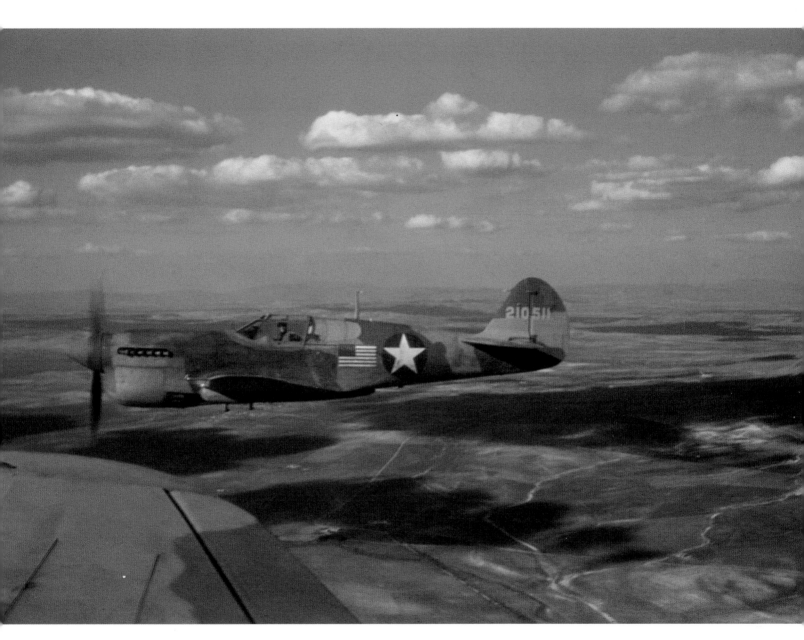

ABOVE

A P-40L operating with the 59th Fighter Squadron,
33rd Fighter Group, flies over Tunisia, North Africa,
in January 1943.

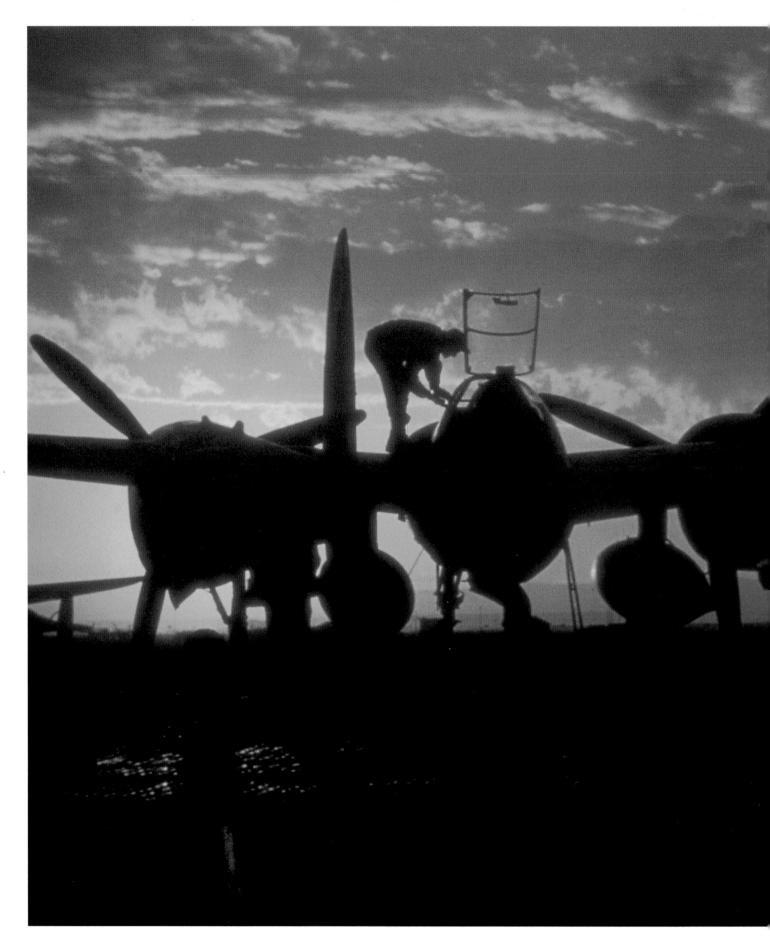

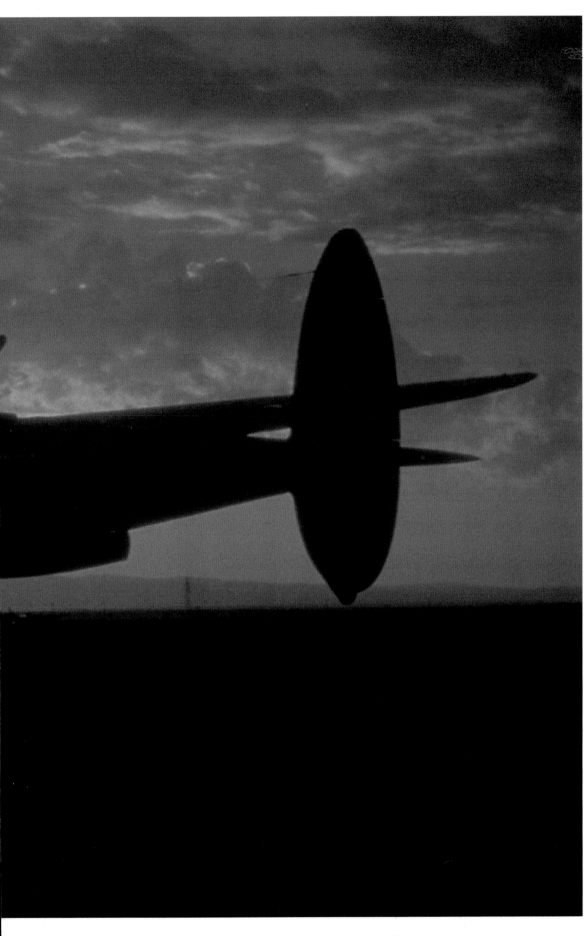

A mechanic works late into the evening carrying out repairs on an aircraft (location unknown, but probably North Africa).

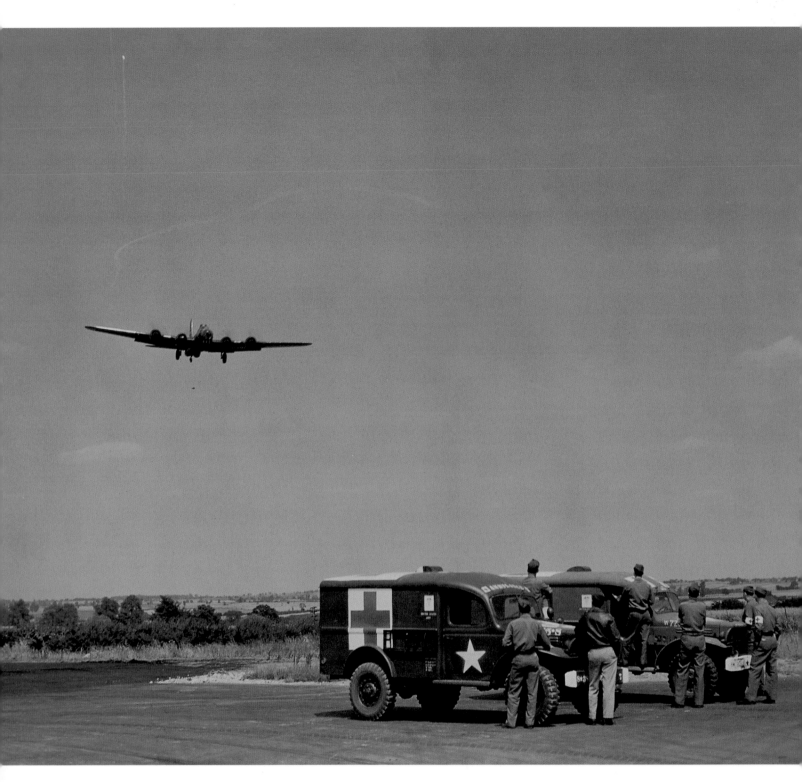

ABOVE

A B-17 comes in to land, having fired wounded flares to indicate that an
ambulance is required. Two Dodge "meatwagons" have responded to the flares.

A member of the Army Chemical Corps fills and stacks 100lb aircraft bombs at the Edgewood Arsenal, Maryland, in 1943. On many occasions non-lethal chemical agents, such as tear gas, were used to train men to deal with chemical warfare in the event that the enemy used toxic gases.

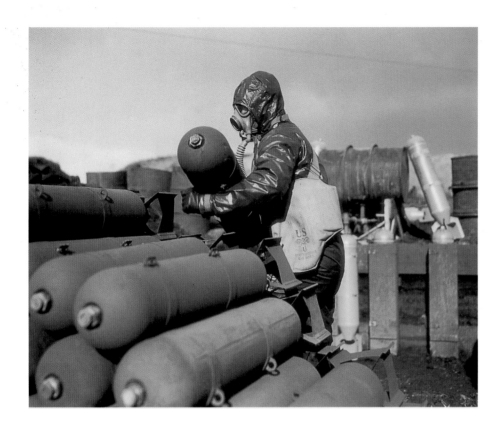

BELOW

Returning from an anti-submarine patrol over the Bay of Biscay, a U.S. Navy PB4Y-1 approaches the chalk cliffs of the English coastline, *circa* July 1943.

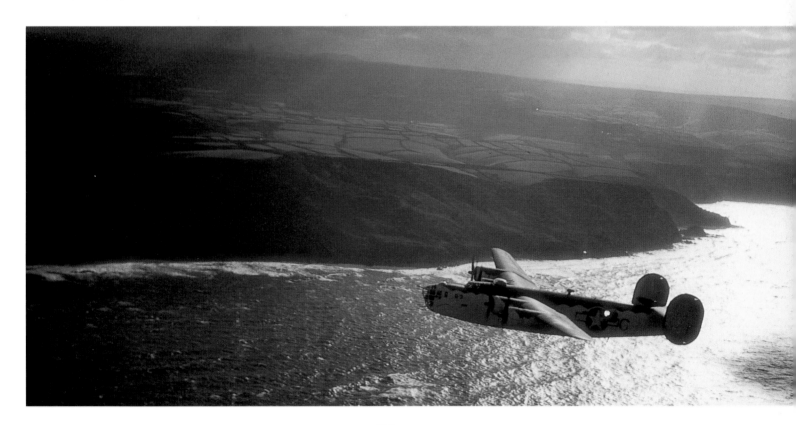

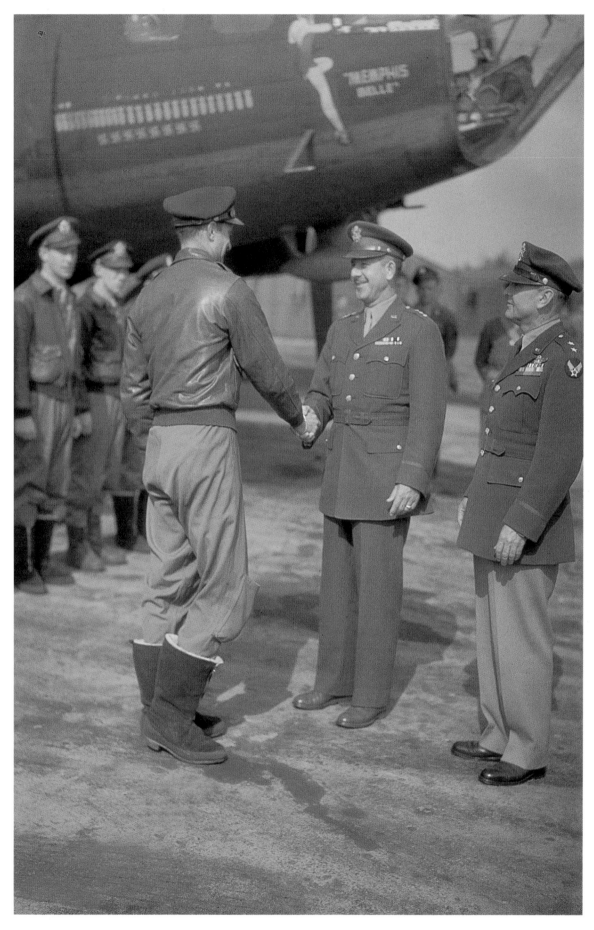

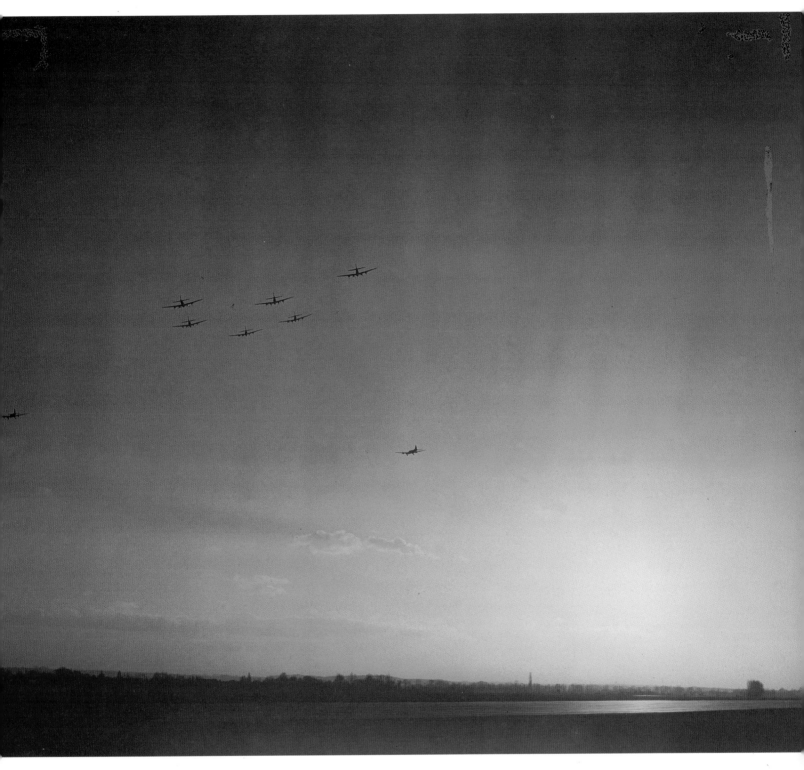

LEFT

June 6, 1943: General Jacob Devers congratulates Robert K. Morgan, captain of the B-17 "Memphis Belle," on completing twenty-five combat missions over occupied Europe. The "Belle" was chosen as the focal point of a war-bond tour in the U.S.A. and was immortalized in William Wyler's Oscar-winning documentary for the Office of War Information, *Memphis Belle*.

ABOVE

B-17s of the 8th Air Force in eastern England silhouetted against the sunset as they return from a bombing mission over occupied Europe, *circa* 1943.

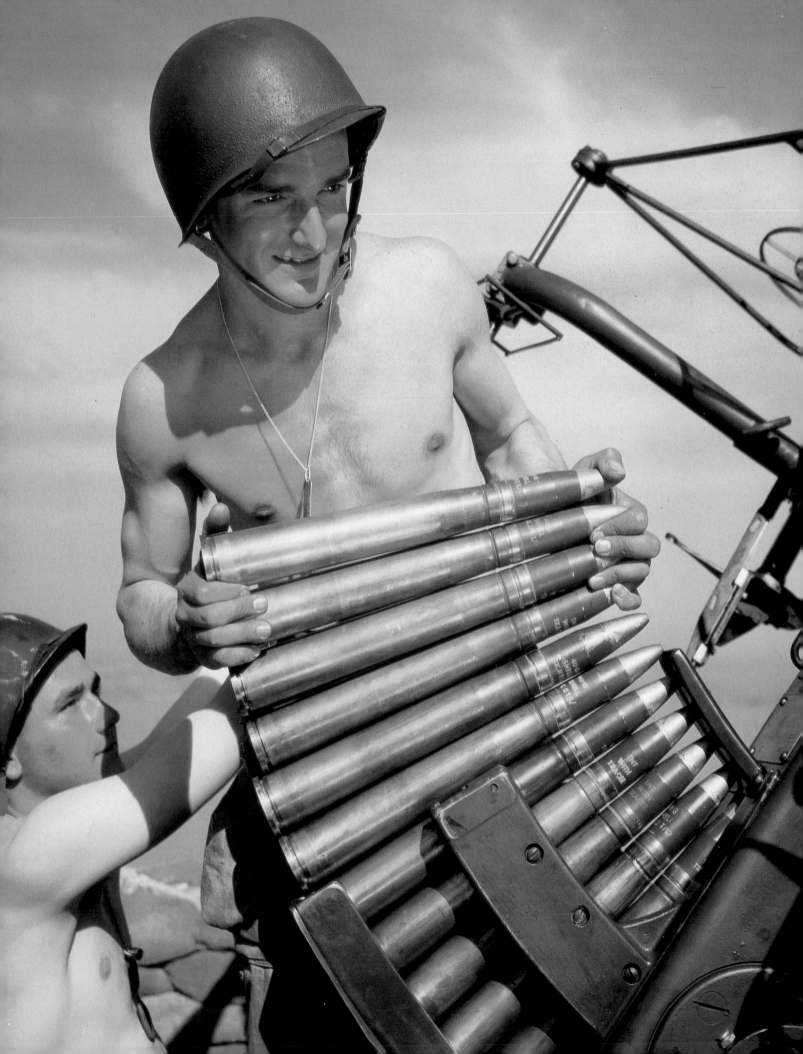

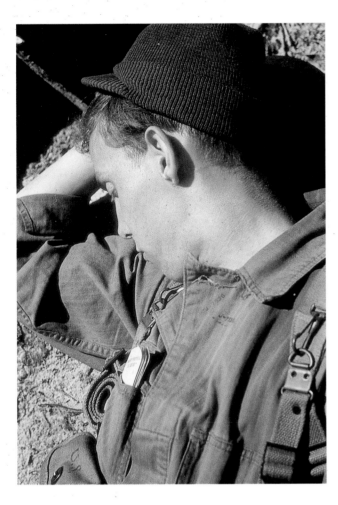

A member of the 397th Bomber Group takes a nap during training at MacDill Field, Florida, in the fall of 1943.

LEFT
Shells are loaded into a Bofors anti-aircraft gun by Private First Class Paul Kaiser of Philadelphia, Pennsylvania, at a U.S. air base in England.

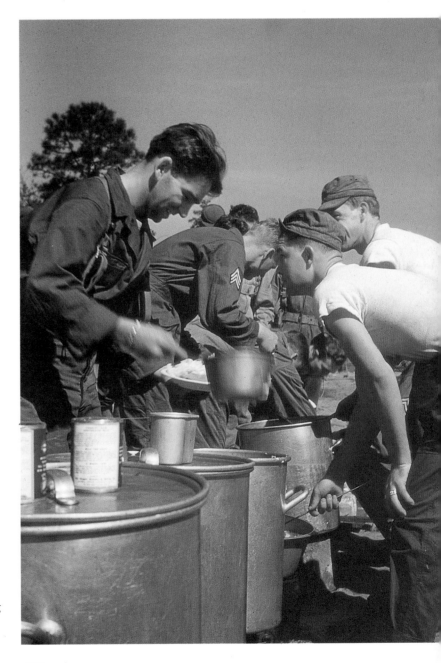

RIGHT
A line for food at a field kitchen at MacDill Field, Florida, during training of the 397th Bomber Group in fall 1943.

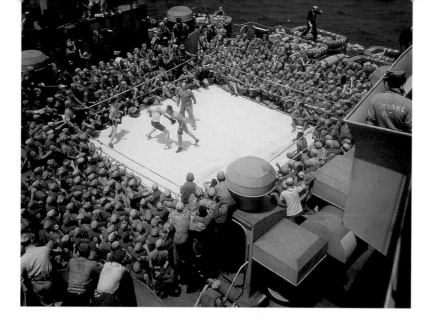

When a Brazilian ship was sunk by the German Navy in 1942, Brazil became the first South American country to declare war on Germany and Italy. The 25,000-strong Brazilian Expeditionary Force served with distinction in the Italian campaign with General Mark Clark's U.S. 5th Army. Here, men of the 2nd Contingent, Brazilian Expeditionary Force watch a boxing bout aboard a troopship en route to Italy.

THE MEDITERRANEAN STRATEGY

The second phase of the Allies' "Mediterranean Strategy" was the invasion of Italy. Churchill's description of this theater of operations as Hitler's "soft underbelly" proved to be very misleading. The Italian campaign was a long and bitter struggle as some of Germany's finest troops used superb defensive tactics to thwart the Allied advance along the Apennine Peninsula.

Troops go ashore on a beach south of Salerno, near Naples.

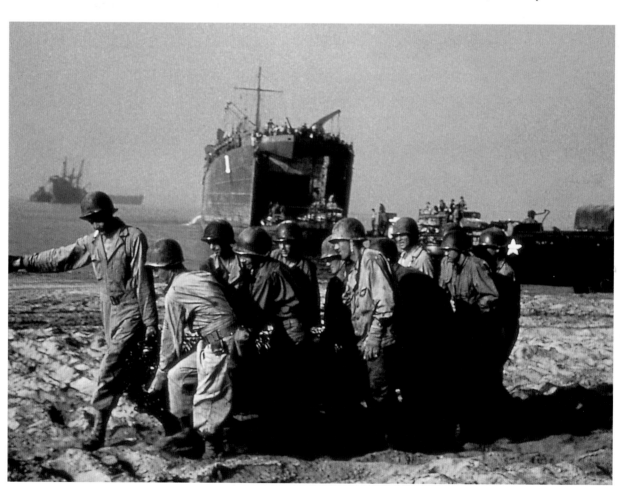

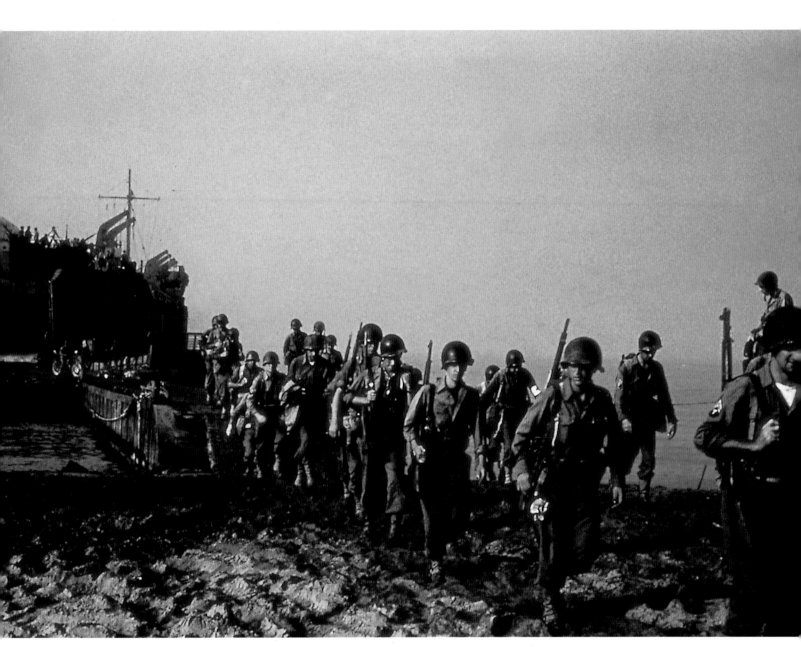

ABOVE

Soldiers disembarking from a landing craft on an
Italian beach meet no resistance.

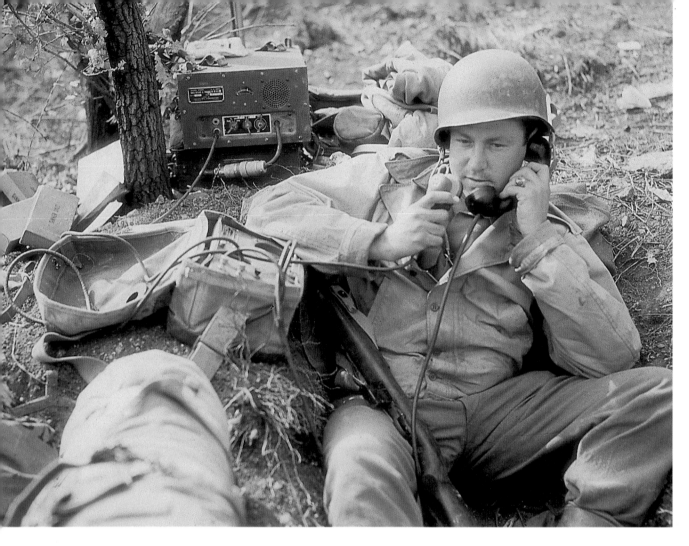

ABOVE

A radio operator relays reports from a remote
control point to an artillery command post.

RIGHT

Signal Corps Cameraman Sergeant
William Dean McWhirter of Atlanta,
Georgia, assigned to the 313th Signal
Service Company, poses with camera
on the Gothic Line (German defensive
position in Italy) in 1943. Before his
three years in the army, he worked
as a freelance photographer on the
Atlanta Constitution newspaper.

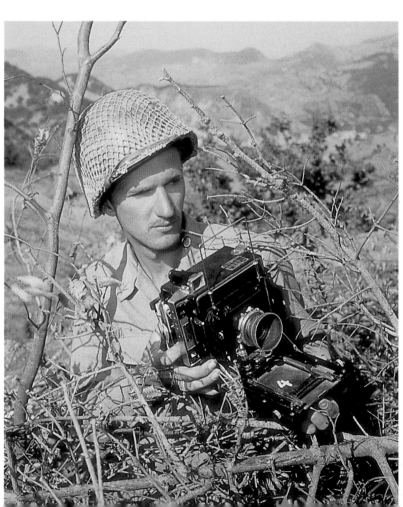

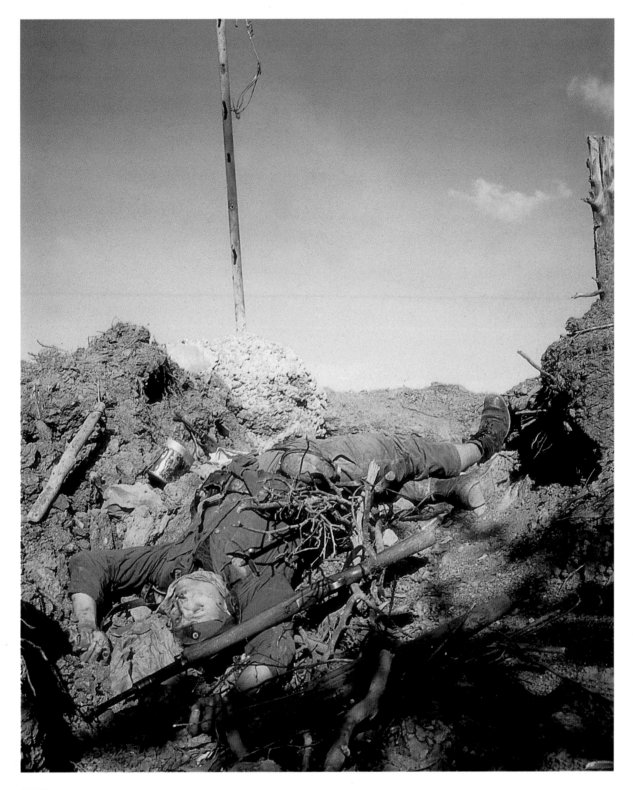

ABOVE

The Allies inflicted heavy casualties on the Germans in Italy.
This German soldier was killed in 1943.

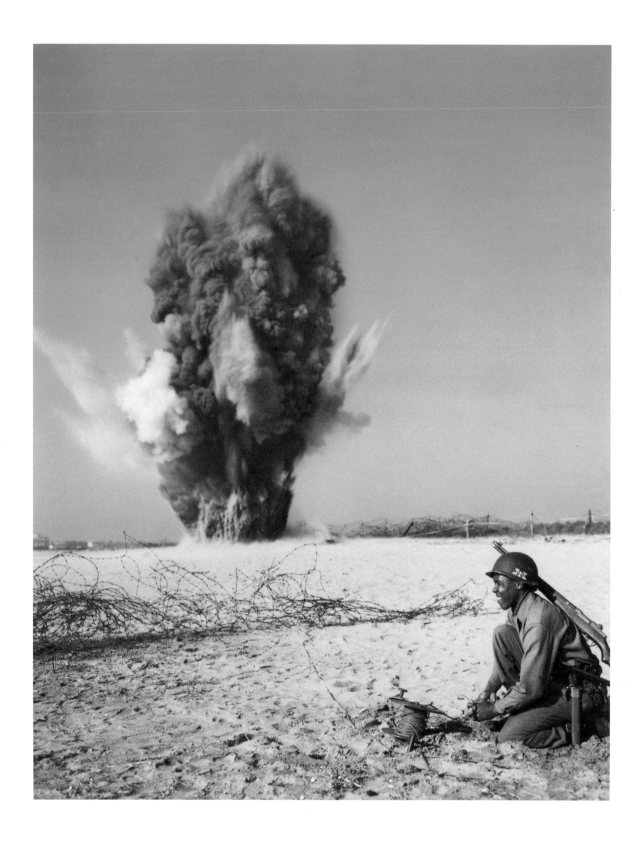

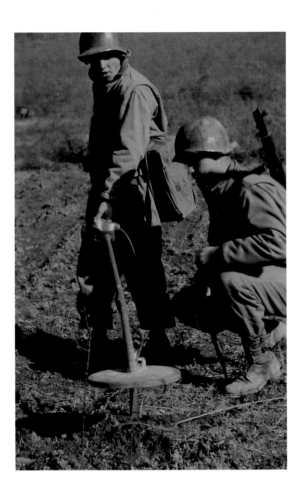

The engineers employed in mine clearance often had to use very basic equipment: here, a mine detector and bayonet.

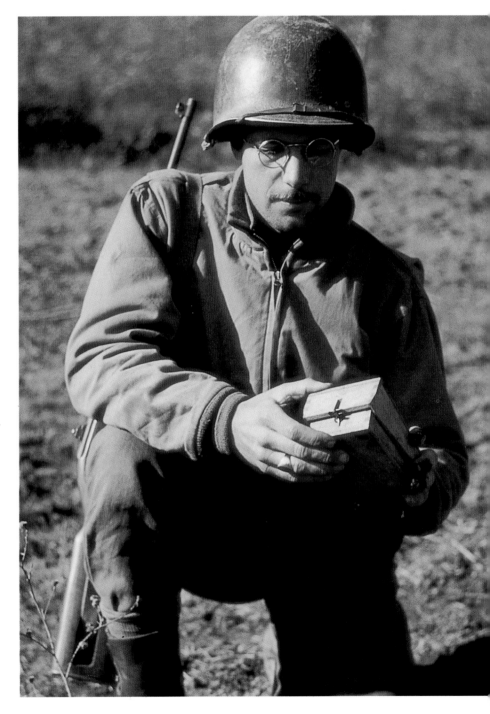

LEFT

Mines being exploded on the beach in Viareggio, Italy, by an engineer of the 92nd (Negro) Division.

RIGHT

A G.I. displays a wooden spring mine, used to avoid discovery by metal detectors.

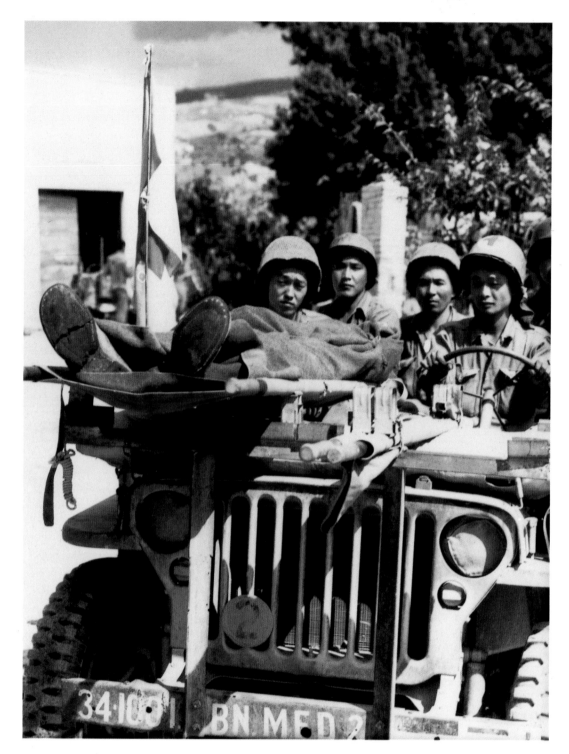

ABOVE

Japanese-American medics with a casualty in Italy.

RIGHT

An alert crew aboard a tank of the 752nd Tank Battalion guarding a vital crossroads on the road to Pisa, Italy.

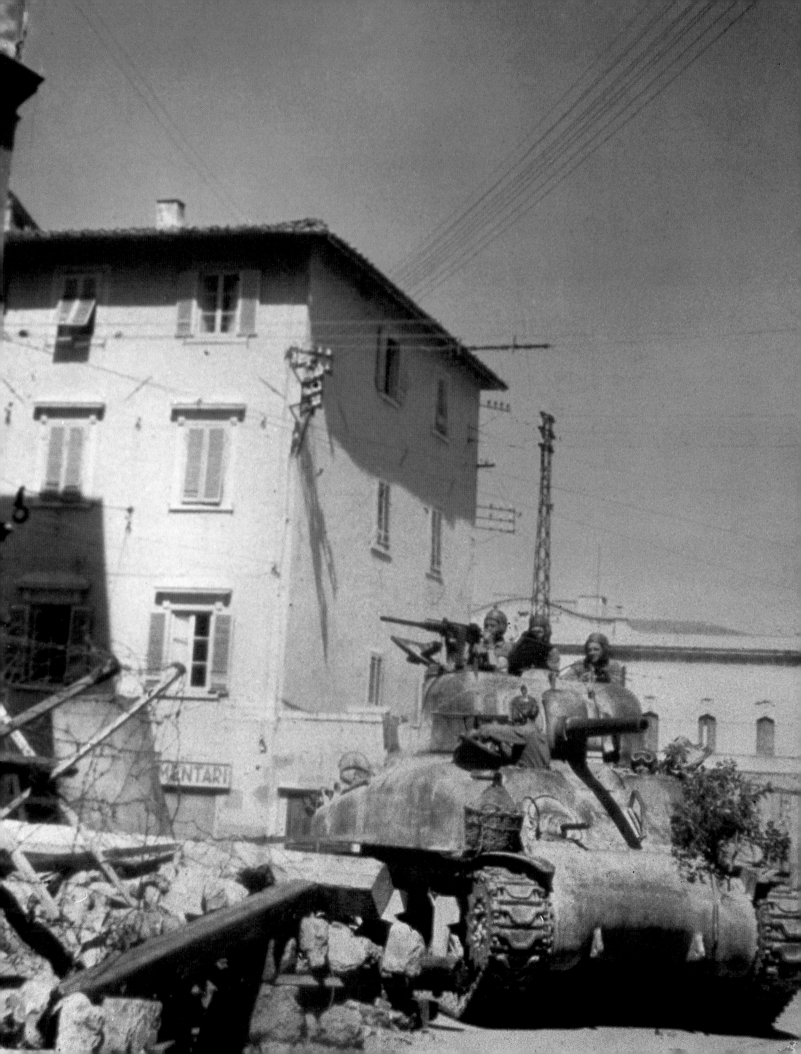

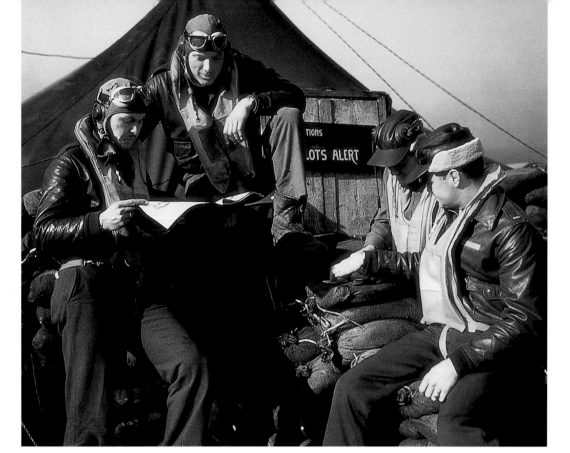

Four U.S. Army pilots discuss their mission outside their tent on the Aleutian Islands, in the northern Pacific.

BATTLE FOR THE ALEUTIANS

Two of the Alaskan Aleutian Islands—Altu and Kiska—were occupied by Japan in June 1942. For the next nine months the Japanese were constantly harassed by U.S.A.A.F. bombing raids from the nearby islands of Adak and Amchitka. The land battle to liberate Altu in May 1943 was particularly vicious, with only 28 Japanese survivors from a force of almost 2,500. When U.S. and Canadian forces landed on Kiska in August, they found that the invaders had evacuated the island without a fight.

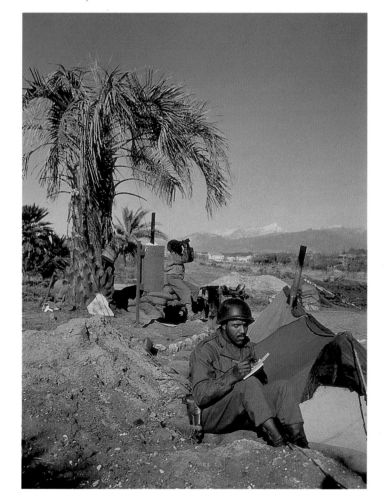

Private Wesley Smith, of Brooklyn, New York, writing home to his mother. He was attached to Headquarters Company, 92nd Division.

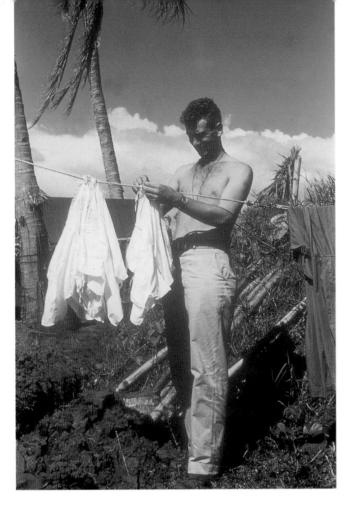

LEFT
The tropical sun helps on wash day.

BELOW
Papua New Guinea: troops stationed there pose with "natives" for a wartime souvenir.

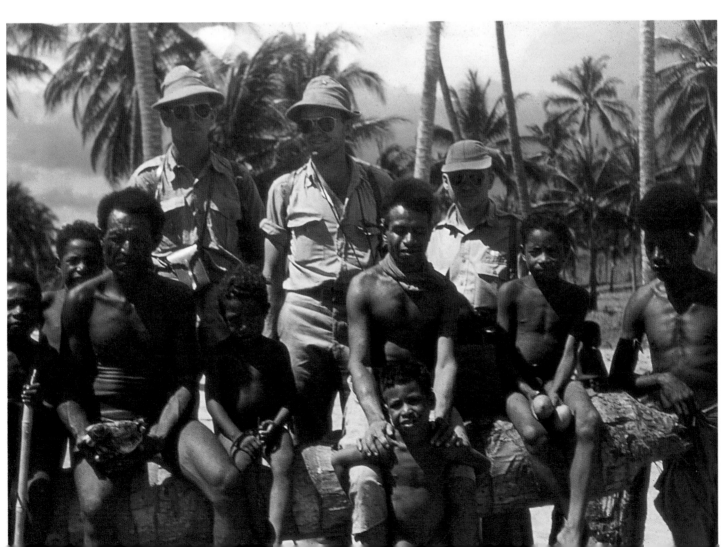

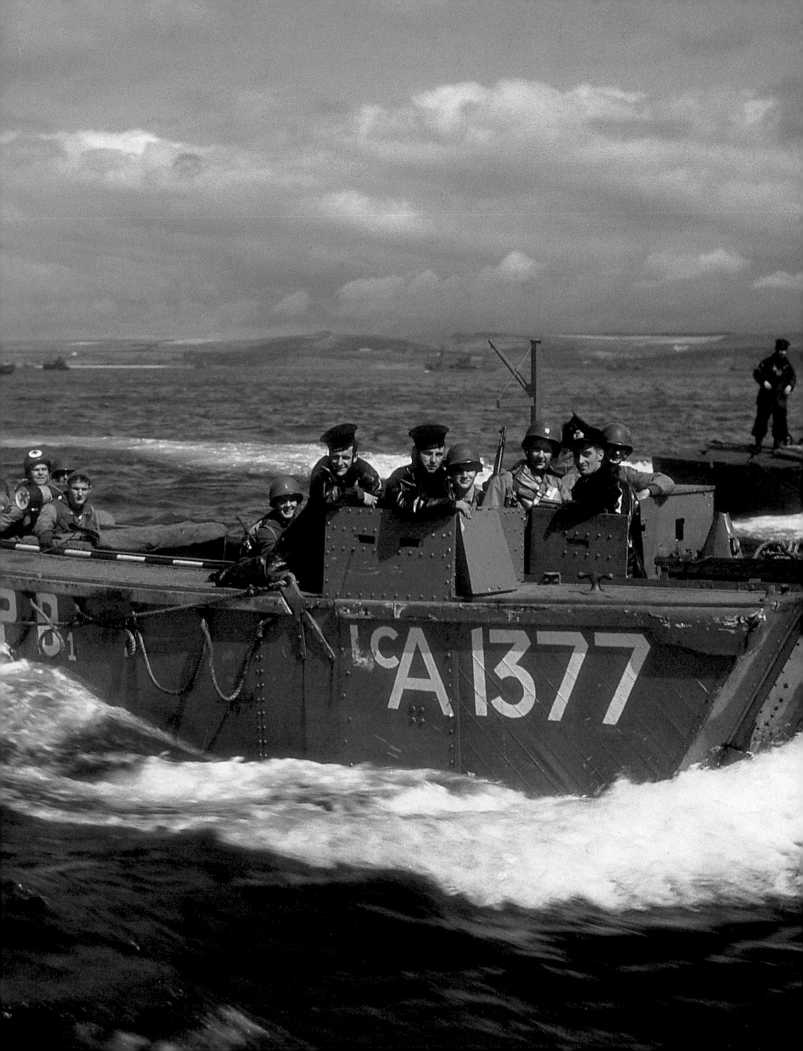

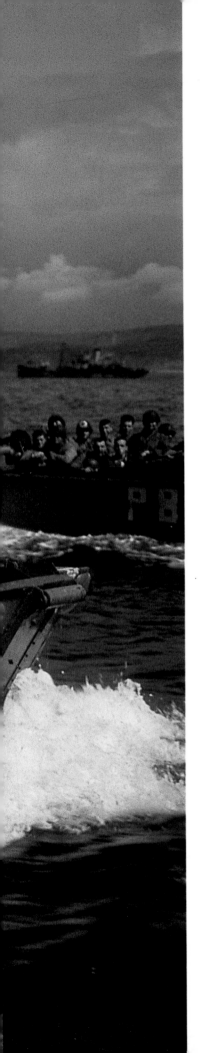

1944

BEACHHEAD TO BERLIN

Aт тне beginning оf 1944, тне writing was оn тне wall for тне Axis powers. Day by day, the military and economic strength of the Allies grew, fed by the great powerhouse of the United States, by the vast resources of Britain and its dominions and empire, and by the inexhaustible Red Army. That Japan and Germany resisted the inevitable for a further eighteen months is a reflection of the fanaticism of their leaders. In January 1944 there were significant break-throughs on the Eastern Front, in the Mediterranean, and in the Pacific.

On November 3, 1943, Hitler had issued a strategic directive acknowledging that the situation on the Eastern Front was serious. But, concerned about the threat of invasion from the west, he had decided not to reinforce his eastern armies until the western invasion had been repulsed. Hitler was prepared to buy time by sacrificing his eastern army and conceding territory on the Eastern Front. His generals must have known the strategy was flawed, but at the slightest hint of dissent they were replaced by younger, more aggressive commanders. The Red Army attacked in the north on January 14, and on January 27 Stalin declared the long siege of Leningrad over, as Soviet forces crossed the Moscow–Leningrad railway line.

In Italy, the Germans had used the winter conditions to establish a series of defensive positions—which the Allies called the "Winter Line"—south of

Rome. In an attempt to outflank the German line, on January 22, 1944, the Allies mounted an amphibious assault north and south of Anzio. It was not their most successful offensive: the U.S. Navy's official historian later said that putting such a modest force ashore was akin to sending a boy on a man's errand. The problems arose not from the landings themselves, which were largely unopposed, but from the attackers' failure to break out from their beachhead. By January 27, when the Allies were ready to advance, the German commander in Italy, Field Marshal Albert Kesselring, had brought six divisions to hold the perimeter. The Allies had over 5,000 casualties by the end of the month, including the

Landing craft in an English estuary churn through the water loaded with G.I.s in a D-Day training exercise in 1944.

greater part of two battalions of U.S. Rangers, wiped out at Cisterna in an ambush. Not until the end of May were they able to break out from their encirclement to join the advance on Rome.

The key to the approach to Rome, and to the relief of the forces stranded at Anzio, was Monte Cassino, a fortified town with, above it, on a rocky promontory, an ancient monastery of great historical significance. The defenders were the best of the German army: panzer grenadiers and paratroopers. Between January and May 1944 there were four battles, featuring both astonishing bravery and gross incompetence. The Allied forces were a truly international mix and the battles and subsequent advance on Rome produced heroic contributions from, among others, Free French troops, New Zealanders and the 2nd Polish Corps, made up of Polish émigrés. On May 17, with their defensive line disintegrating around them, the Germans withdrew, allowing the Poles their moment of glory in capturing the hill. Sadly, the sixth-century Benedictine monastery had been reduced to rubble by Allied shelling. The Allies now seized the initiative, and on June 4 General Mark Clark and the U.S. Fifth Army captured Rome. It was an historic moment: though the Italians had surrendered the previous year, Rome was the first Axis capital city to fall.

It was many months since Hitler's "soft underbelly" had been pierced in a campaign intended to preoccupy him and deflect his forces from the main objective: the invasion of France and liberation of Europe.

U.S. forces had been building up in Britain for two years, and by spring 1944 over a million G.I.s had arrived. The call to arms in America had been phenomenal. In 1939, U.S. armed forces personnel totaled less than 350,000—by the end of the war they numbered 12 million. This was a huge accomplishment. Not only had they to be recruited, they had to be equipped, clothed, fed, entertained, and kept reasonably happy. Most importantly, they had to be trained to resist and overcome two remarkably belligerent enemies, the like of which the world had never seen before. That U.S. forces acquitted themselves so well is a tribute not only to their own skill and tenacity, but also to the legion of civilians back home who supported them. The U.S. fighting machine had been built almost from scratch and had learned the rules as it went along.

In Britain, the G.I.s were both welcome and unwelcome. The cry "Overpaid, oversexed and over here" succinctly expressed British resentment at the impact the flamboyant young Americans had on a war-weary nation.

Historical inevitability is one thing, but battles still have to be won and wars have to be brought to a conclusion with the minimum of casualties. This was the challenge for General Dwight D. Eisenhower and his fellow planners in 1944. Failure in the Allied invasion of northern Europe would have delayed the end of the war by many months, perhaps even years, and cost countless lives. Two key elements had to be guaranteed: overwhelming numbers and resources, and surprise. The former meant that the whole of southern England had to be transformed into an armed camp; the latter required a web of intrigue and fabrication which would have been comical had it not been so serious.

The obvious place to attack was across the narrowest part of the English Channel, towards Calais, so the Allies endeavored to persuade the Germans that this was the objective. General Patton was chosen as the decoy force's commander and dummy camps, tanks, men, equipment, and intelligence information were constructed to convince the German High Command. Set-builders from the film industry were employed to make cardboard tanks and barracks look authentic. Allied ULTRA intelligence, by intercepting German military communiqués, confirmed that the bait had been swallowed. The Germans, under Field Marshal Rommel's command, built massive defenses along the Pas de Calais—Rommel believed the battle would be won or lost on the beaches—closely supported by armored units.

Meanwhile, the real invasion was planned for Normandy, further to the west. Operation Overlord was much more than a beach assault: it involved sustained bombing of German positions, prolonged information-gathering and sabotage by the French Resistance, and an airborne assault behind enemy lines to disrupt defenses and destroy lines of communication.

The invasion was set for June 5, but bad weather forced a day's delay. June 6, 1944, became D-Day, the "beginning of the end" for Nazi Germany.

Nearly 7,000 ships took the troops across the Channel. Overhead, massive aerial support guaranteed aerial supremacy. Ahead of the main invasion force, over 23,000 British and U.S. airborne troops had already landed on the flanks of the chosen beaches, which were code-named Utah, Omaha, Gold, Juno, and Sword. As in all crucial battles, there was terrible carnage: Some U.S. units, in the first wave of landings at Omaha beach, suffered 90 percent casualties. The bombing of German positions had been too deep and had missed its targets, German reinforcements were better-quality troops than expected, and the low tide meant that many craft could not get close inshore, so that the G.I.s had to cross a vast expanse of open beach under overwhelming enemy fire. Nevertheless, the men fought heroically, and eventually succeeded in establishing a beachhead.

Though a terrible price had been paid—Allied dead numbered nearly 2,500—by the end of the war's "longest day" over 150,000 men were ashore: the "Beachhead to Berlin" had been secured. But now further disadvantages of landing in Normandy became clear. The surrounding countryside was a mixture of woodland, intricate field systems, narrow lanes, and ditches and hedgerows, all of which provided ideal defensive positions for the Germans. It took almost four months to reach and liberate Paris.

In Asia in 1944, the Allies' main aim was to continue the advance in the central Pacific, westward from the Marshall Islands to the Marianas and, ultimately, to the Philippines.

In addition, U.S. personnel lent support in the main British theater of operations on the Asian mainland, to which Burma was the key. British and Indian troops bore the brunt of the fighting, but Generals "Vinegar Joe" Stilwell and Claire Chennault organized two significant American contributions. Chennault's airmen provided a crucial air link to China over the Himalayas, and aerial support for the British and Indian forces on the ground; while Stilwell assisted General Chiang Kai-Shek's Chinese nationalists in their struggle against the Japanese. Among Stilwell's troops in Burma from March to August 1944 was the Galahad volunteer U.S. commando force, nicknamed "Merrill's Marauders" after their commander, General Frank. D. Merrill, which included Sioux and Japanese-American soldiers. The Marauders fought with great distinction behind Japanese lines, in parallel with British General Orde Wingate's Chindits.

By the beginning of 1944, U.S. forces had retaken huge areas of the Pacific. General MacArthur was making steady progress in New Guinea, with the Philippines as his ultimate objective. The next major targets in the Pacific were the crucial Mariana Islands—particularly Tinian, Saipan, and Guam—which would bring Japan within range of B-29 heavy bombers for the first time.

The battle for Saipan, in June 1944, was fierce. The 30,000 Japanese troops, under General Saito, were well dug in and a large fleet was on hand to wreak havoc on the U.S. assault fleet. It took over three weeks to subdue the island at the cost of over 3,000 American lives. The horrendous—over 23,000—Japanese losses included many civilians who, terrified by stories of rape, torture and death, threw themselves off the island's northern cliffs.

Guam and Tinian were captured in the following weeks. On Guam, the main force of defenders was weakened by accurate air and sea bombardment, but pockets of resistance remained for some time. Incredibly, it was not until 1972 that the last soldier surrendered after he was discovered still hiding in the jungle. Tinian fell in just twelve days, though some Japanese die-hards held out for over three months.

The retaking of the Marianas was the final straw for General Tojo, the Japanese prime minister, and he resigned from office. Perhaps even more significant than the islands' capture was the accompanying naval battle, the Battle of the Philippine Sea. Five Japanese aircraft carriers and their accompanying vessels faced seven U.S. carriers. The Japanese hoped their pilots would inflict such severe damage on the U.S. fleet that it would be unable to support the landings. They were wrong. The U.S. fleet picked up the Japanese ships on radar and was well prepared when the attacking aircraft appeared. The Japanese lost 350 planes, more than ten times the U.S. losses, and three aircraft carriers (two to U.S. submarines), and were unable to mount a serious carrier threat for the rest of the war.

The tide that had turned in 1943 was now running strongly in the Allies' favor. There had even been an assassination attempt on Hitler, plotted by senior members of the armed forces, but it had narrowly failed. By the end of 1944 Allied forces had liberated almost the whole of France and Belgium and, despite the ill-fated circumstances of Operation Market Garden (airborne assaults and armored advance across the Rhine at Arnhem), they held a strategic salient in Holland.

In the Pacific, U.S. forces went on from the Marianas to land in the Philippines at Leyte. The landings were accompanied by the Battle of Leyte Gulf, the "greatest naval battle in history," involving over 230 Japanese and American warships and almost 2,000 planes. There were heavy losses on both sides, but the Japanese could afford them far less than the Americans and suffered yet another mortal blow, despite the actions of a new and terrifying weapon, the suicide pilots of the "divine wind," kamikaze.

PREPARATIONS FOR WAR IN WESTERN EUROPE

By early 1944, preparations were well advanced for the invasion of western Europe. The biggest task facing the Allies was to try to gain an element of surprise for an attack that both sides knew to be inevitable and imminent.

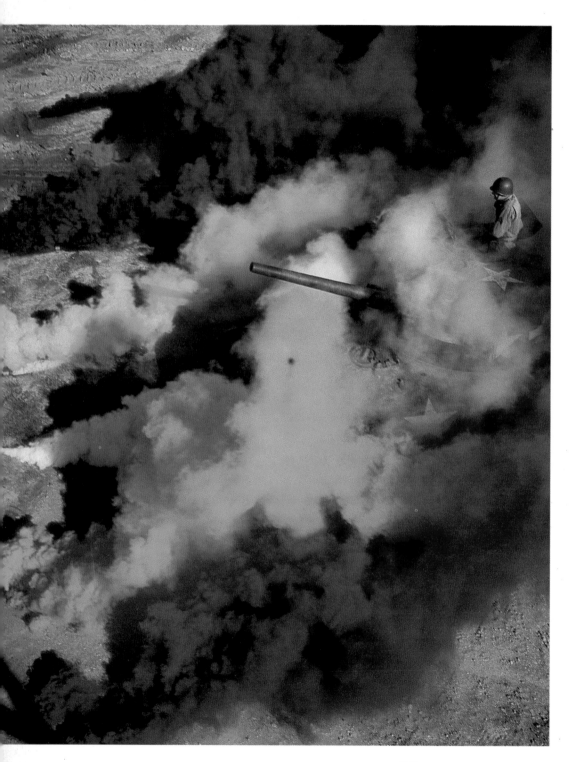

LEFT
Colored smoke grenades surround a Sherman tank in a test carried out by the Chemical Warfare Service at Edgewood Arsenal, Maryland. Six different colors were found to be identifiable from an altitude of 10,000 feet, thus minimizing the incidence of casualties caused by "friendly fire."

RIGHT
With the aid of searchlights an ack-ack battery fires at night.

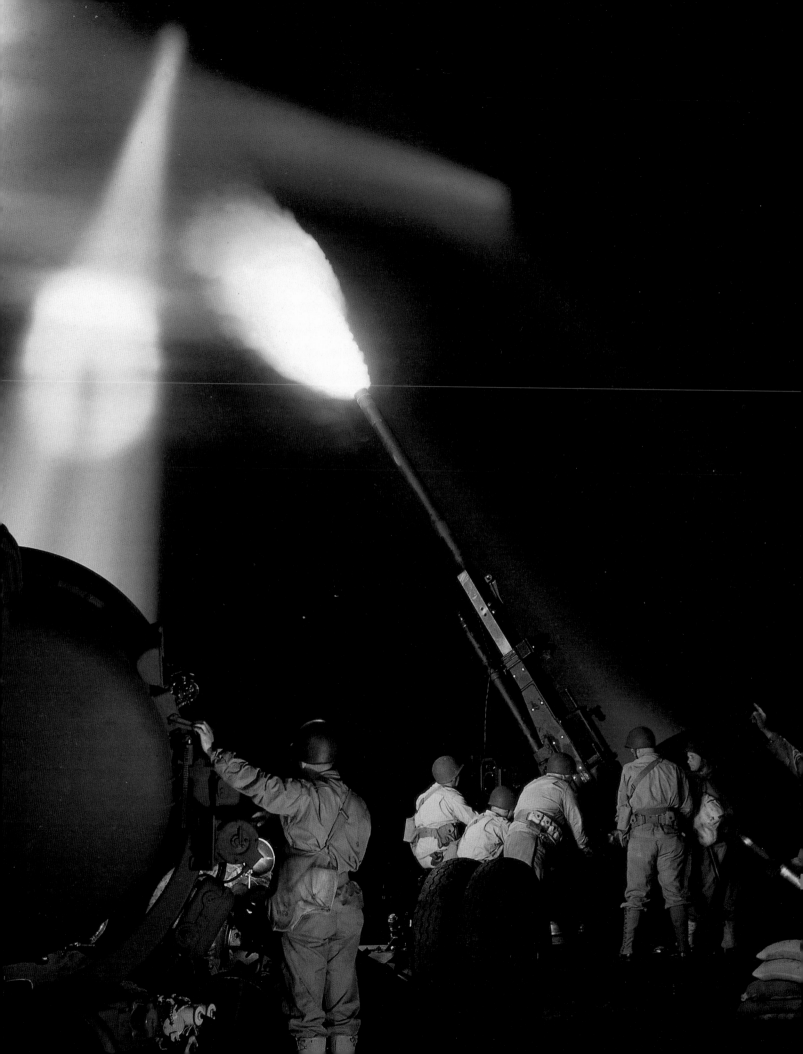

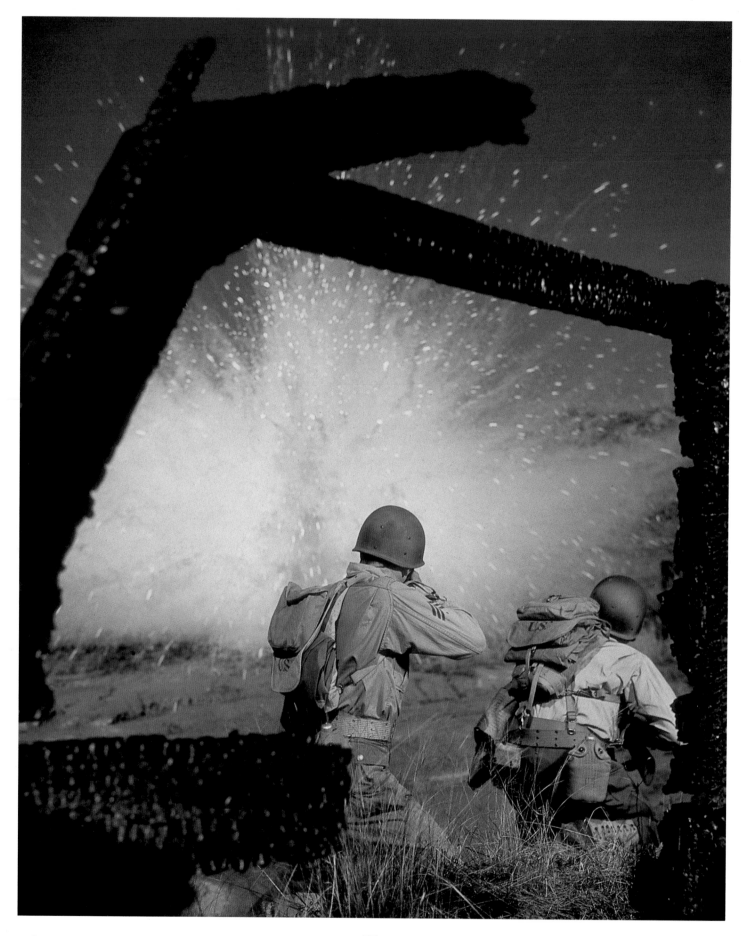

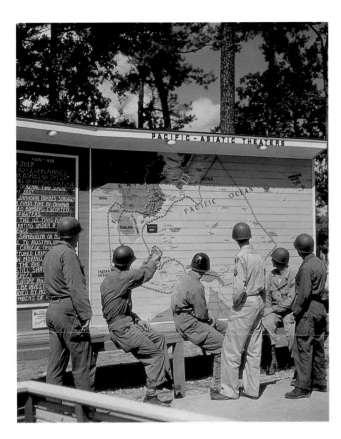

LEFT

In 1944, new recruits look at a world map to keep up to date with activities in the Pacific and Asian theaters in the war against Japan.

LEFT

Phosphor grenade training at the Edgewood Arsenal, Maryland. White phosphor was used in bombs, shells, and grenades because the smoke it produced offered the greatest "TOP" (total obscuring power).

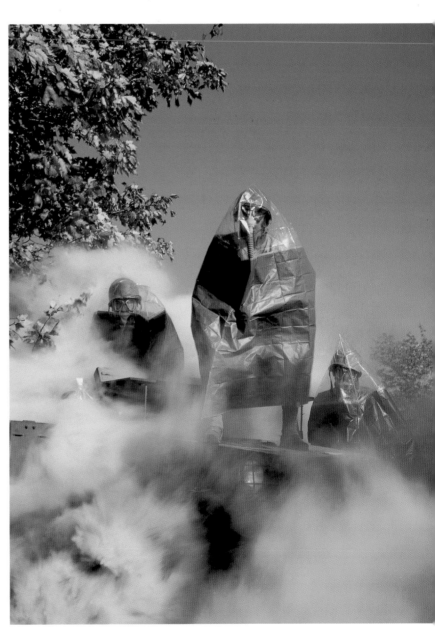

RIGHT

Special suits worn by infantry to protect against possible attack by chemical warfare weapons.

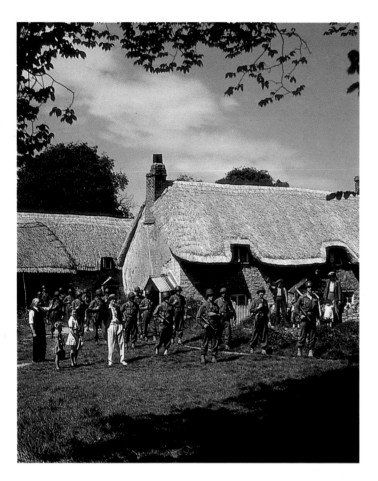

Lieutenant Ben Clemints leads his patrol through an English farmyard on a pre-D-Day exercise in May 1944.

PREPARATION FOR D-DAY

Stringent security measures were introduced to maintain secrecy in the lead-up to D-Day. All plans were given the classification of BIGOT and all those privy to them were said to be "BIGOTed." A coastal strip, 10 miles deep, across southern England—from the Wash to Land's End—was closed to all except authorized travelers. The D-Day planners believed that the scale of the attack made daylight visibility essential for the assault forces, and that the pre-invasion airborne attack needed a full moon. This meant that there was an extremely narrow window of opportunity from June 5–7. June 5 was chosen, but bad weather forced a days delay.

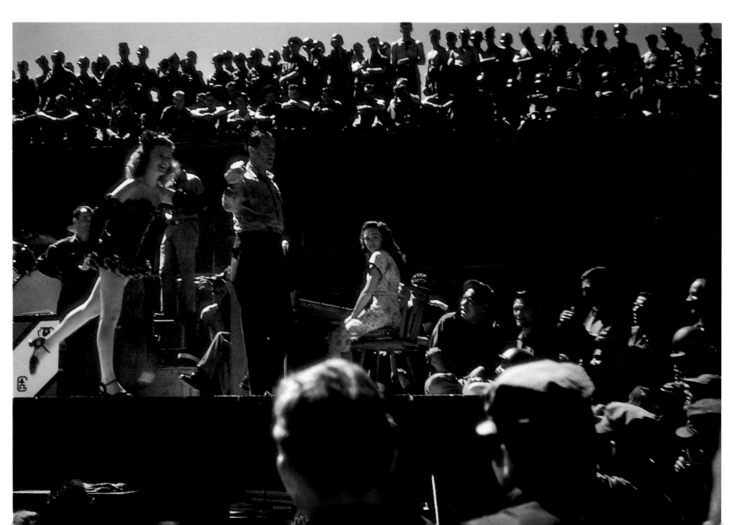

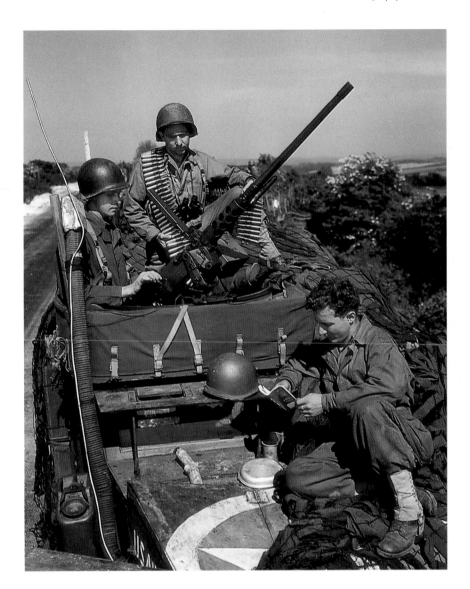

LEFT

(L–R) Corporal John Hartlage, of Brees, Illinois, Corporal Edward L. Smith of St. Paul, Minnesota and Private George Roberts of Herndon, Virginia, photographed in a half-track parked in southern England shortly before embarkation for D-Day in summer 1944.

BELOW

In spring 1944, as a rehearsal for the invasion of France, several amphibious assault exercises were held on Slapton Sands, Devon, England. This elevated shot shows three landing craft on the beach. It reveals little of the tragedy, during "Operation Tiger," in April 1944, when over 600 U.S. troops were killed when their assault craft were attacked by German motor-torpedo boats.

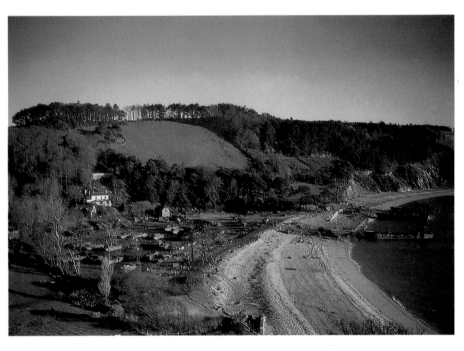

LEFT

Entertainer Bob Hope introduces dancer Patty Thomas to members of the 55th Fighter Group at an open-air concert in England.

THE NORMANDY LANDINGS

D-Day, June 6, 1944, the crucial day of Operation Overlord—the Allied invasion of France—was the greatest amphibious invasion in history. Over a million men prepared for this assault on the Normandy beaches. Three airborne divisions (two American, one British) proceeded to secure the flanks of the landings on five beaches, *Utah* and *Omaha* for the Americans and *Gold*, *Juno* and *Sword* for the British and Canadians.

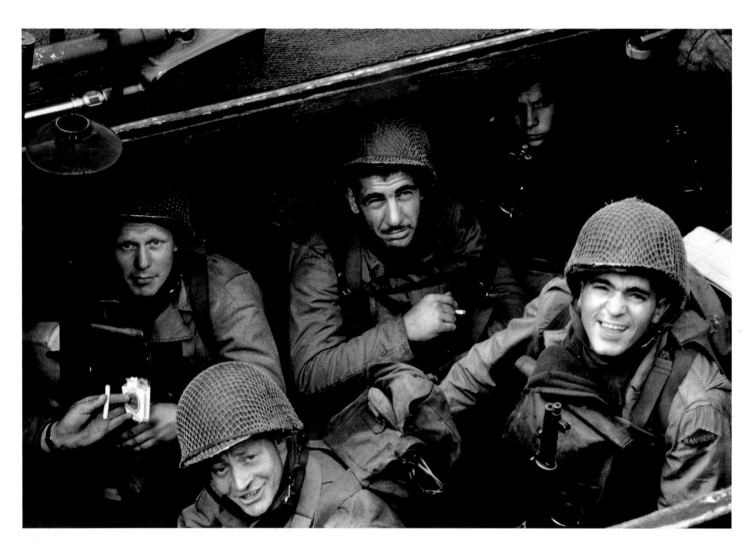

ABOVE

Troops in an L.C.A. at Weymouth harbor, England, attempt a smile for the lens of a Signal Corps combat photographer's lens.

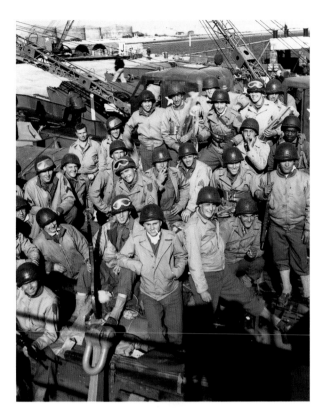

ABOVE

Troops, possibly of the 1st Infantry Division, pose on a landing craft in Weymouth harbor in June 1944, before setting sail. The African American soldier on the extreme right is probably attached to the unit from an engineer battalion.

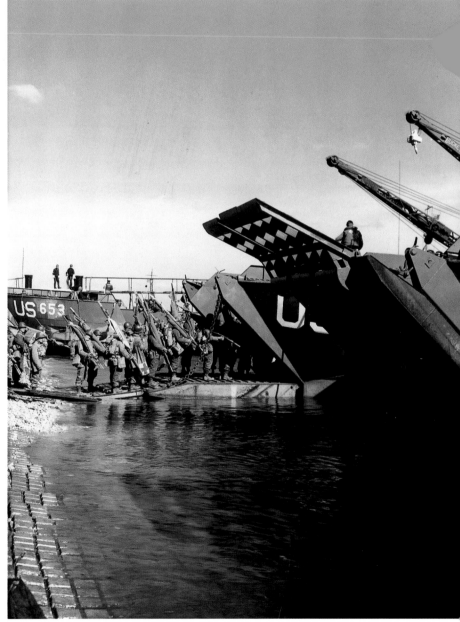

RIGHT

Medics and stretcher bearers board landing craft in Weymouth harbor on June 5, 1944. There was an unwritten code of ethics on the battlefield, whereby German and Allied troops would not target medics aiding wounded comrades. This was in sharp contrast to the policy of the Japanese army, which regarded medics as primary targets.

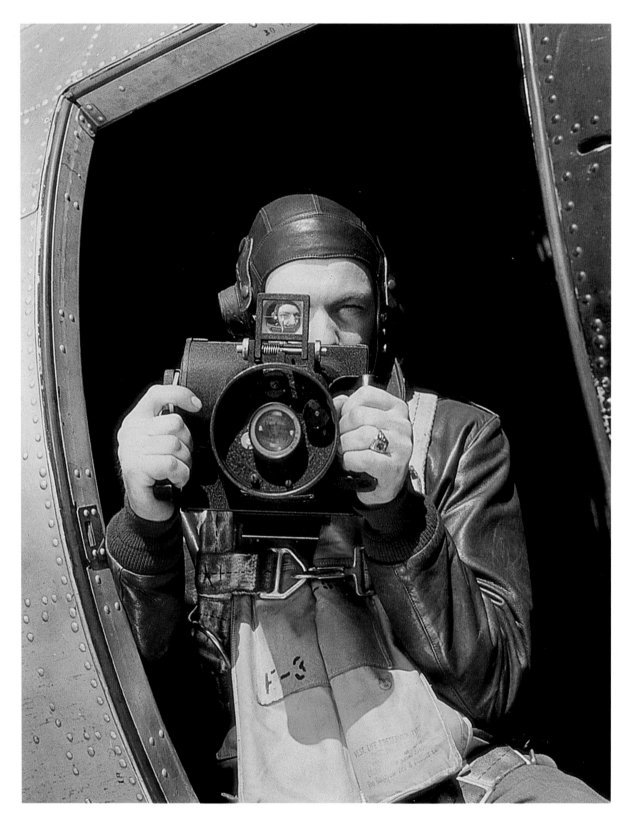

ABOVE

Staff Sergeant Brush of the U.S.A.A.F. poses
with a K20 aerial reconnaissance camera at the
waist-gun window of a B-17 bomber. The first
aerial pictures of the invasion flotilla and
beachheads were taken with this camera.

BELOW

A Normandy beachhead as D-Day—June 6, 1944—draws to a close.
Although ultimately successful, the landings were hampered by fierce
resistance from German positions in the sandy cliffs and the loss of many
of the tanks, meant to accompany the assaulting infantry, in the choppy
waters. Here, Allied troops are still coming ashore, whilst a temporary
enclosure for German prisoners of war has been erected in the foreground.

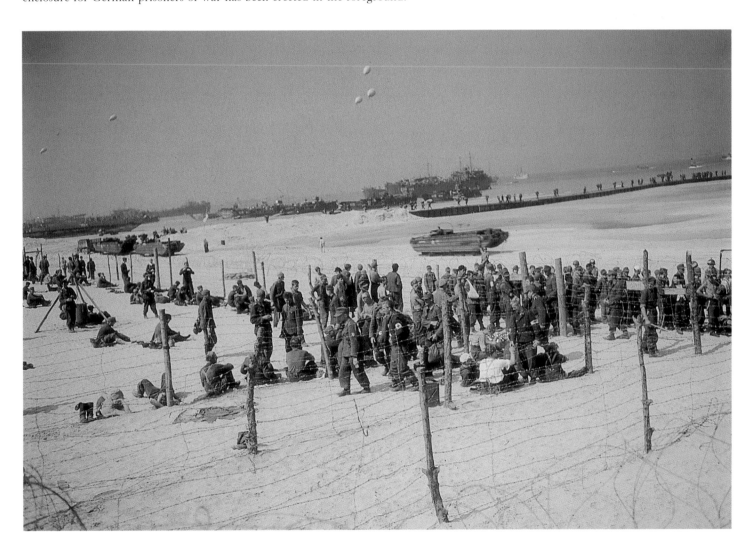

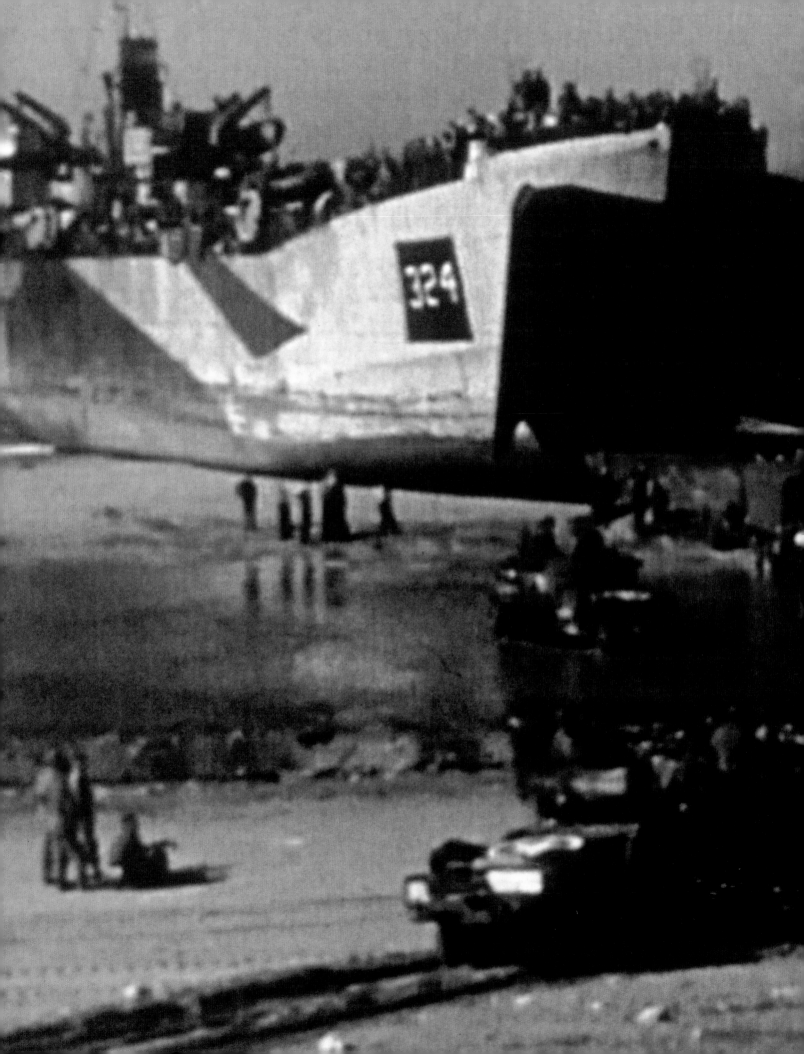

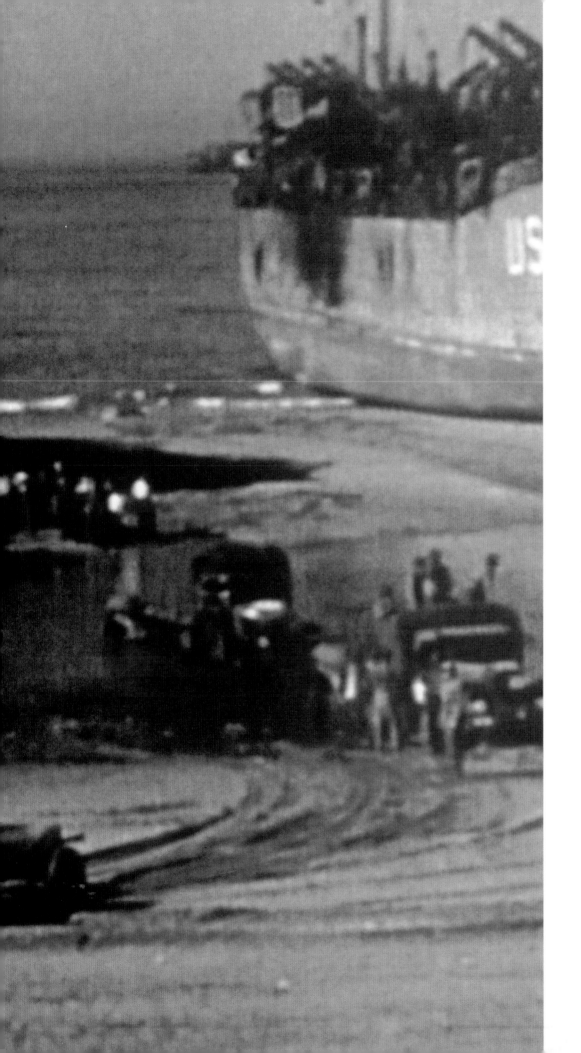

LEFT
The Normandy Landings
were a logistic operation of
unprecedented scale. Here,
Allied troops in trucks
disembark from a landing
craft on a beachhead.

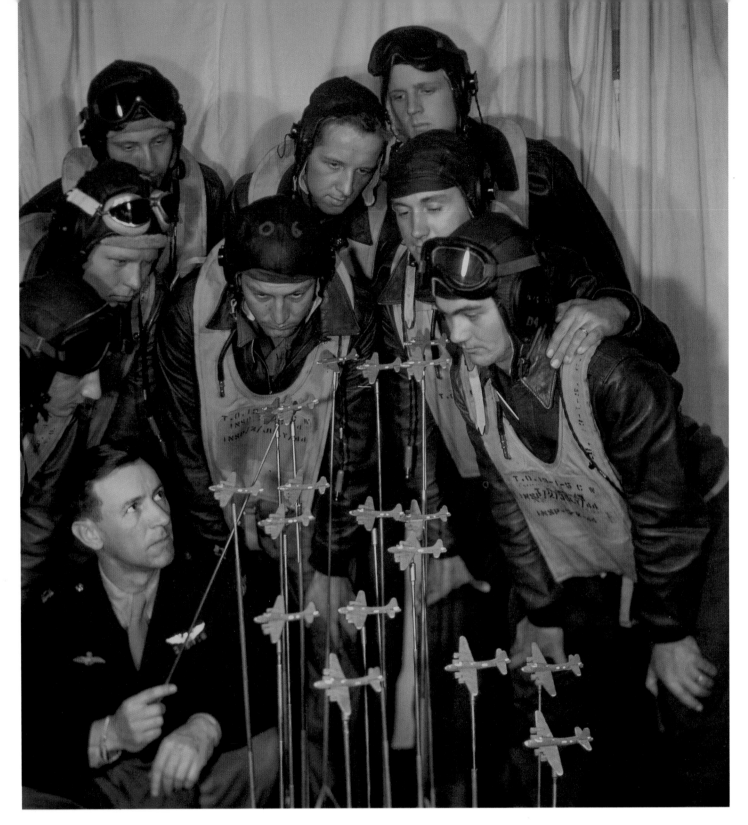

AERIAL BOMBARDMENT

As the circle of Allied forces closed around Hitler's Germany, Allied air power and the bombardment of German cities and manufacturing became a more and more important factor in destroying the German people's ability and will to resist.

Captain Jack Westward of Lewiston, Idaho, instructs aircrew on details of formation flying, in 1944.

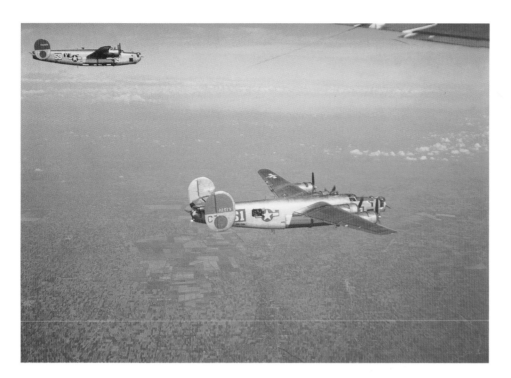

ABOVE

Consolidated B-24 "Liberator" bombers of the
15th Army Airforce en route to bomb the
Oswiecim Oil refinery, 60 miles from Krakow,
Poland, then under German occupation. The town
is better known by its German name, Auschwitz.

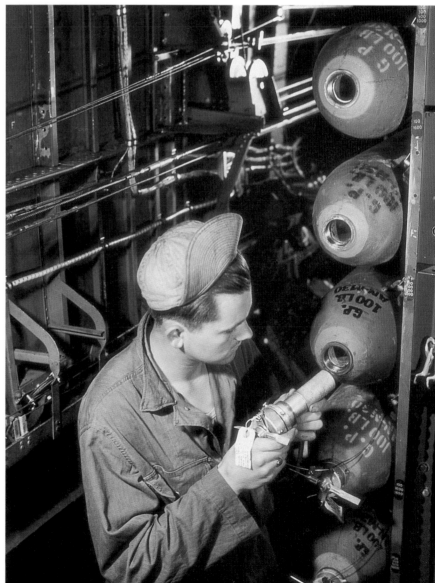

RIGHT

Fuses are inserted into 100lb bombs on a B-24 bomber.

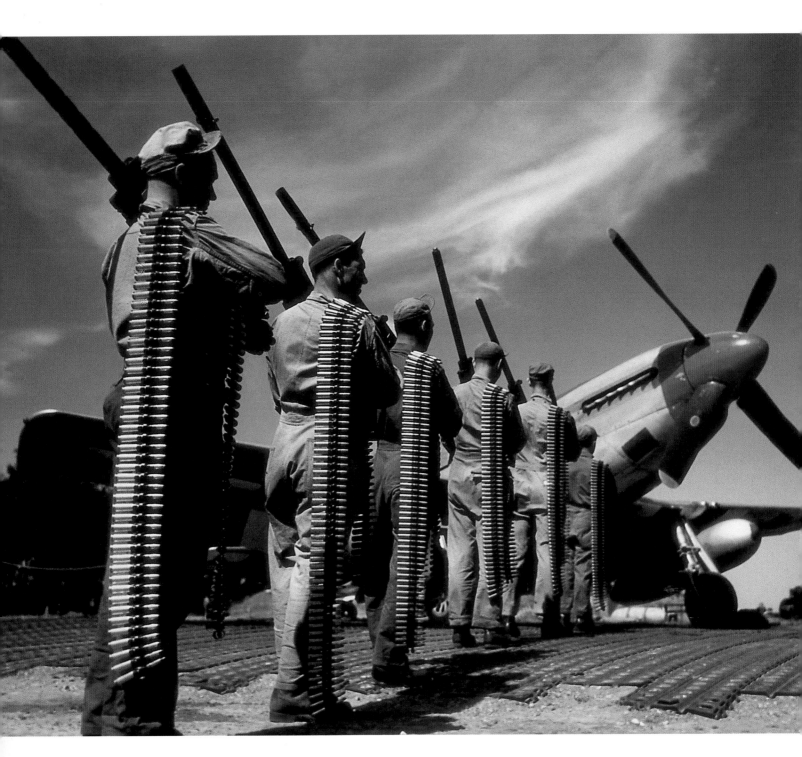

ABOVE
Canon shells being carried to a P-51 Mustang in
summer 1944. This amount of ammunition is a
sixth of that required by just one of its six guns.

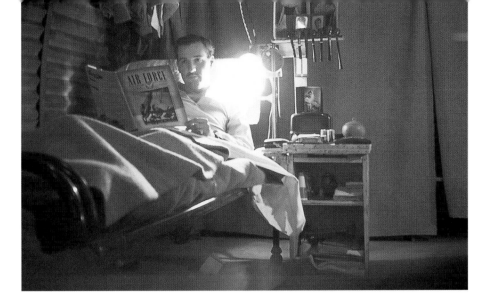

9th Air Force Marauder pilot
Jack Havener in his bed at
camp in Stanstead, England.

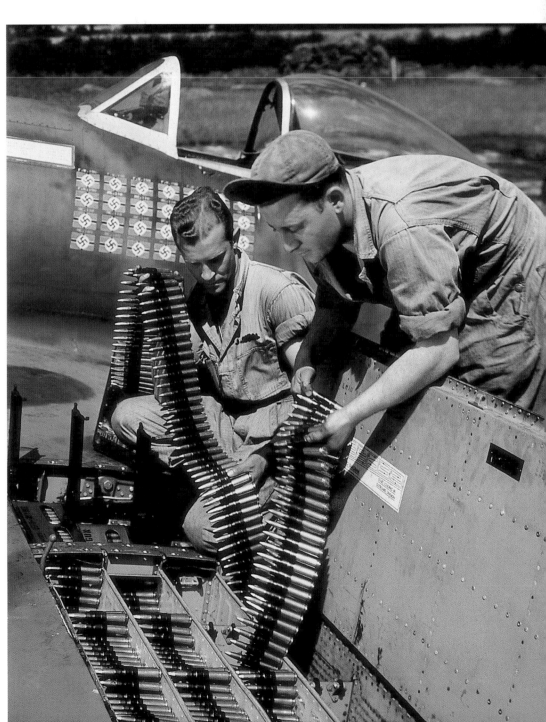

0.50-caliber machine-gun shells
being loaded into the wings of
a P-47 fighter in summer 1944.
Incorrect loading could lead to gun
jams and perhaps the death of a
pilot. This aircraft was flown by
the leading ace of the European
theater, Lieutenant Colonel Fram.

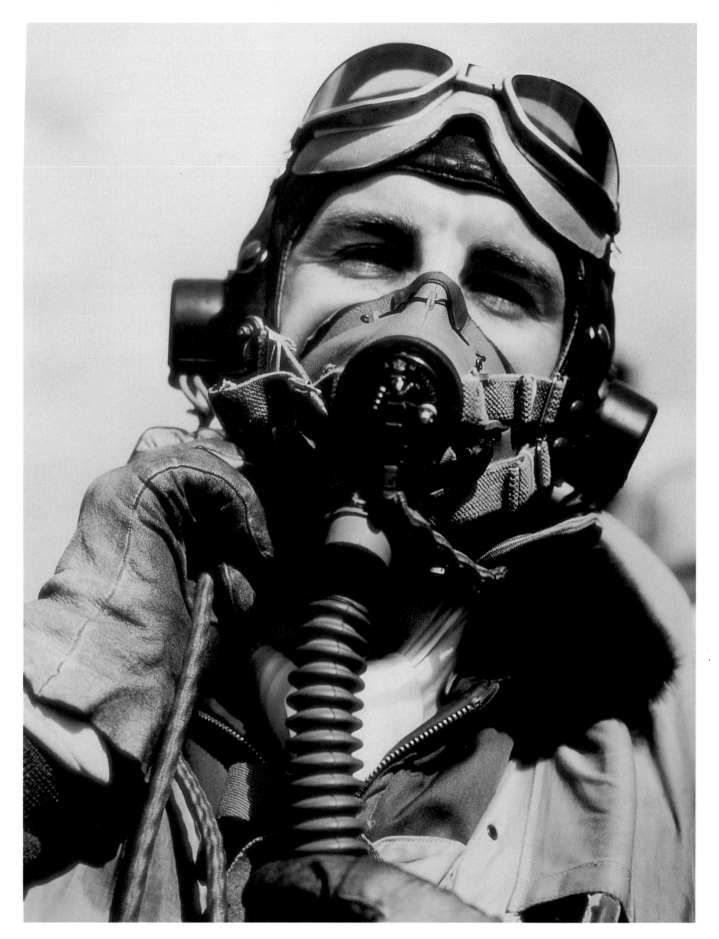

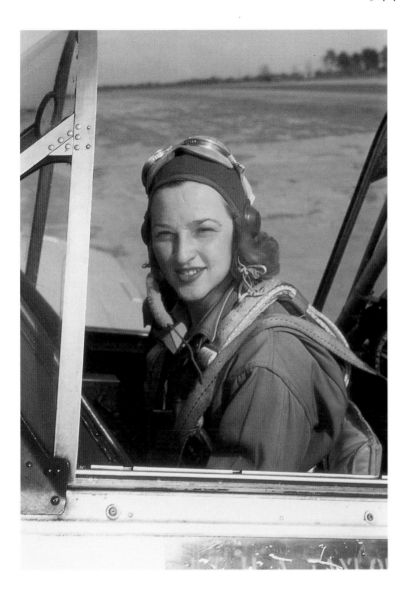

LEFT

A female ferry pilot smiles for the camera at Napier Air Force Base in February 1944. The Women's Auxiliary Ferrying Squadron (W.A.F.S.) was reformed in July, 1943 to become the Women's Airforce Service Pilots (W.A.S.P.s).

BELOW

Fighters from the 356th Fighter Group pass through contrails from bombers they are escorting over Germany.

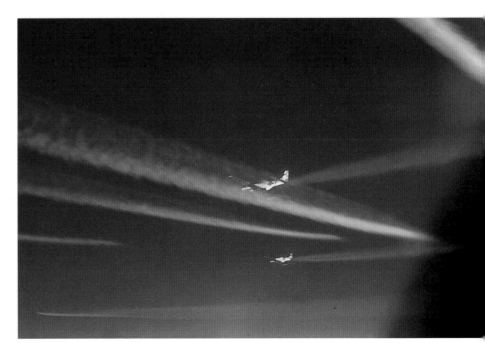

LEFT

P-47 fighter ace Lieutenant Colonel Francis S. "Gabby" Gabreski of the 56th Fighter Group. He recorded a total of 28 "kills."

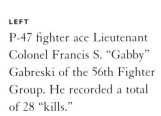

INVASION OF ITALY

The rapid collapse of Italian resistance to the Allies, and Mussolini's fall from power in mid-summer 1943, were an inevitable consequence of the weakness of the fascist cause in Italy. Unlike Hitler, Mussolini had been unable to effectively mobilize the Italian nation for the war effort, nor had he been able to suppress his opponents. When the end came for Mussolini and his regime, the blows were struck by the Italian people, not by the Allies.

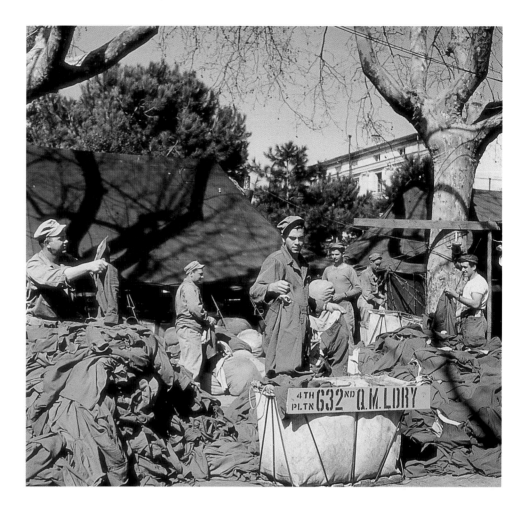

ABOVE

Mobile laundry kit exchange of 4th Platoon, 632 Quartermasters Laundry. The supply of clean uniforms and clothing was a major factor in maintaining troop morale in combat zones, as well as preventing disease and infection.

LEFT

Two army nurses pose by their washing line at a field hospital on the Italian Front, in winter 1944.

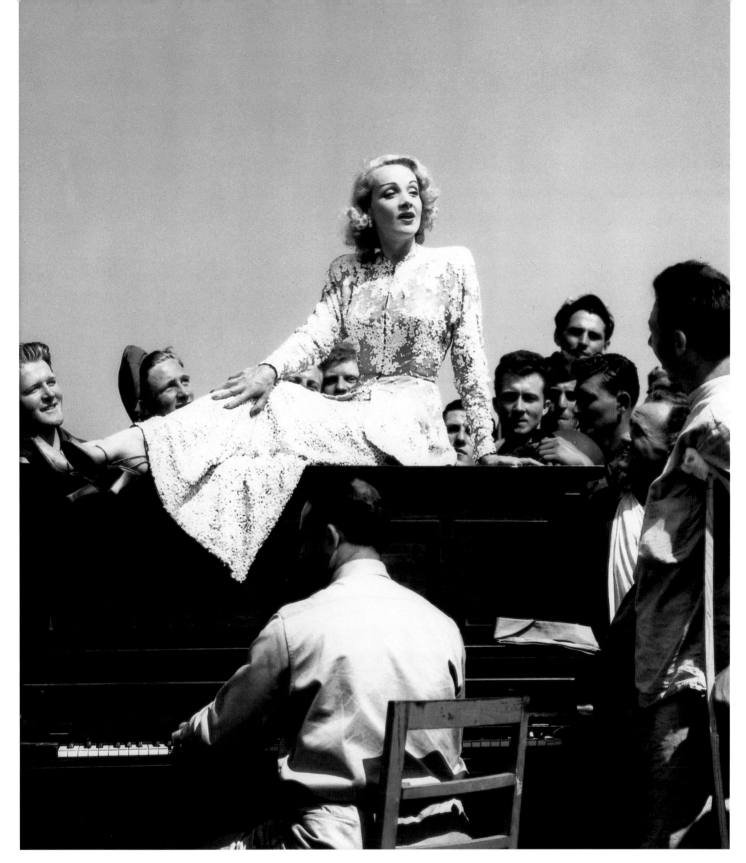

A characteristic pose by Marlene Dietrich, surrounded by
wounded troops at an evacuation hospital on the Italian
Front in May 1944. She had left Nazi Germany shortly
before the outbreak of war and moved to the U.S.A.

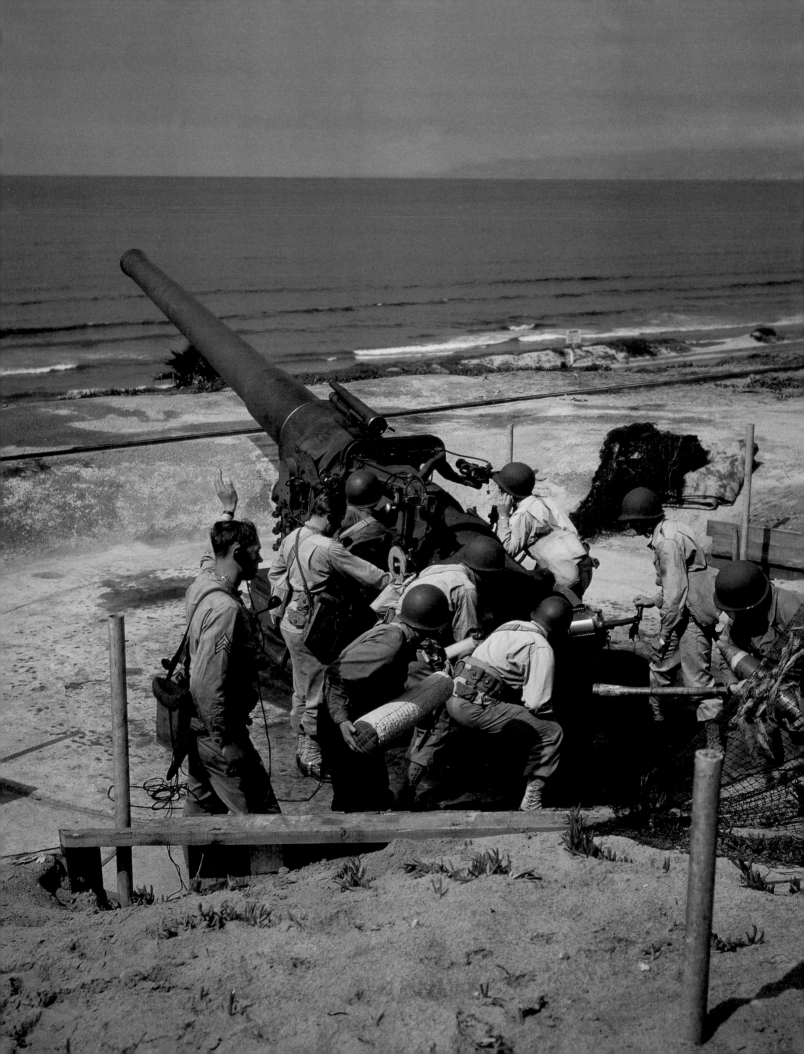

LEFT

A gun crew load a 155mm coastal defense gun on a beach in the United States. Although the threat of invasion had diminished, German U-boats still patrolled off the Eastern seaboard and continued vigilance was necessary.

RIGHT

Two G.I.s inspect the results of ferocious artillery fire on German positions on the Gothic Line, in a forest in the Apennine mountains, Italy.

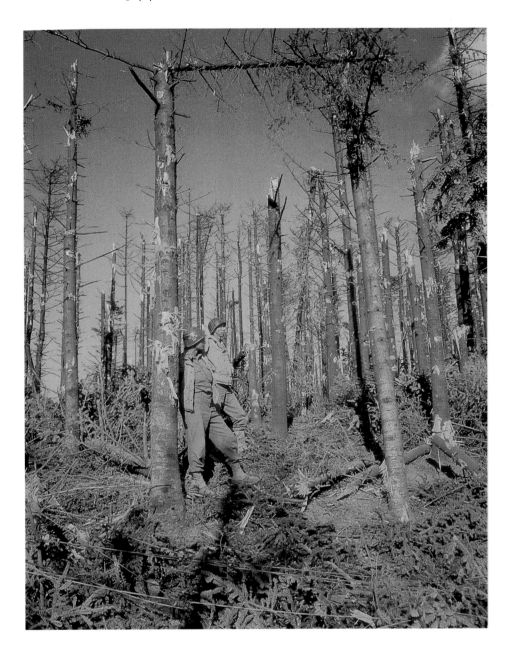

LEFT

An army truck passes an overturned Panzer tank, abandoned by the retreating Germans during the Italian campaign.

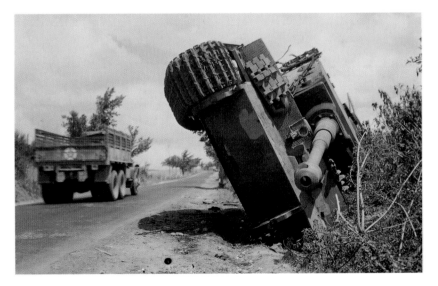

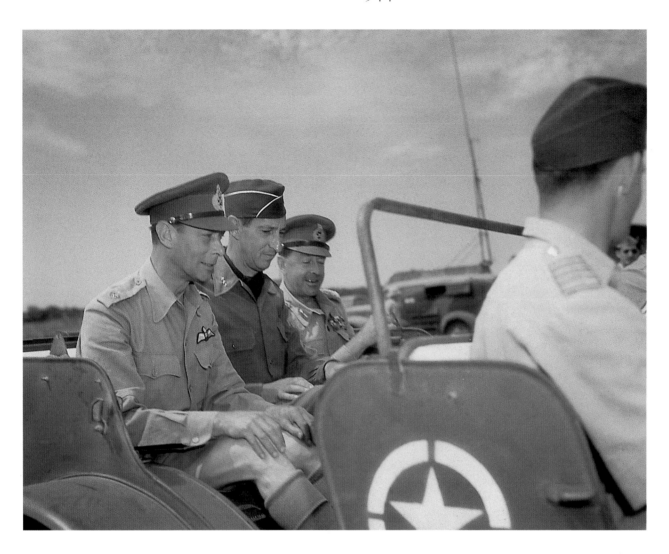

ABOVE

King George VI of Britain (left), Lieutenant General Mark Clark, Commander of the U.S. 5th Army (center), and British General Sir Harold Alexander (right) in a command car prior to a New Year inspection of the 5th Army in Italy.

RIGHT

A soldier of the 791st Ordnance, part of 91st Division, Private E. R. Williams of Raleigh, North Carolina, helps serve food to the liberated civilians of Monghidoro, near Bologna, Italy, on November 10, 1944. Food shortages during the German occupation had led to considerable malnutrition in Italy's civilian population.

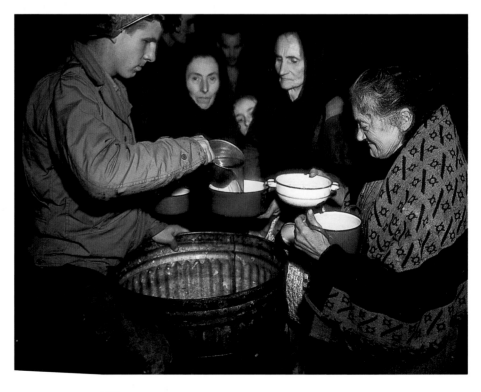

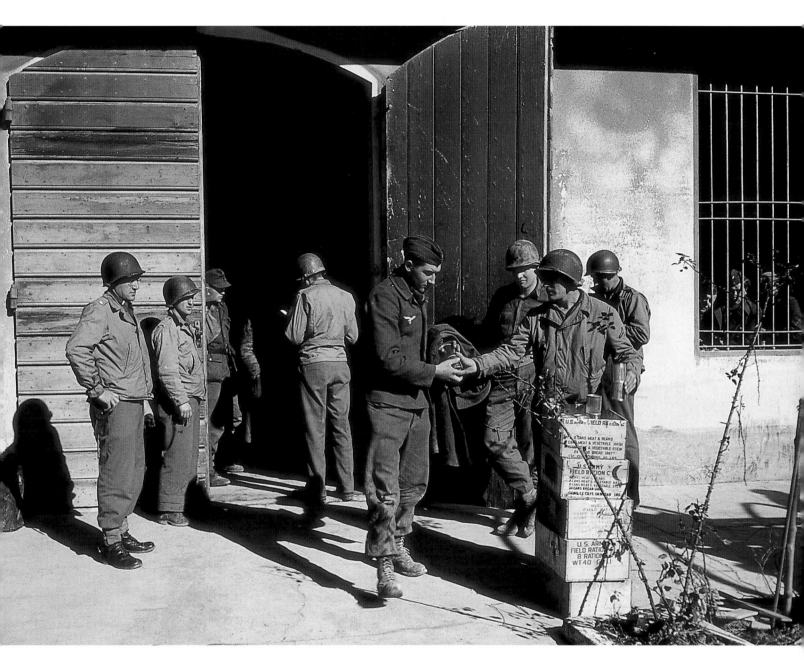

ABOVE

A German prisoner of war receives his rations before boarding a truck bound for Anzio, in early spring 1944, while other prisoners look on from behind bars.

RIGHT
Private Chester Kolano of the U.S. 5th
Army, from Buffalo, New York, kneels
by the grave of his fallen lieutenant, a
fellow Buffalonian.

BELOW
Army Air Corps Nurse Lieutenant
Frances Sale of Boise, Idaho, speaks with
an evacuated patient, Private First Class
Raymond Labell, in June 1944. He had
been wounded in the left shoulder and
was awaiting transport to Naples, Italy.

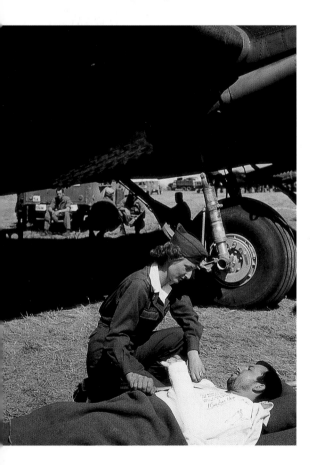

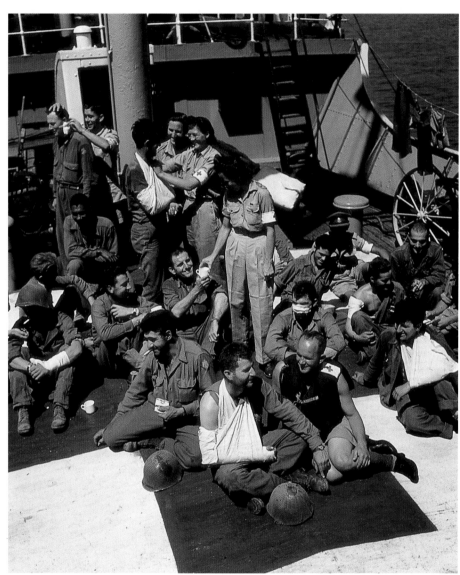

ABOVE
Wounded G.I.s and civilians being evacuated
from the Italian Front aboard a British
hospital ship in June 1944. The large red cross
painted on the deck was intended to present
clear identification to enemy aircraft.

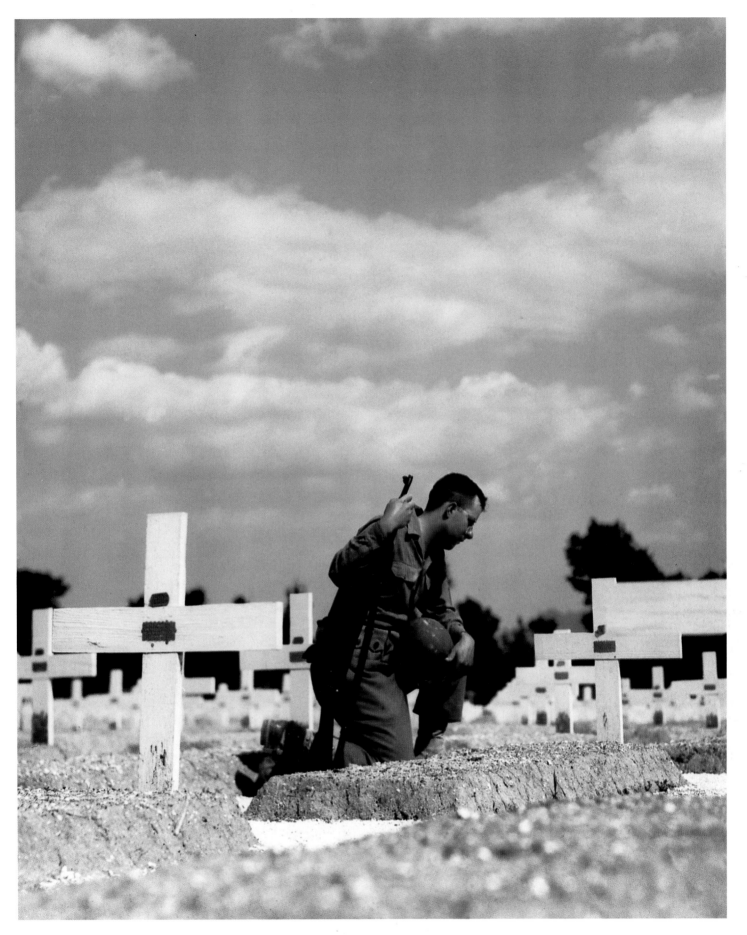

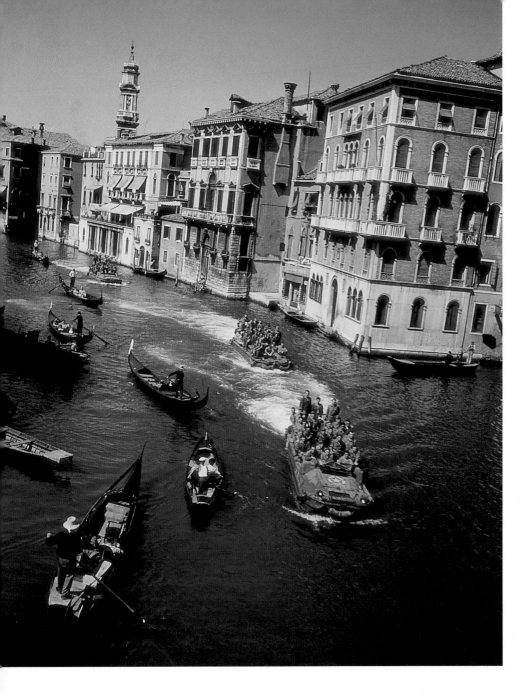

LEFT
DUKWs (amphibious six-wheeled trucks), previously utilized on the Anzio beachhead, were used as tour vehicles for G.I.s on the canals of Venice.

RIGHT
Pope Pius XII is mobbed by G.I.s at a Vatican audience, which he had granted so that he could give them his personal thanks for their role in the liberation of Rome. Although he welcomed the troops, he had previously sent a request to the Allies that Rome should not be garrisoned by black troops after its liberation.

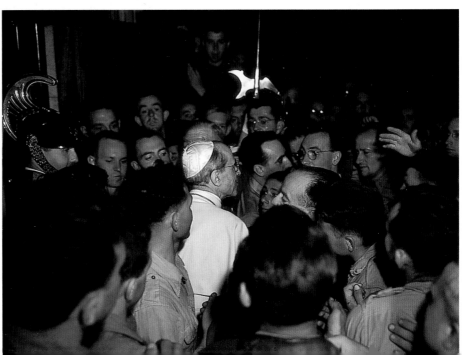

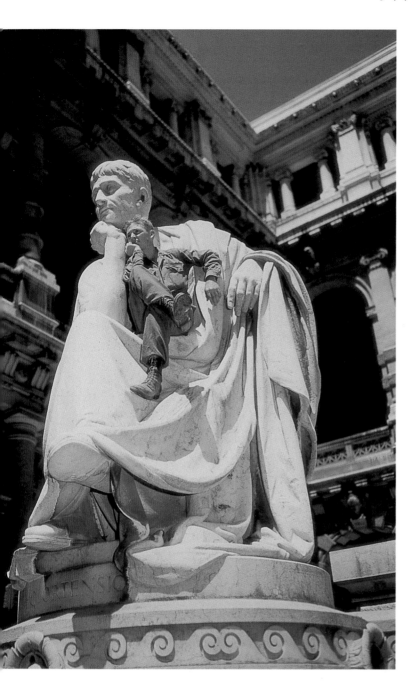

RIGHT

Two soldiers chat with a British "Tommy" beside a fountain in St. Peter's Square, Rome, in June 1944.

LEFT

Private Sisto A. Ganz of the 3rd Division, 5th U.S. Army, mimics the pose of a statue outside the Palace of Justice in Rome, in June 1944.

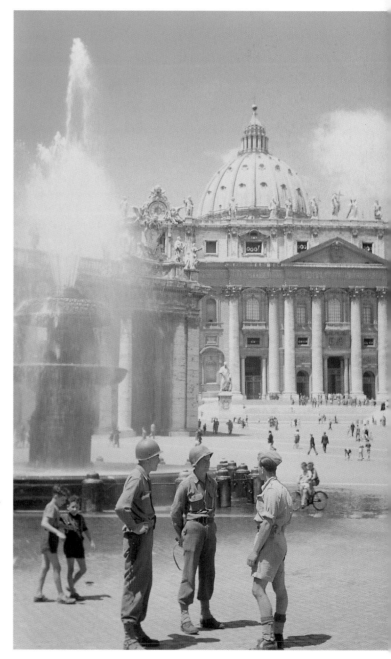

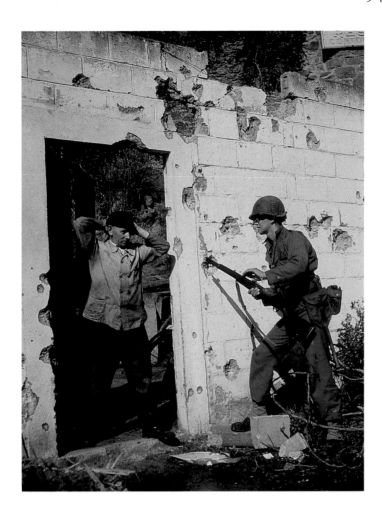

Private First Class Walter T. Stankowski, from Baltimore, Maryland, challenges a French civilian in Dinard, Brittany, a newly liberated area, in 1944.

LIBERATION OF EUROPE

The liberation of Europe was greeted with great relief by the civilian populations, most of whom had suffered greatly under German occupation. Many also had to bear the brunt of bombing and destruction inflicted by both retreating Germans and advancing Allies.

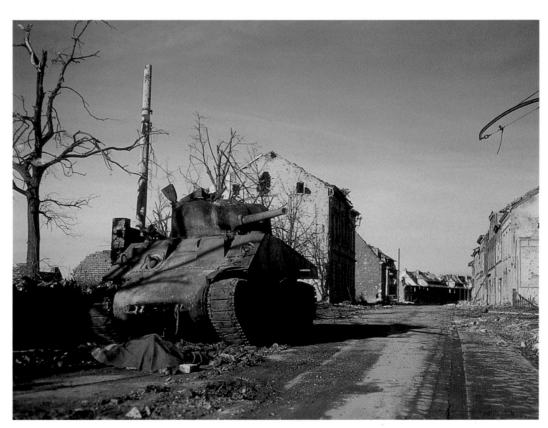

A tarpaulin covers the body of a dead American soldier, in front of his destroyed Sherman tank, in the wake of the continuing Allied advance through northern France.

BELOW
A convoy snakes through the ruins of Saint-Lo.
The damage is typical of that inflicted on many
towns and cities in Normandy by the Allied
bombing of German positions.

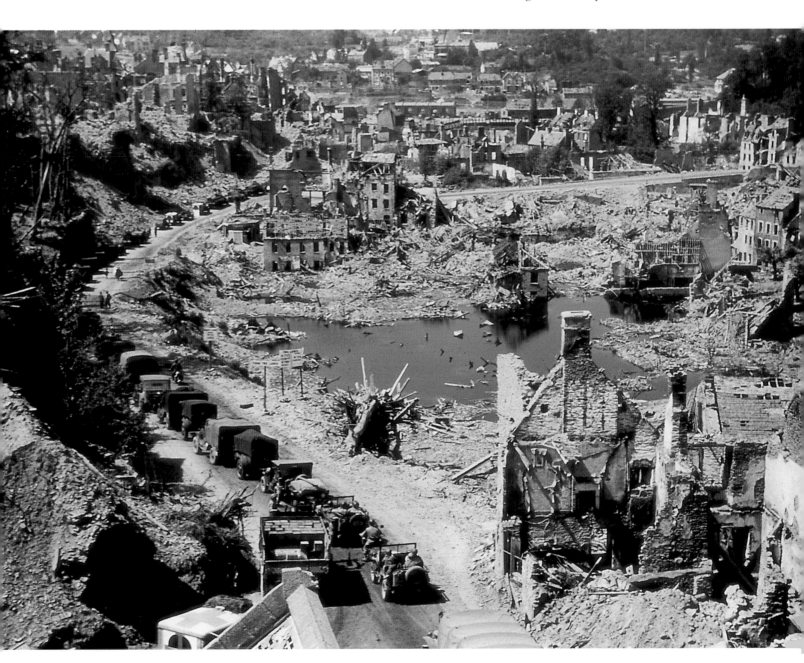

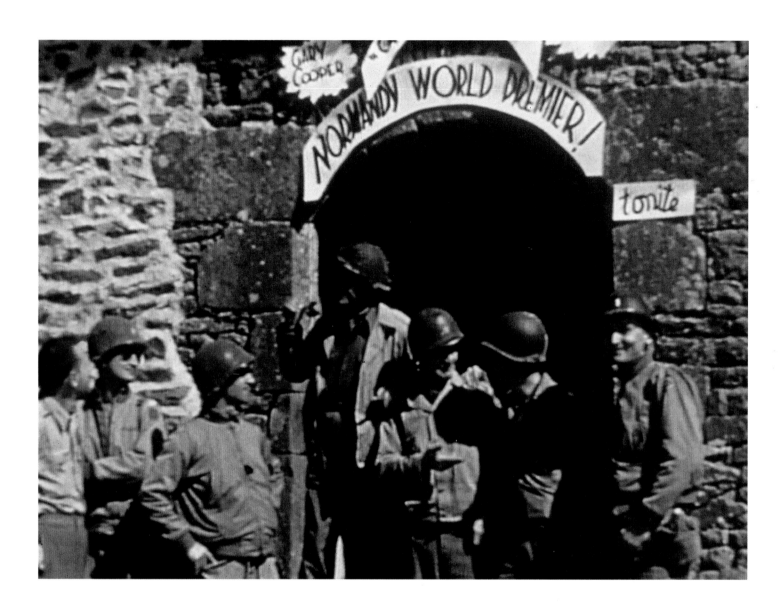

ABOVE
A group of U.S. soldiers relax in front
of the entrance to a makeshift cinema,
where a Gary Cooper movie is playing,
in Normandy, in July 1944.

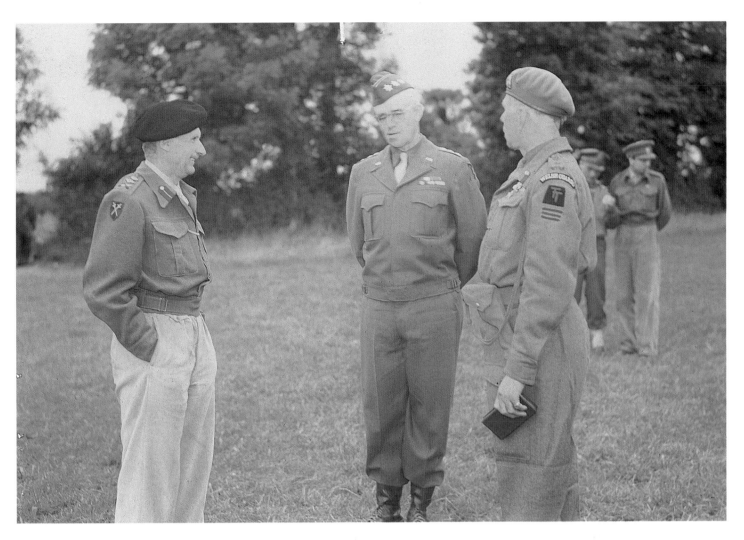

American Decorations for British officers at General Montgomery's Headquarters on July 13, 1944: General Sir Bernard Montgomery with the Commander of the U.S. 1st Army, General Omar Bradley (center) and Brigadier Sir Alexander Stanier at General Montgomery's Headquarters in Normandy. General Stanier had just received the Silver Star from General Bradley on behalf of President Roosevelt.

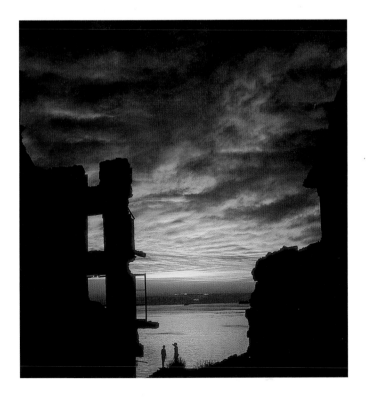

LEFT

The sunset sharply outlines the ruined seafront of St.-Malo, Brittany, after its liberation from German occupation in summer 1944.

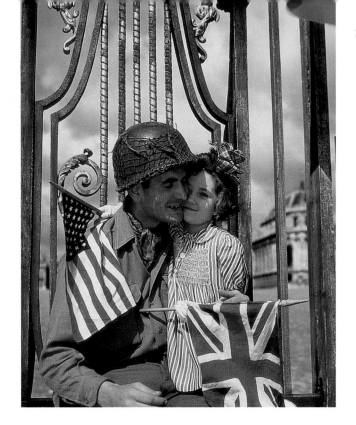

LEFT

Chris S. Gikas of Boston, Massachusetts, receives a hug from Florence Le Noray, outside the gates of the palace of Versailles, near Paris, in September 1944.

RIGHT

Liberated Paris, 1944. Enjoying the pleasures of a traditional sidewalk café are (L–R) Corporal Ortho Hoffman, of Moline, Illinois, Corporal Marlyn Shanebrook, of Pontiac, Illinois, Private John Vetter, of Buffalo, New York, Corporal Worthy Lucas, of Tonkawa, Oklahoma, and Corporal Floyd Mascard, of Lawton, Oklahoma.

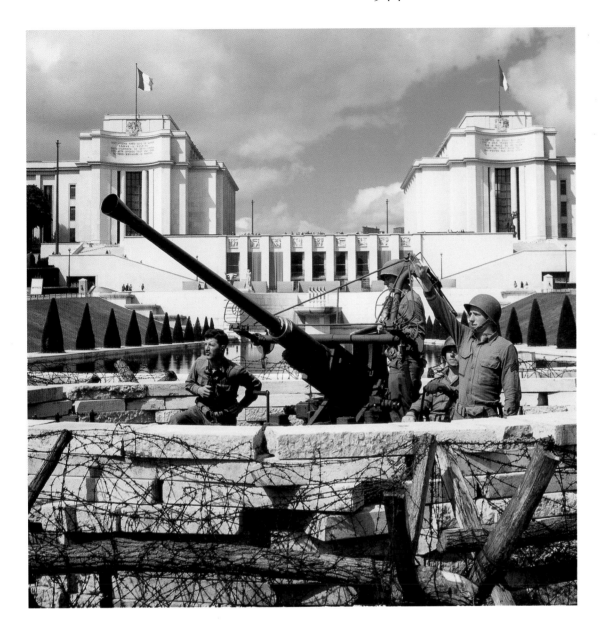

LEFT

A 40mm Bofors ack-ack battery unit guarding the skies above Paris in September 1944, with the Trocadero in the background. The gunners are (L–R) Private First Class Spiro Lano, of Portland, Maine, Corporal Edward McGee, of Waco, Texas, Private First Class Frederick Baird, of Waitsfield, Vermont, and Sergeant David Robbins, of Hollywood, California.

RIGHT

The official Liberation Day parade in Paris on August 26, 1944.

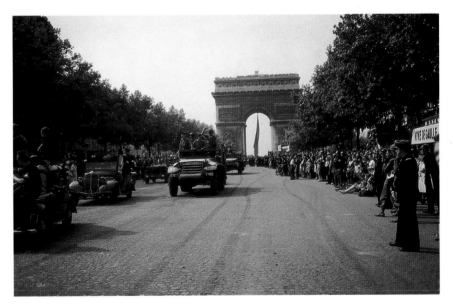

FIGHTING CONTINUES

Although Paris was liberated by the Allies in August 1944, there were still many months of hard fighting to come. Not until May 1945 did Germany finally surrender.

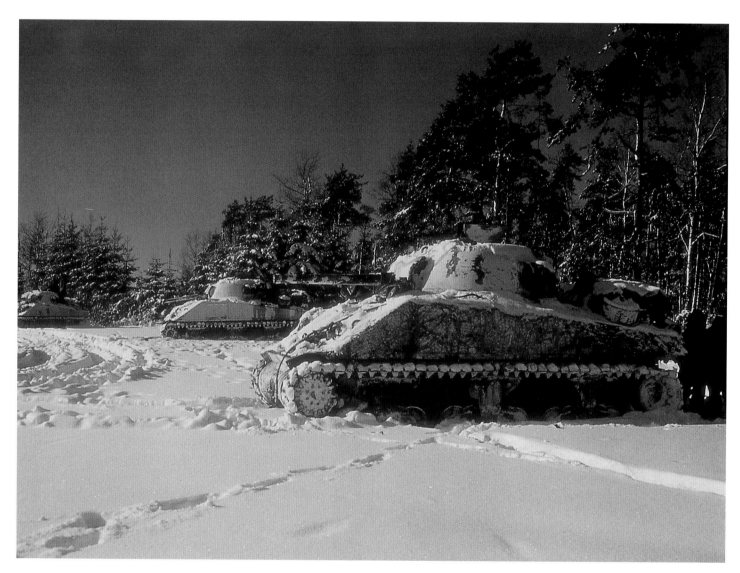

ABOVE

Lined up in the snow-covered fields of Belgium, near Saint-Vith, in winter 1944–5, are M-4 Sherman tanks of the 10th Tank Battalion.

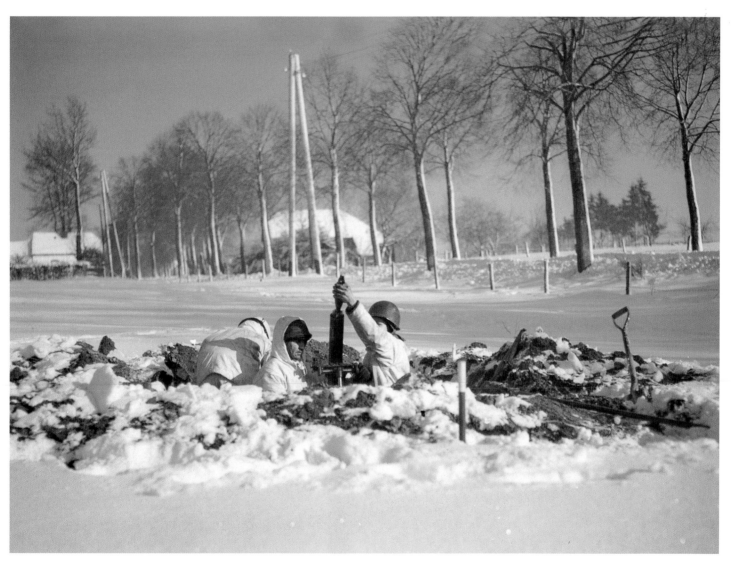

ABOVE

A mortar position near Saint-Vith, in winter 1944–5. It is
manned by (L–R) Private R. Pierdo, from Wyahoga Falls, Ohio,
Staff Sergeant Adam Calinca, from Windsor, Connecticut,
and Tank Sergeant W. Thomas, from Chicago, Illinois.

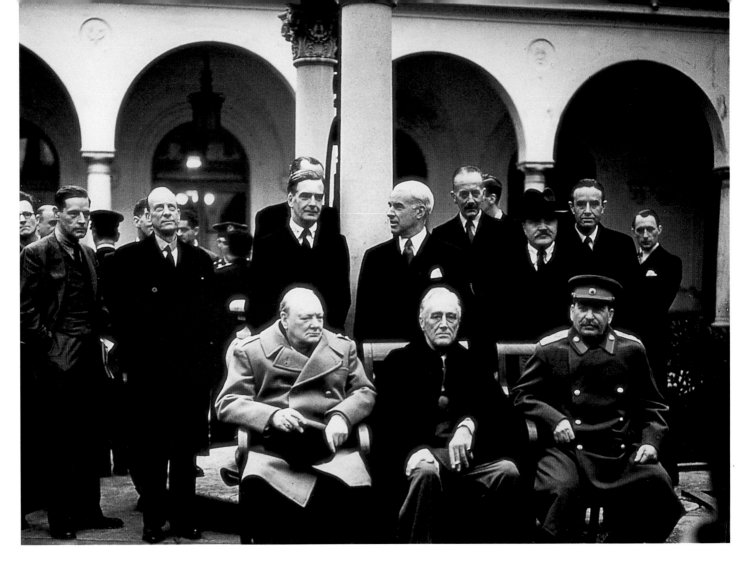

ABOVE

The Yalta Conference in the Crimea, in February 1945, at which the Allies carved up postwar Europe. Seated are (L–R) the "Big Three:" British Prime Minister Winston Churchill, President Roosevelt, and Soviet premier Josef Stalin. Standing behind them are British Foreign Secretary Anthony Eden (behind Churchill), Secretary of State Edward R. Steffinius (behind Roosevelt) and Soviet Foreign Minister Vyacheslav Molotov (behind Stalin). Averill Harriman, an interpreter at the meeting, stands behind Molotov's left shoulder.

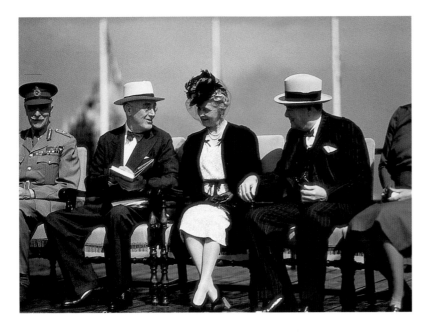

LEFT

President Roosevelt and Prime Minister Winston Churchill chat with Britain's Princess Alice (granddaughter of Queen Victoria) at a pause for photographs during the Quebec Conference in September 1944: the British Governor-General of Canada, Lord Athlone, looks on.

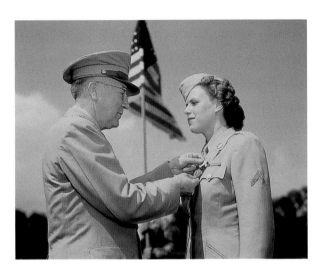

ABOVE

July 25, 1944: Major General Harry C. Ingles decorates Private First Class Mary Jane Ford of the Signal Corps, with the Soldier's Medal, in recognition of her attempts to save the life of a drowning soldier. Private Ford, from Los Angeles, California, was the first W.A.A.C. (Women's Army Auxiliary Corps) to receive the decoration.

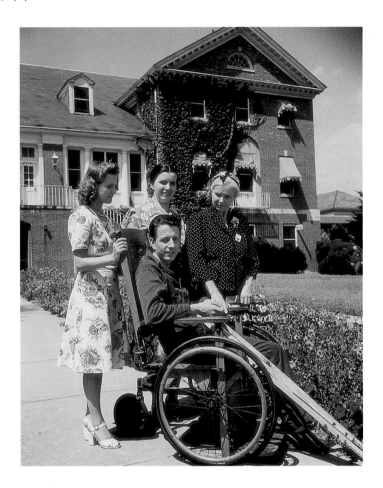

ABOVE

A wounded soldier poses with his family outside the Walter Reed General Hospital, Washington, D.C.

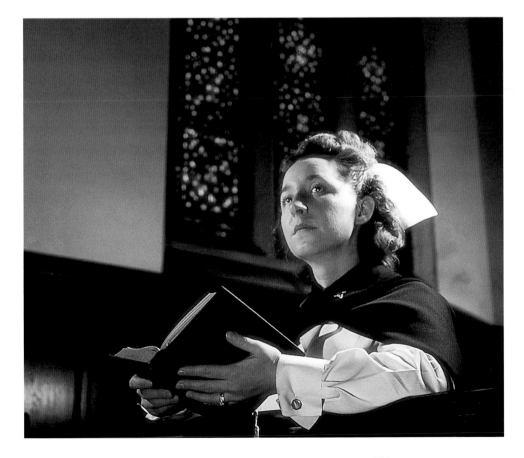

LEFT

An army nurse in the chapel of the Walter Reed General Hospital in Washington, D.C.

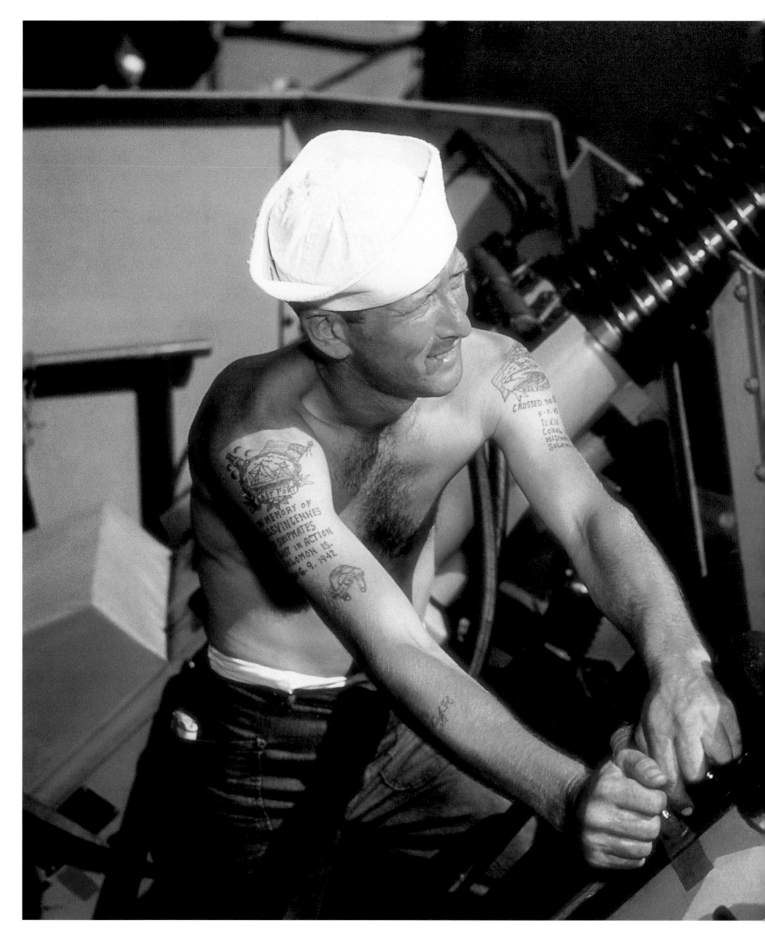

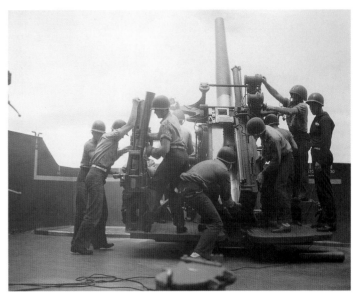

THE TIDE TURNS IN THE PACIFIC

U.S. naval supremacy, won back painstakingly after the crippling blow of Pearl Harbor, was vital to the success of the campaign in the Pacific. With the Japanese Imperial Navy unable to defend the remote islands of its empire successfully using sea and air cover, it was only a matter of time before the U.S. Marines and infantry were able to recapture the territory.

ABOVE
A gun crew in combat aboard the
U.S.S. *New Mexico*.

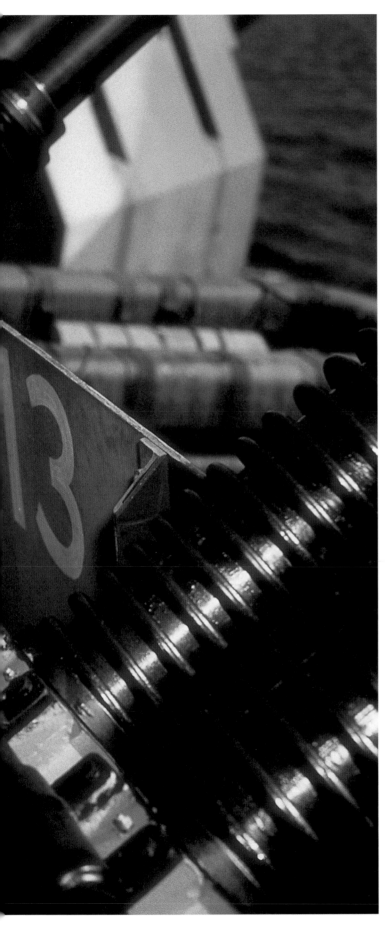

LEFT
Charles J. Hansen works on a 40mm
"quad" gun aboard the battleship
U.S.S. *Missouri* in July 1944.

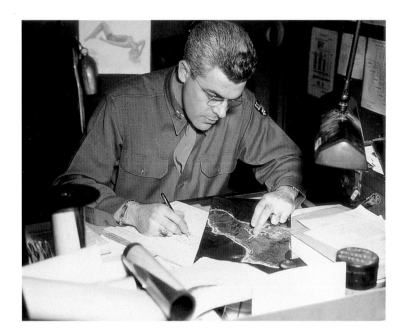

LEFT
Captain Hils Peterson, of Johnson City,
Tennessee, a photo reconnaissance interpretation
specialist, based on the Aleutian Islands, west of
Alaska, studies a picture of an island in the
Kuriles, north of Japan.

BELOW
Russell Price, a photographic technician, hands out
mail aboard a ship in the Pacific.

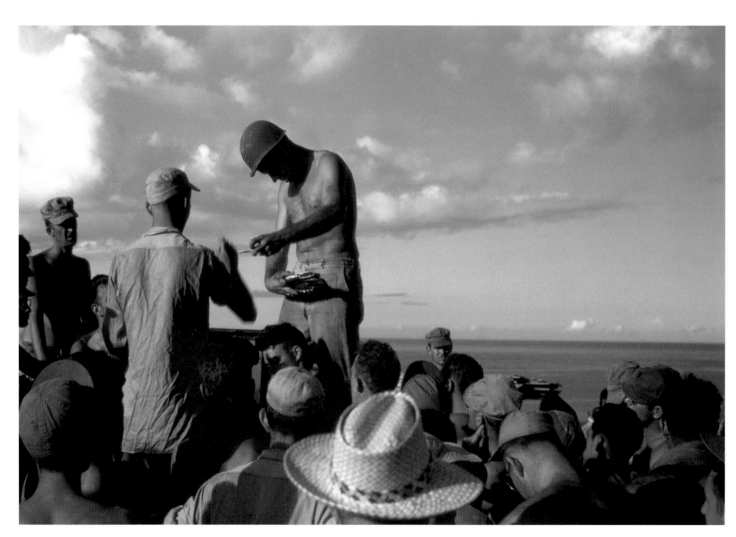

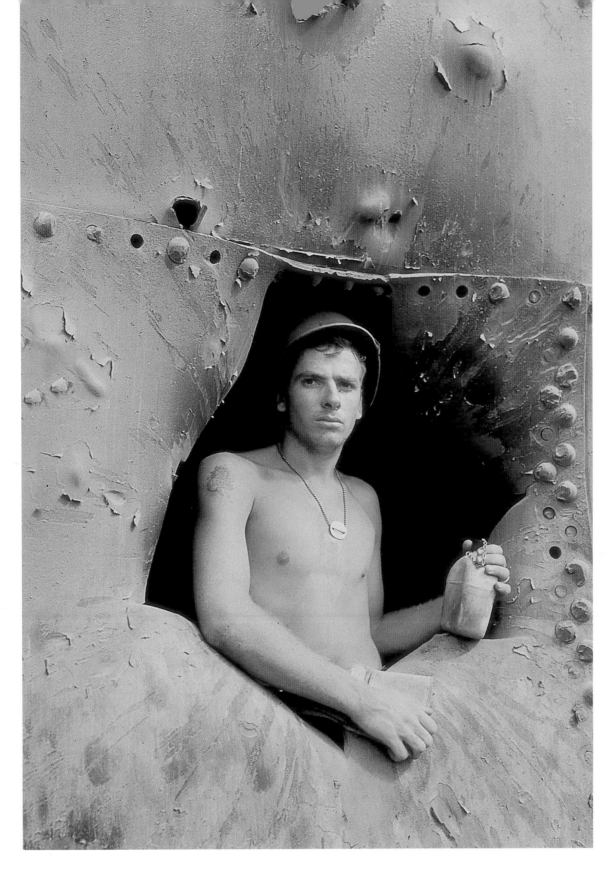

A U.S. Marine poses in a shell hole in a
Japanese storage tank on Kwajalein, one of the
Marshall Islands, after its recapture from the
Japanese in March 1944.

RIGHT
Dead Japanese lie amid the wreckage on a Kwajalein beach in the Marshall Islands following their liberation by U.S. forces in March 1944.

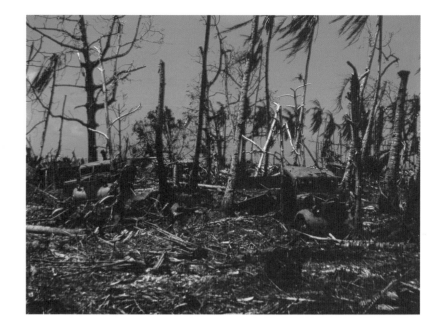

BELOW
A flame-thrower in use against Japanese positions on Bougainville in the Solomon Islands, in April 1944, while a rifleman covers the attack.

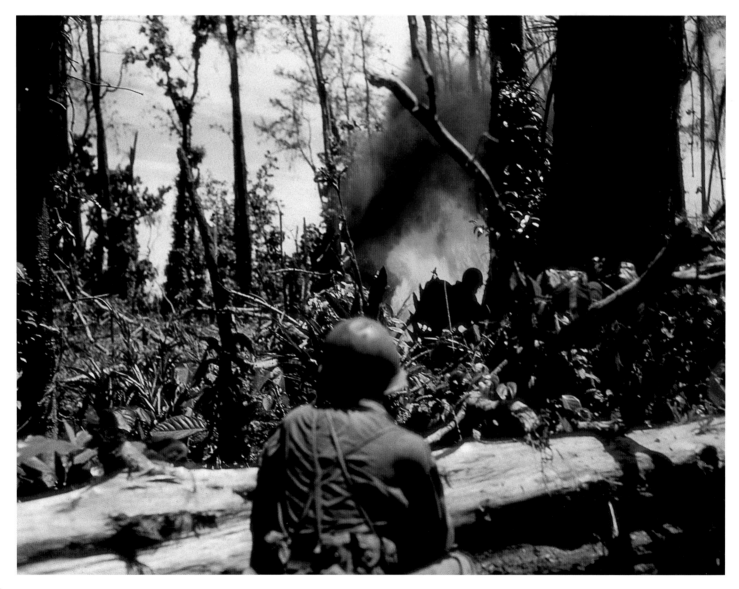

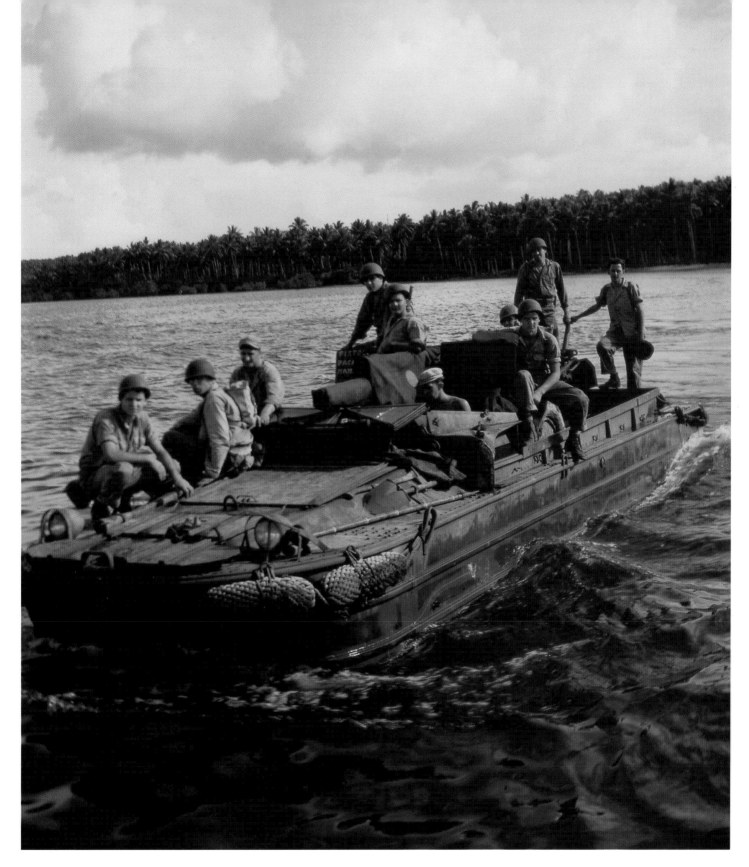

Marines transport heavy artillery aboard an
amphibious truck off Pavuvu, in the Russell
Islands, on August 20, 1944.

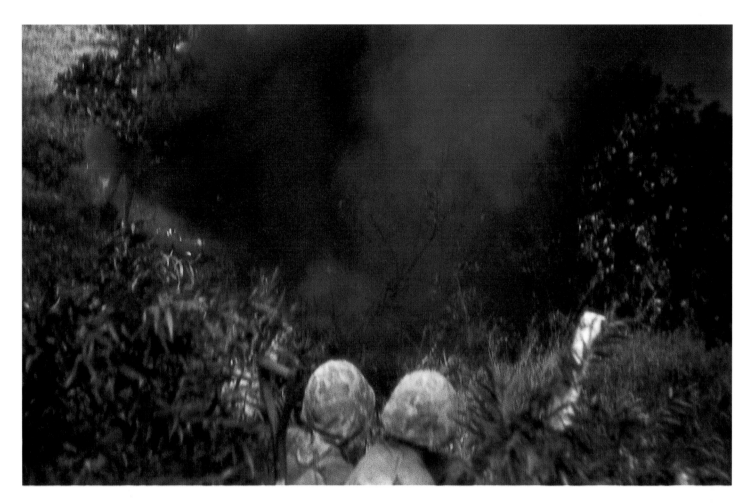

BATTLE FOR THE ISLANDS

The war in the Pacific was merciless, with very high casualty rates in the intense battles from island to island. Over 55,000 U.S. Marines and infantry were killed in the campaign, and over 100,000 were wounded. Japanese losses are thought to have been as high as ten times that number.

ABOVE
Marines use grenades to flush out Japanese troops from underground positions on July 8, 1944.

RIGHT
Marines examine the body and papers of a Japanese soldier killed in the battle for Saipan, one of the Mariana Islands, central Pacific, on July 8, 1944.

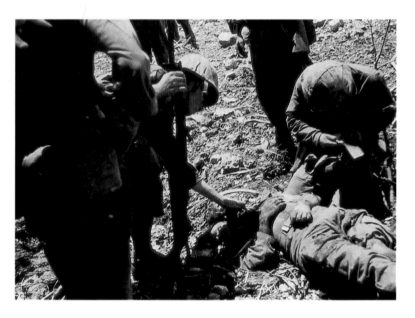

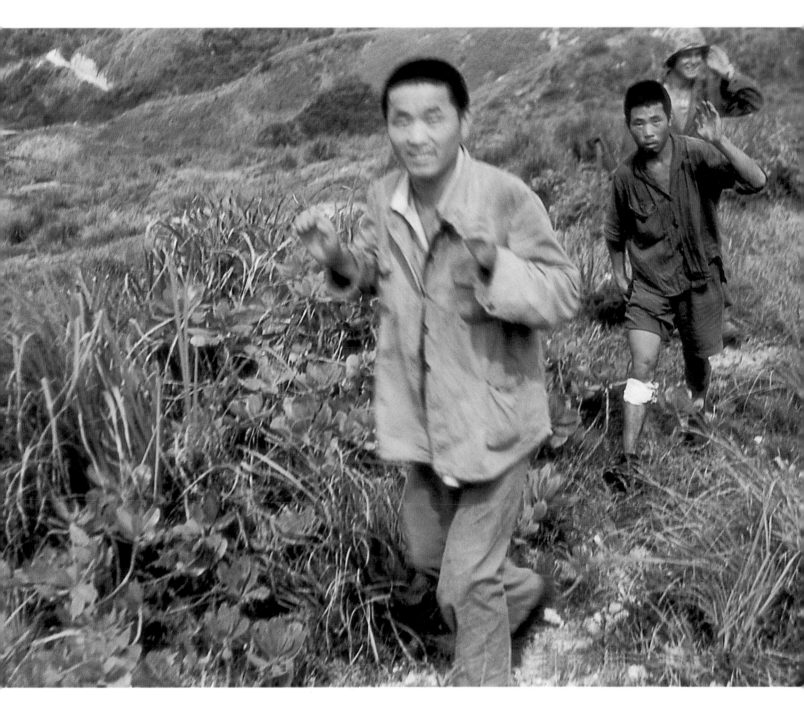

ABOVE

Marines bring in Japanese prisoners taken on
Saipan on Independence Day 1944.

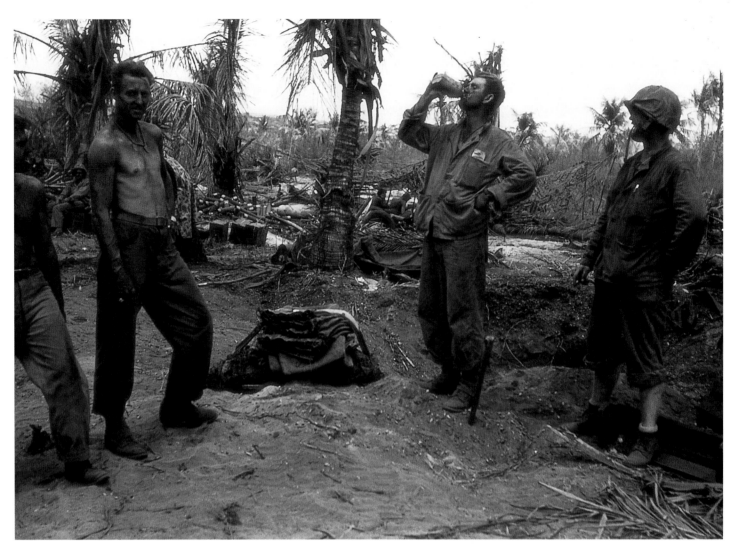

ABOVE

A lull in the fighting for Saipan in June 1944:
(L–R) Private First Class Robert O'Connell,
from Rhode Island, Private First Class
Torrence Caebell, from South Carolina,
Private First Class George Richers, from
Wyoming, and Staff Sergeant John Nation,
from Montana.

RIGHT

Sergeant Ed Barrett provides a
pillow for Corporal Jack Fruk,
sleeping in Hollandia New Guinea,
en route to the Philippines. Both
men served with the 17th
Reconnaissance Squadron.

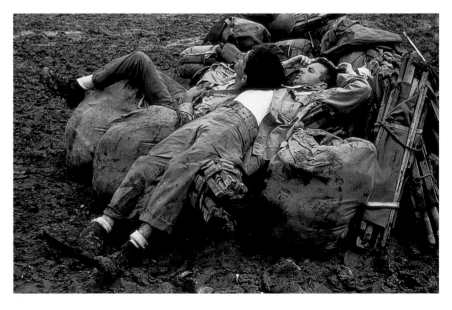

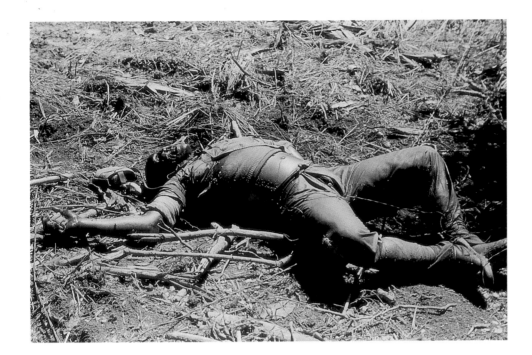

LEFT

The bloated corpse of a dead Japanese soldier on Guam in the central Pacific, photographed in August 1944.

BELOW

Marine Corporal F. E. Wilbur, of Downer's Grove, Illinois, snatches a rest under a tree in Guam in July 1944. All his worldly possessions are around him.

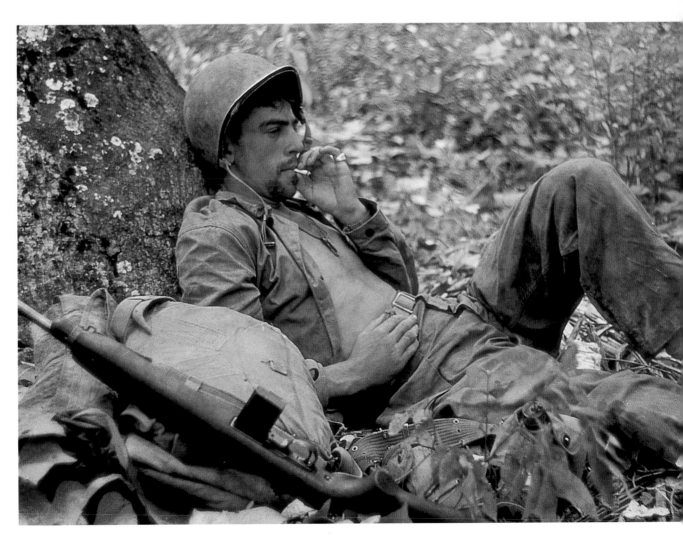

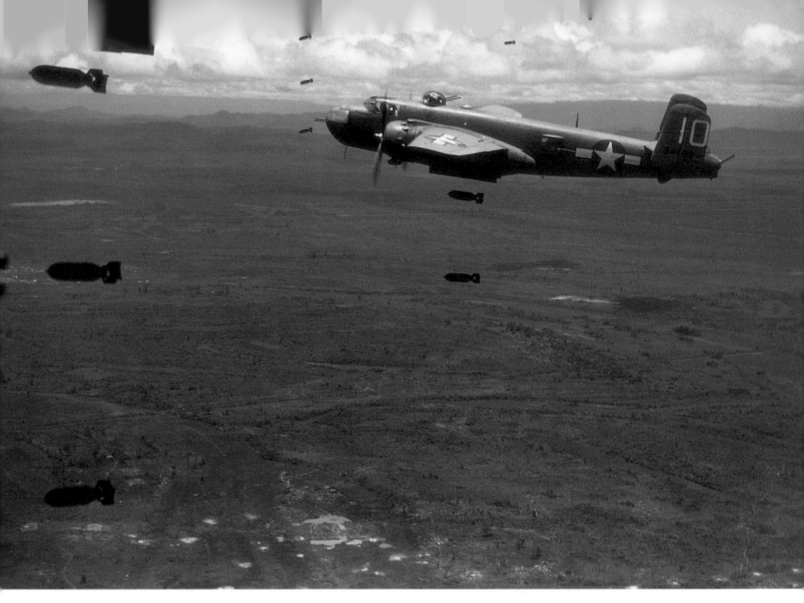

July 23, 1944, flying from Fenny,
India. Aircraft of the 12th Bomb
Group drop their payload on to
Myitkyina, Burma.

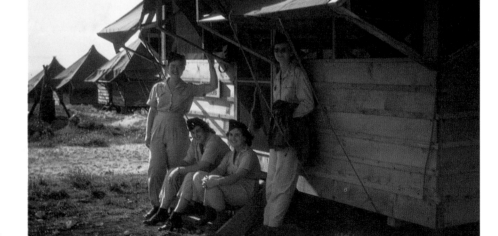

RIGHT

Army nurses enjoy the shade at a
camp in Saipan where they served
during combat operations.

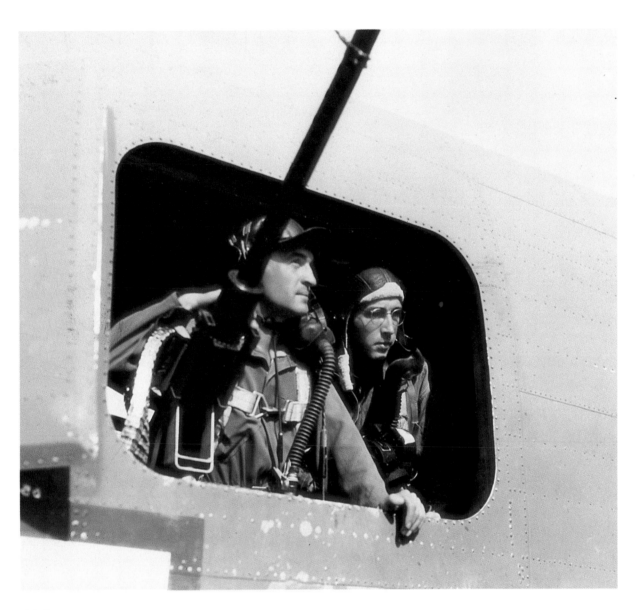

ABOVE

A waist gunner and aerial photographer
of the 16th Combat Camera Unit in
position in their aircraft port in the
Pacific theater.

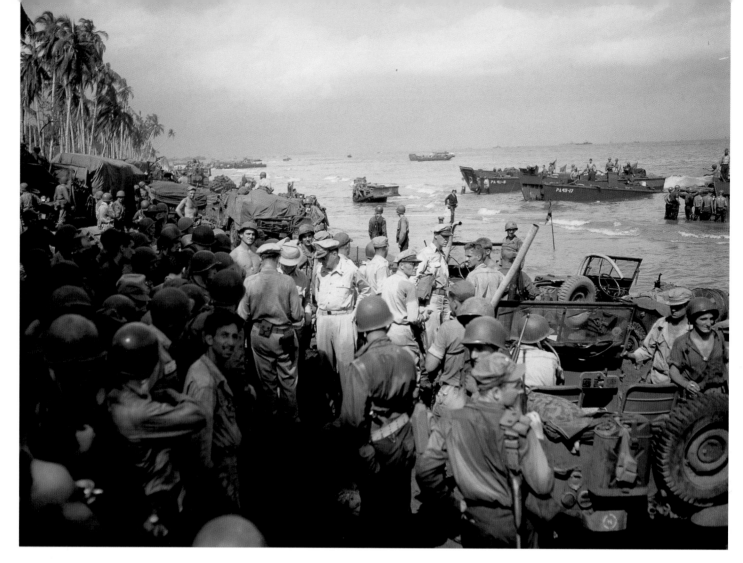

ABOVE

October 20, 1944: General Douglas MacArthur inspects the beachhead on Leyte Island in the Philippines, accompanied by Lieutenant General George Kenny, Lieutenant General Richard Sutherland, and Major General Verne Mudge.

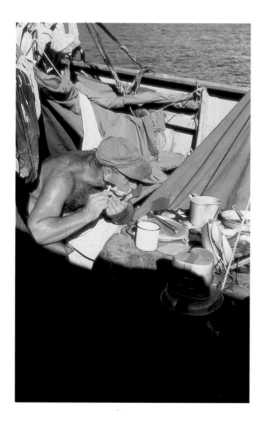

LEFT

G.I. Russell Sage shaves on-board a Liberty ship between New Guinea and the Philippines.

RIGHT

RIGHT

A welcome coffee break for nineteen-year-old Private First Class Faris Touhy (left) and two other Marines. They are dirty and weary after two continuous days and nights of fighting on Eniwetok Atoll, in the Marshall Islands, in February 1944.

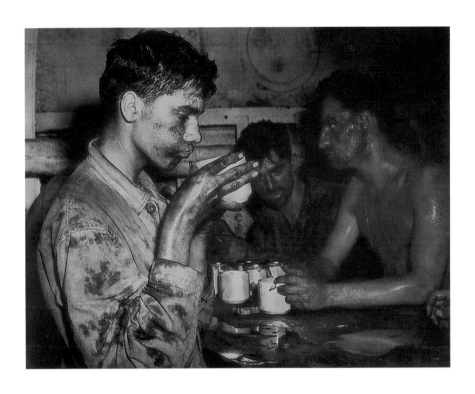

BELOW

W.A.V.E.S. (Women Accepted for Volunteer Emergency Service—the U.S. Navy's Women's Service) wrap Christmas gifts for convalescing men of the Navy and Marine Corps at the Bethesda Naval Hospital, Maryland, in December 1944.

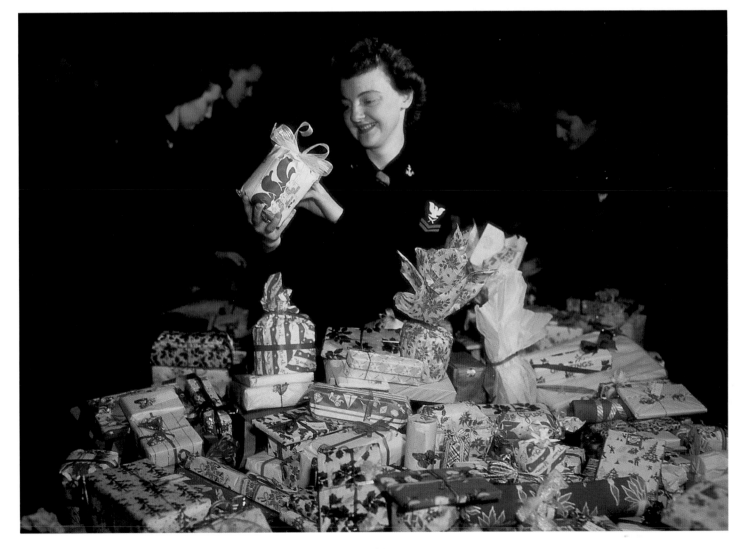

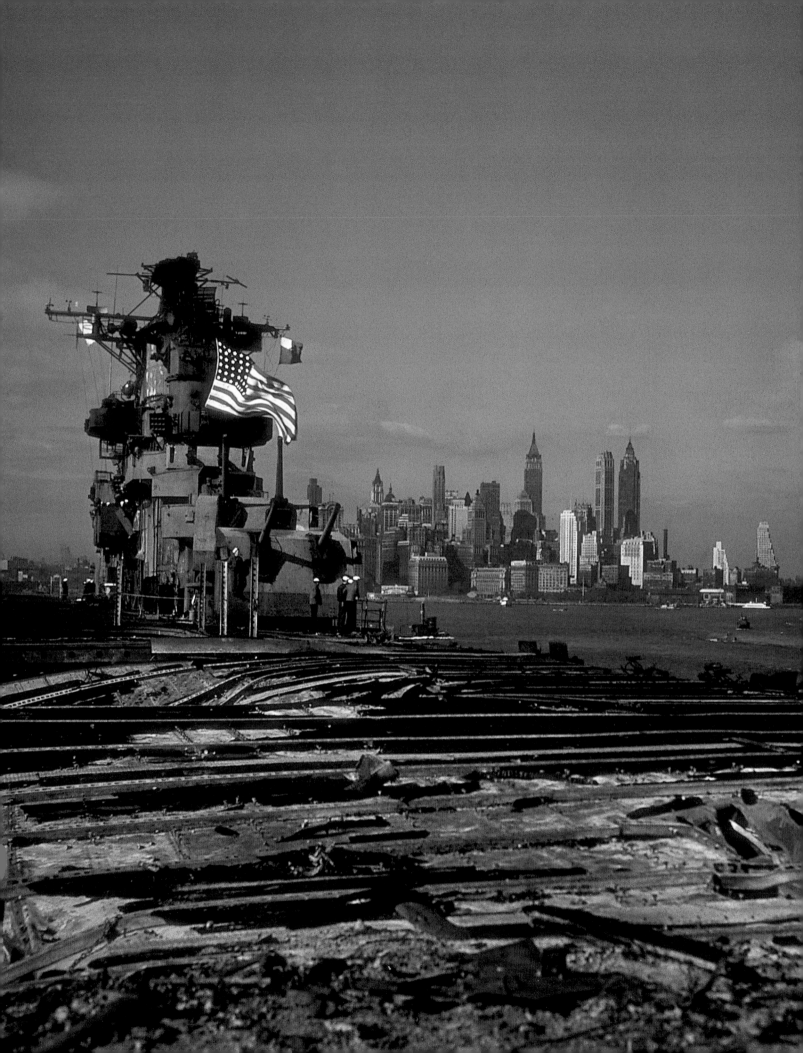

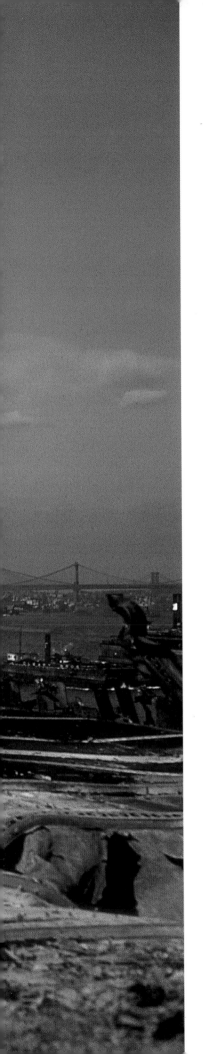

1945

THE TERRIBLE RECKONING

For all the Allied advances, 1944 ended with a sharp sting in its tail. On December 16, in the Ardennes—scene of the German attack that had led to the fall of France in 1940—Hitler had thrown his last dice. Typically, the plan was bold and daring, but also was over-ambitious and lacked adequate supply lines and reinforcement. He managed to muster some thirty divisions, and exhorted his most fanatical and loyal troops to make one last charge.

General Sepp Dietrich's Sixth S.S. Panzer Army led the attack. Lieutenant Colonel Otto Skorzeny's paratroopers included some who spoke fluent English and who penetrated U.S. lines in G.I. uniforms to cause havoc and confusion.

The attack took the Allies by surprise and knocked a sixty-mile hole in their line of advance, near the German border; this "bulge" gave the battle its name. Only the rapid, brave response by U.S. troops under Generals Patton and Hodges halted the advance. By the New Year, the Allies were pushing the Germans back. Hitler lost over 100,000 of his half-million men and almost all his armor, critical losses from which he never recovered. Churchill said the Battle of the Bulge was the greatest American battle of the war. The Ardennes campaign also produced one of the many atrocities that marked the conduct of the war by both Germany and Japan. At Malmédy on December 17, an S.S. unit executed seventy-one American soldiers and several civilians. After the war,

Dietrich and several fellow S.S. officers were imprisoned for war crimes.

In February, Roosevelt (newly inaugurated for an unprecedented fourth term), Churchill, and Stalin met at Yalta, in the Crimea. The Allied forces were still in shock after the Battle of the Bulge, but the Red Army was within a hundred miles of Berlin, having liberated most of Eastern Europe. Churchill and Roosevelt had little to bargain with, and, moreover, Roosevelt needed Stalin's troops to move against Japan, once the war in Europe was over. Stalin won major concessions. Thus were created the postwar political boundaries between democratic West and communist East, and the ideological divide that engendered the "Cold War."

LEFT

The aircraft carrier U.S.S. *Franklyn*—severely damaged in a kamikaze attack in the Sea of Japan on March 19, 1945—limped back to New York, via the Panama Canal, for repairs at the Brooklyn Navy Yard.

Roosevelt's failing health had been an issue in the 1944 presidential election. Now he was fading fast, but the seriousness of his condition was kept secret. The long trip to Yalta did not help, and during March his health worsened. He died of a stroke in Warm Springs, Georgia, on April 12, 1945. America's grief was deep, sincere, and long-lasting. The cause of freedom had lost a dear friend. Churchill said, "Not one man in ten millions, stricken and crippled as he was, . . . would have tried, not one in a generation would have succeeded, not only in entering the [political] sphere, not only in acting vehemently in it, but in becoming indisputable master of the scene."

*

The brutalities of the end of the war in Europe were matched by those in Asia. Each side portrayed the other as monstrous, murderous, subhuman, and each believed its own propaganda. The hatred had led to atrocities on both sides.

Nearly 70,000 U.S. troops landed at Luzon in the Philippines on January 9, 1945. Despite stiff resistance from a quarter of a million Japanese defenders, the capital, Manila, fell on March 4. The whole Philippines campaign was over by July.

On February 15, the focus of U.S. attack in the Pacific shifted to the small, but significant, island of Iwo Jima. It was within a thousand miles of the Japanese mainland, and could be used by P-51 Mustangs to give vital fighter protection to B-29 planes bombing Japan. But Iwo Jima was a hard nut to crack, its thick black volcanic sand concealing 20,000 troops and an extensive network of gun positions, bunkers, minefields, and tunnels. Yet again, the Marines had to fight yard by bloody yard to extract the stubborn defenders.

On February 23, in a truly symbolic moment, the Marines hoisted the Stars and Stripes atop Mount Suribachi. But that symbolism had cost almost 7,000 U.S. lives. General Holland Smith said it was the toughest action in the Marines' 168-year history. Once again, few Japanese troops surrendered; most fought to the death.

The next target was Okinawa, which—though 350 miles from mainland Japan—is part of the Japanese homeland; the assault would give an indication of how the increasingly desperate Japanese might react to an attack on their main islands. Dismantling Japan's empire, piece by piece, was costing hundreds of U.S. lives per square mile. Kamikaze attacks typified the Japanese response to impending defeat: better death than defeat. The planes needed little speed or sophistica-

tion, their pilots little training; and defense against them was difficult. These "human bombs" raised the specter of increasingly fanatical defenders of the emperor, as U.S. forces neared Tokyo.

In the attack on Okinawa, kamikaze accounted for 36 ships sunk and 368 damaged, at a loss of 5,000 U.S. servicemen. It is estimated that over 2,500 Japanese pilots died in these attacks by the end of the war.

The amphibious landings on Okinawa, on April 1, were the last significant conventional military operation of the Pacific war, involving some half-million Marines and infantry and 1,200 warships. The Japanese commander, General Mitsuru Ushijima, concentrated his force of 100,000 inland, out of range of the ships' guns; he hoped for a prolonged battle which would inflict huge casualties on the invaders. By the end of April, only the southern tip, around the capital city, Naha, still held out. After fierce fighting, Naha fell at the end of May, but Ushijima fell back to a last redoubt on the Oroku peninsula. The final encounter was the costliest of all the U.S.'s Pacific battles: 7,600 Marines and infantrymen died, and only 7,500 Japanese troops surrendered. General Ushijima and his staff committed ritual suicide and ordered the civilian population to do the same. Many thousands obeyed.

The fall of Okinawa left Japan defenseless, especially against air raids. B-29 bombers, whose loads included napalm bombs, inflicted huge damage and killed hundreds of thousands of people. On the night of March 9, a firestorm engulfed Tokyo when over 300 planes dropped incendiaries, killing at least 100,000 people. But Japan's leadership steadfastly refused to surrender, still clinging to a vast land-based Asian empire which included the key cities of Seoul, Beijing, Saigon, Hong Kong and Singapore. At that point, it seemed as if the Allies—the Soviets from the north, the British from the west and the U.S. from the south and east—might have to wage a massive land war to clear mainland Asia of Japanese troops, while staging a bitter campaign on mainland Japan. The issues arising from the dilemma, and the solution to it, would, for the new President, Harry S. Truman, pose the most difficult ethical question of the war.

As Japan suffered under relentless air attacks, a similar price was being paid in Germany. On February 13–15, 1945, British and American bombers attacked the lightly defended city of Dresden; the resulting firestorm destroyed virtually the entire city center. It is estimated that more than 50,000 people were killed; questions about the morality of such attacks were still being asked, over fifty years later.

Events began to move rapidly in Europe, as Germany suffered the humiliation and pain of total defeat. It became a tragedy of unimaginable proportions, as the full extent of the horror of Hitler's Germany began to emerge: the revelation of the enormity of the Nazi policy of genocide. It was a crime on an unimaginable scale, committed not only by hundreds of thousands of Germans, but also by hundreds of thousands of active and passive collaborators throughout occupied Europe.

From the oppression and arrests of the 1930s, to the concentration camps and the death squads of the early years of the war, to the extermination camps of the "Final Solution," Nazi Germany had systematically murdered over six million European Jews, as well as Gypsies, Slavs, socialists, homosexuals, the physically or mentally disabled, and other "undesirables." The horror will forever live in history as the Holocaust.

As the Allied armies closed in on the German heartland, the awful truth emerged. The Red Army had liberated Auschwitz at the end of January, and on April 11, the day before Roosevelt's death, the U.S. Army reached the concentration camp at Buchenwald, where the surviving prisoners had already liberated themselves. One U.S. Ranger, who discovered the furnaces used to burn the dead, described what he saw. "Heavy metal trays had been pulled out of the openings. On those trays were partially burned bodies. On one tray was a skull, burned through, with a hole in the top; other trays held partially disintegrated arms and legs. And the odor, my God, the odor!"

On April 25, the U.S. and Soviet armies met at Torgau, on the River Elbe. The end was only days away. On April 28, Benito Mussolini and his mistress were shot by Italian partisans, their bodies strung up for public ridicule. Two days later, after marrying his mistress, Eva Braun, Hitler shot himself in his Berlin bunker. In a squalid and sordid funeral scene, in total contrast with the mythical fantasies he had envisaged for himself, his body was burned in a shell hole. The S.S. fought on to the bitter end, as the capital city of what had once been envisaged as a "Thousand Year Reich" descended into an orgy of killing and revenge.

The war in Asia was also nearing its end. In late July, the Conservative Party was defeated in the British general election, and Churchill was replaced by Clement Attlee at the Potsdam Peace Conference. Although Churchill had already endorsed a positive decision, President Truman now had to think the unthinkable. The Red Army was about to strike into China and Korea, but there was still no sign of surrender from Tokyo. An atomic bomb had been successfully tested at Alamogordo, New Mexico, a few weeks earlier, and the president had to decide whether to use the terrifying new weapon. Military planners had predicted that an invasion of the Japanese mainland would entail huge losses on both sides. Truman had little choice but to use the A-bomb and try to end the war quickly.

The first bomb was dropped on Hiroshima on August 6, the second on Nagasaki on August 9. Whatever the morality of the decision, the Japanese surrender did come: it was broadcast by radio, on August 15, by Emperor Hirohito himself, the first time his voice had ever been publicly heard. He remained on the throne (and thus, technically, part of a conditional, rather than unconditional, surrender) but it marked the end of his "divinity" and the beginning of modern Japan.

The formal surrender was signed aboard the U.S.S. *Missouri*, in Tokyo Bay, on September 2, 1945, six years and a day after German panzers had rolled into Poland, and almost four years after Pearl Harbor. Over 50 million people had died in the fight against European fascism and the tyranny of the Japanese Empire. Thirty million people were homeless. Most of the dead and destitute were Russians, Poles, and other Eastern Europeans. Several countries, including Japan and Germany, were completely devastated, and many more had suffered damage which it would take decades to repair.

The United States had suffered less than most. But it was, after all, not a party to the forces that had created the whirlwind. When it did join the fray, it did so with remarkable commitment, tenacity, and bravery, and it was U.S. involvement which, in the early days of the war, tipped the balance and made the Allied victory inevitable. This remains true, even with the greatest respect to the astonishing bravery of the people of the Soviet Union, the redoubtable courage of Britain and its empire, and the heroic support of many other nations and countless individuals.

Over 400,000 Americans died in World War II, and 670,000 were wounded. Almost 140,000 servicemen were taken prisoner; many of them suffered hardship, hunger, and torture. Countless more were scarred for life by the experience and are still haunted by it. Freedom had been secured, but at a terrible price.

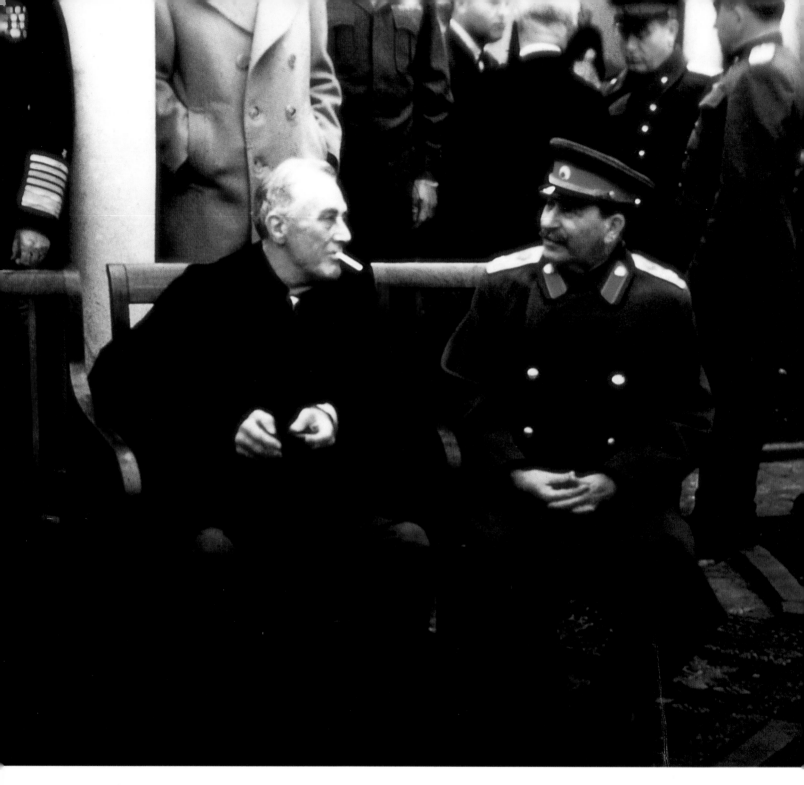

ROOSEVELT AND STALIN

President Roosevelt and Premier Stalin were engaged in a macabre dance of political paradox throughout World War II. They had to trust and support one another and conduct a unified strategy against Hitler, whilst at the same time vying with one another for the vital strategic positions, which would in the future become the Cold War boundaries. As Stalin acknowledged, "It is not difficult to keep unity in time of war, since there is a joint aim to defeat the common enemy. The difficult time will come after the war when diverse interests tend to divide the Allies."

ABOVE
President Roosevelt lights a cigarette whilst the Soviet premier, Josef Stalin, chats on the terrace of the Lividia Palace during a recess in the Yalta Conference in the Crimea, in February 1944.

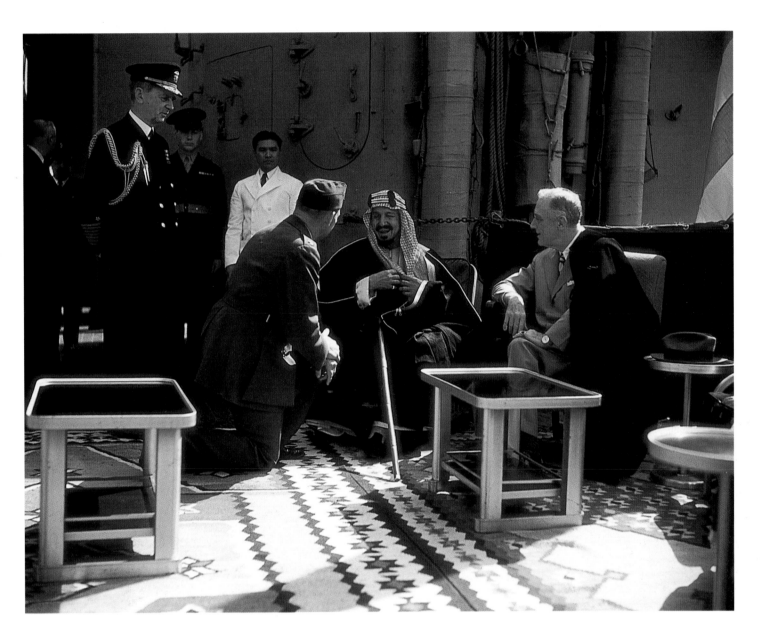

ABOVE

President Roosevelt meets with King Saud of
Saudi Arabia aboard a U.S. battleship docked
in Cairo, Egypt, in 1945. A Marine Corps
officer kneels as he listens to King Saud,
while Admiral William Leahy looks on.

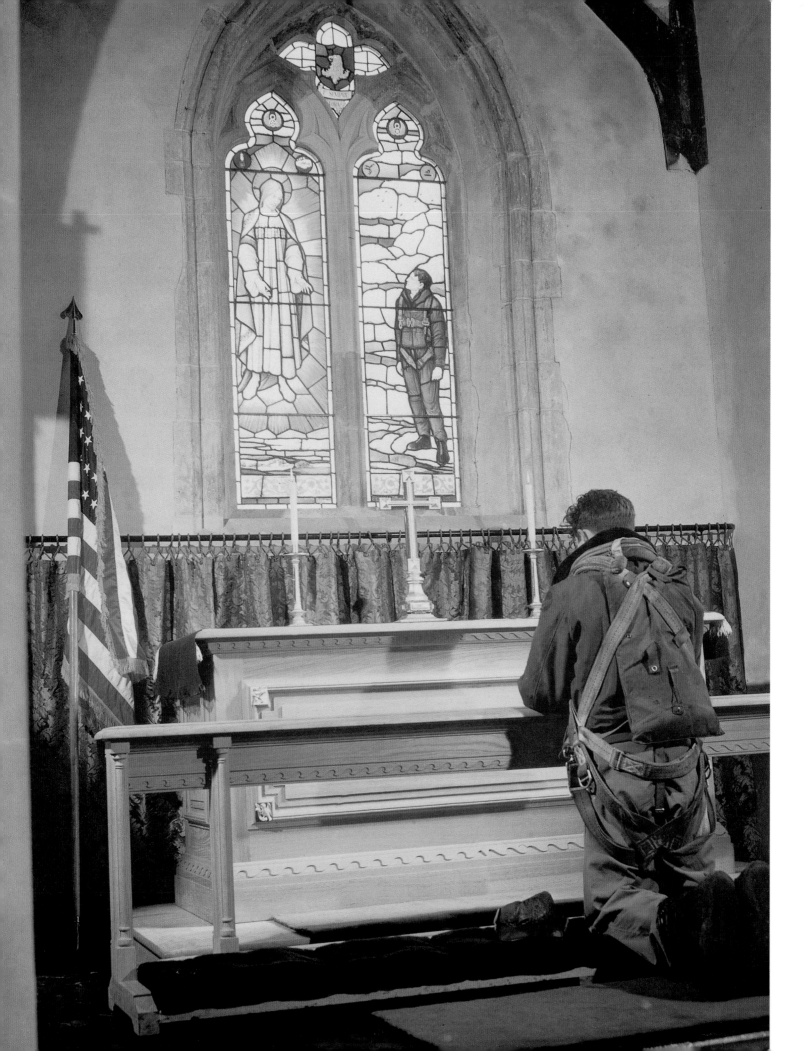

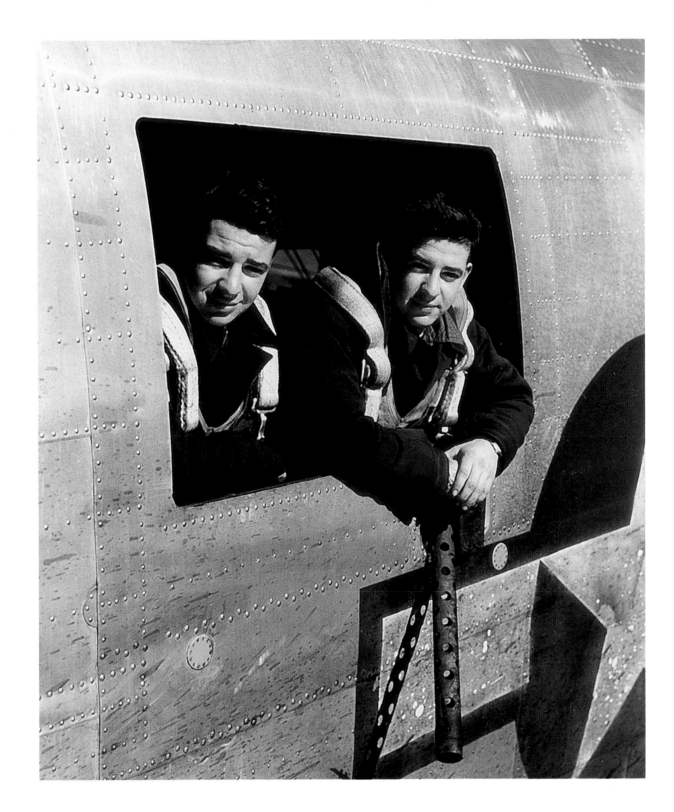

Twenty-three-year-old Sergeant Thomas Barber, of Seattle, Washington, prays in the twelfth-century Chapel of St. Andrew. The memorial window, dedicated to airmen of the 96th Bombardment Group, 8th Army Air Force, killed during the war, was purchased with over $1,600 of contributions from airmen.

Staff Sergeants John E. and Don E. Echols, twin brothers, at the waist-gun port of a B-17 bomber.

COMBINED BOMBER OFFENSIVE

During 1944 the Americans established increasing air superiority over Germany's *Luftwaffe,* and in 1945 the combined bomber offensive rolled on with enormous destructive momentum. Allied bombing raids crippled the German transport system, caused severe fuel shortages, and leveled most major towns, eventually devastating the German economy. In one American and two British raids on the German city of Dresden, February 13–14, 1945, one hundred and thirty five thousand people lost their lives.

BELOW

Lieutenant William Groseclose, of Pierre, South Dakota, climbing into the cockpit of his Mustang. Standing by the wing is his ground-crew chief, Staff Sergeant Harry E. East, of Omaha, Nebraska.

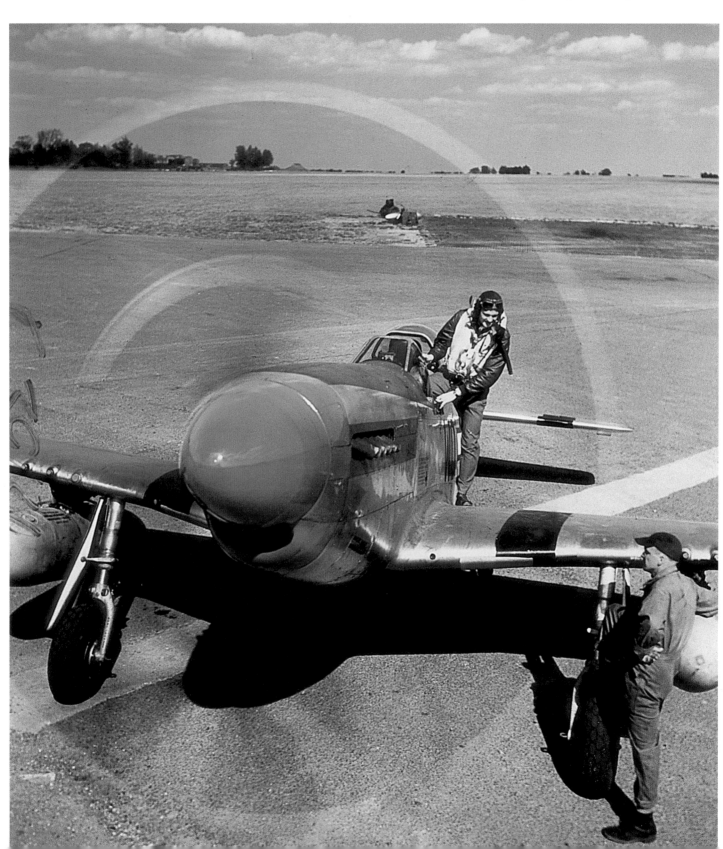

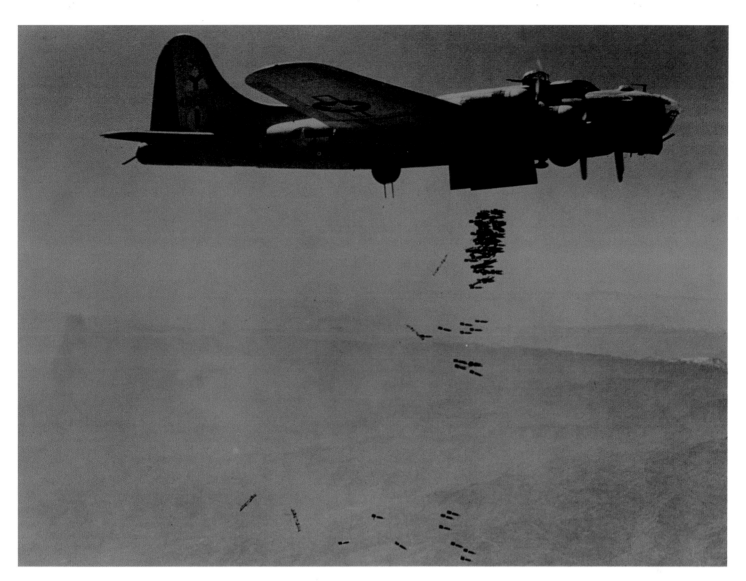

ABOVE

A 15th Air Force "Flying Fortress" drops fragmentation bombs on German positions on the Italian Front in spring 1945.

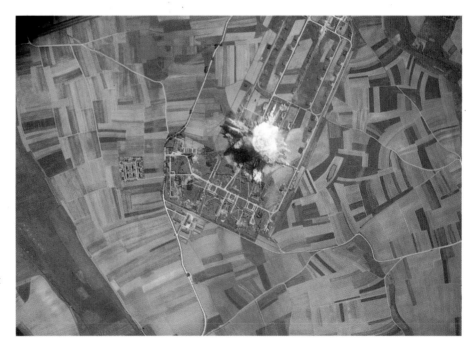

RIGHT

Photographed in 1945 from a B-17 over Ingoldstadt, Germany—a direct hit is scored on an ammunition dump by the first wave of bombs dropped in a U.S.A.A.F. raid.

ITALY

The Allies were prevented from completing the conquest of Italy in 1944 by a combination of bad weather, dogged German defense and the diversion of Allied troops to southern France. They began their main attack in April 1945, crossing the River Po and taking Bologna on April 21, and Verona on April 26.

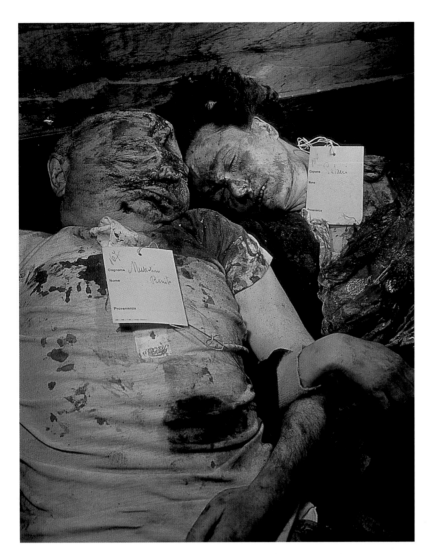

LEFT

The bodies of the Italian dictator, Benito Mussolini, and his mistress, Clara Petacci, in a Milan morgue in May 1945. Their bodies were strung up by the heels in Milan's Piazza Loretto for public degradation. Mussolini, who had been rescued from arrest by the Germans on September 12, 1943 and placed at the head of the puppet Italian Social Republic, was captured and shot by partisans on April 28.

RIGHT

Italian partisans surrender their weapons to U.S. Military Police in the Piazza Vittorio Emmanuele, Bologna, following a formal disbandment ceremony.

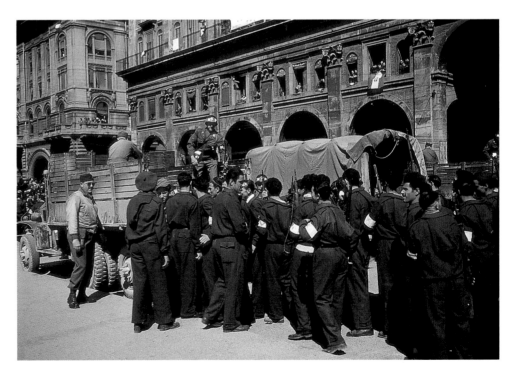

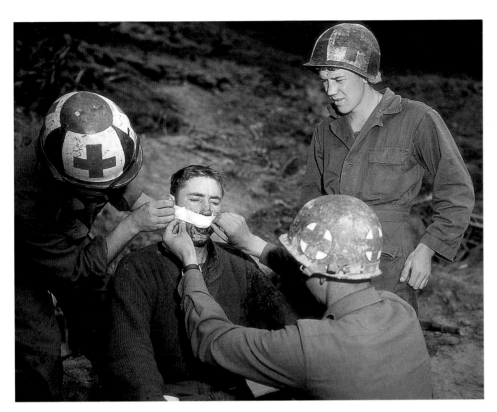

ABOVE

Medics of the 10th Mountain Division in
Italy treat a G.I. wounded during the 5th
Army's push on Bologna in April 1945.

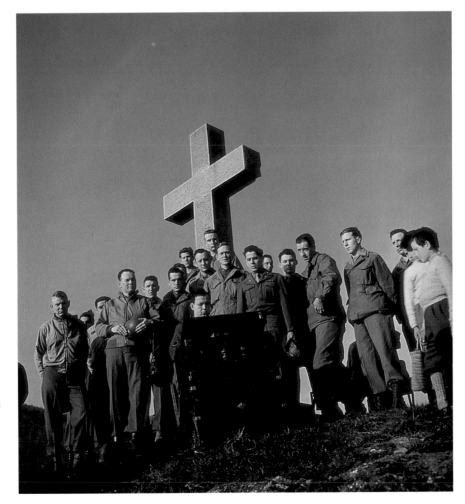

RIGHT

High in the Apennine mountains
of Italy in 1945, soldiers of
the 5th Army participate in
an Easter Day sunrise service,
accompanied by organist Staff
Sergeant William D. Wilkins.

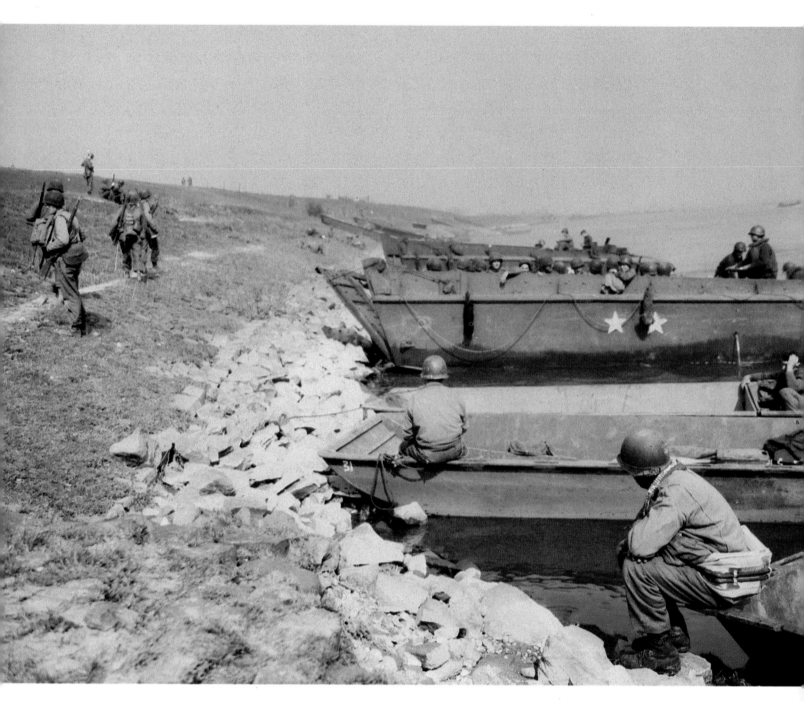

CROSSING THE RHINE

On March 7, 1945 American troops crossed the Rhine, thus breaching Hitler's last natural defense in the west. Eisenhower was keen to avoid a race for Berlin, despite its political and symbolic significance. From their Rhineland bridgehead his 9th and 1st Armies joined east of the Ruhr, capturing over 400,000 German prisoners. His 6th Army swung southward towards Switzerland and Austria, whilst the 12th Army Group marched eastward to the Elbe to meet with the Russians.

ABOVE
Men of the 1st Battalion, 314th Infantry, 79th Division, leaving landing craft to cross the River Rhine at Orsoy.

A stretch of the Siegfried Line, the German defensive line along the border with France, in August 1945. The concrete "dragon's teeth" were intended to prevent movement by tanks and other military vehicles—the distant mountains performed much the same function.

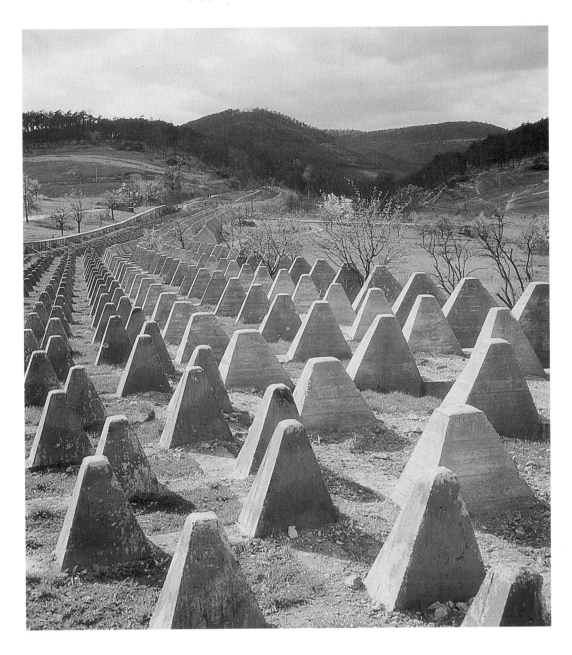

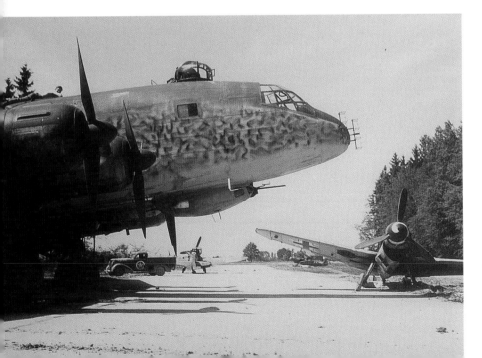

Aircraft abandoned by the Luftwaffe on an autobahn near Salzburg, Austria, during the relentless Allied advance. The bomber in the left foreground is a Junkers 290. The fighter on the right is probably a Messerschmitt 109, around 35,000 of which are estimated to have been produced for use by the Luftwaffe and other Axis air forces.

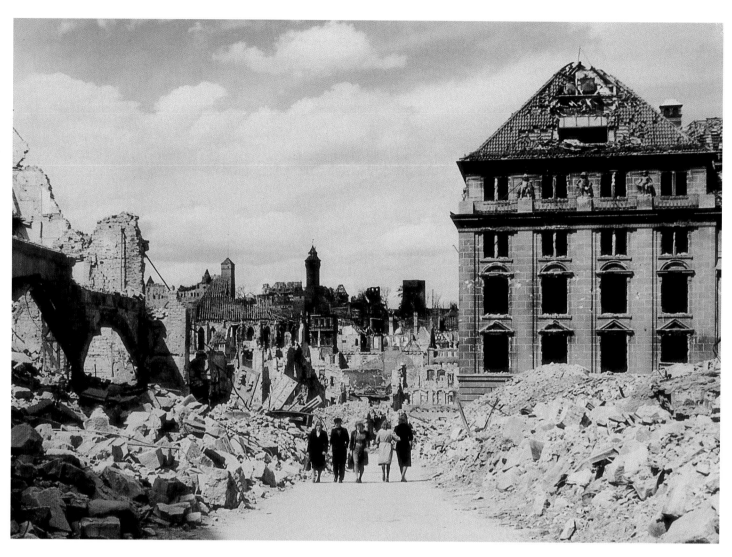

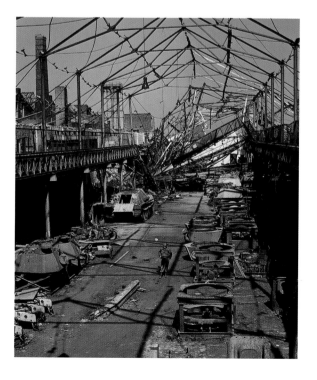

ABOVE

Nuremberg, Germany, in summer 1945. It had been extensively damaged, and the city wall (on the left) destroyed, in Allied bombing raids.

LEFT

A U.S. soldier is dwarfed by the wreckage of a German tank production plant in summer 1945.

RIGHT

Private Hershel L. Brookey, of Hugo, Oklahoma, and Private James J. Dixon, of Murfreesboro, North Carolina, pause to contemplate the ruins of Cologne Cathedral, Germany.

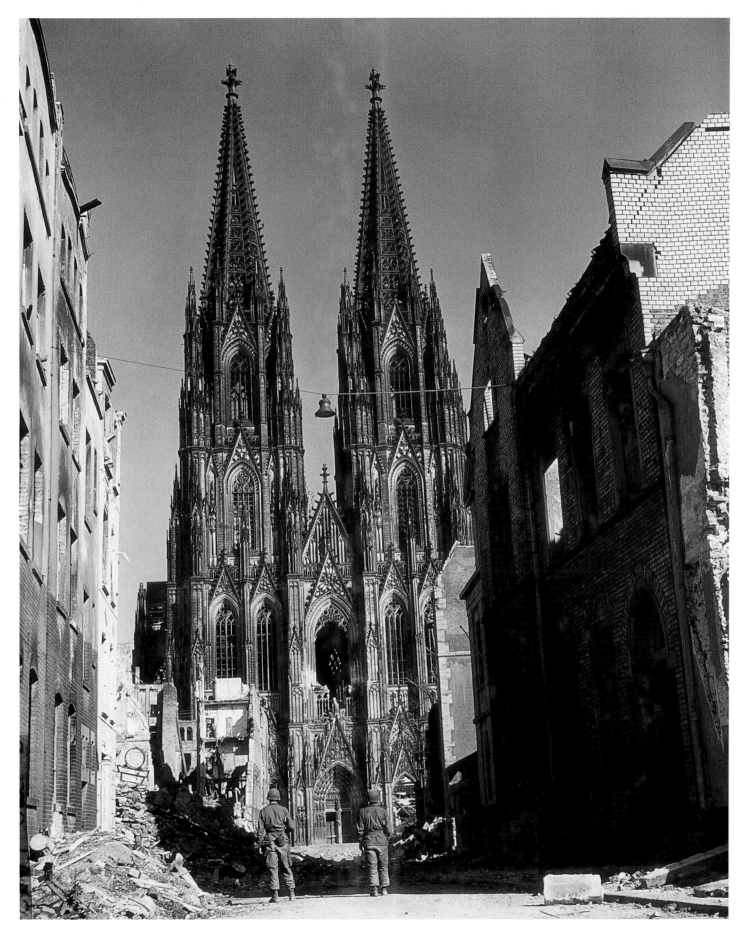

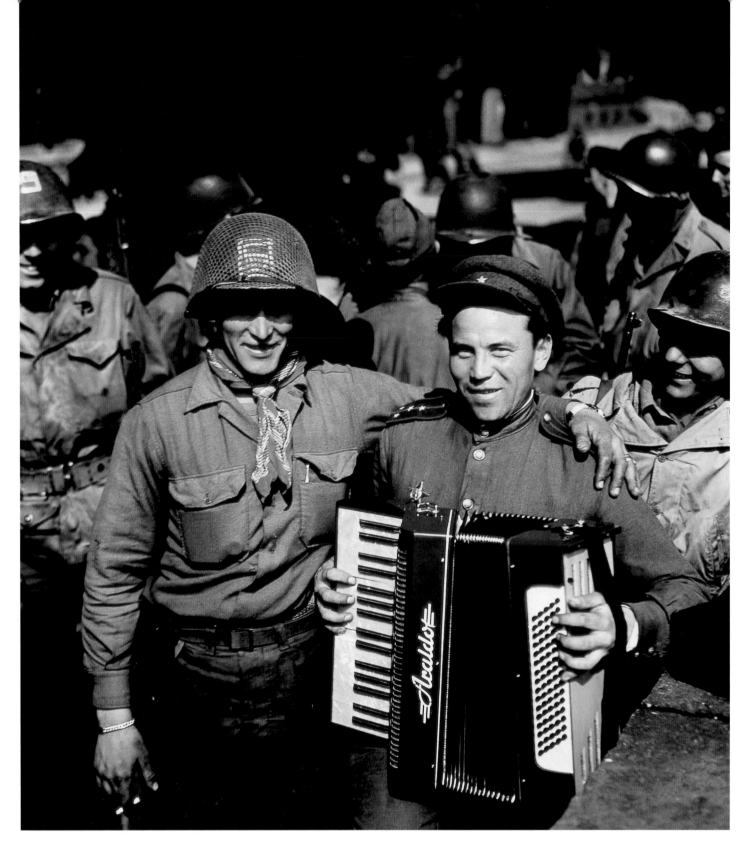

Men of the U.S. 69th Infantry Division celebrate with members of the 98th Guards Division, 1st Ukrainian Army, at Torgau on the River Elbe in Germany, on April 27, 1945. The first meeting between the Allies had occurred two days earlier, when a foot patrol of the 69th, led by Lieuteunant Albert Kotzebue, met a lone Soviet cavalryman near the village of Stehla. Kotzebue's radio report to his command post concluded with "No casualties," reflecting fears that fighting might break out between the U.S. and Soviet armies.

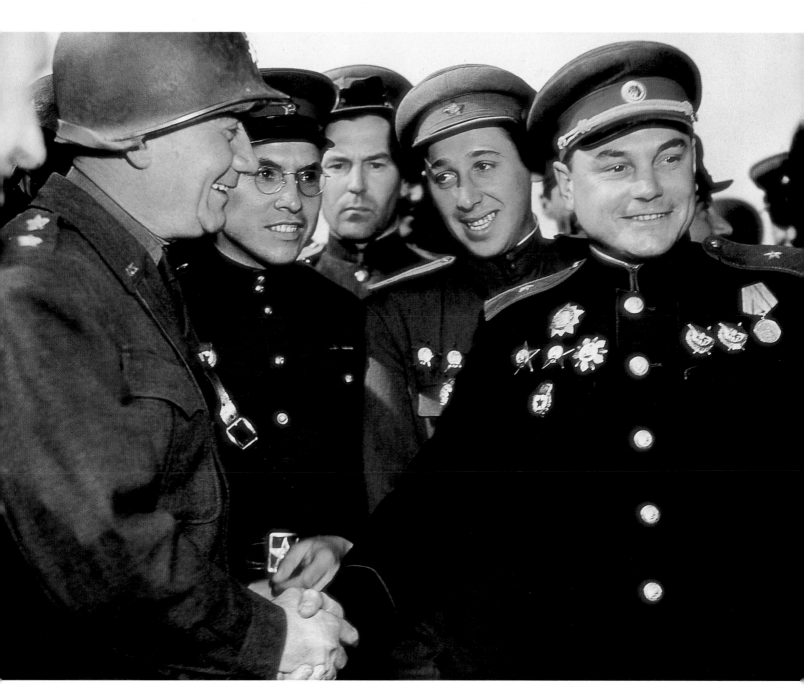

Major General E.F. Reinhard of the 69th Infantry
Division meets Major General Rusakov of the 58th
Guards Division, 1st Ukrainian Army, at Torgau in
a "photo opportunity" arranged for the Press Corps
on April 27, 1945.

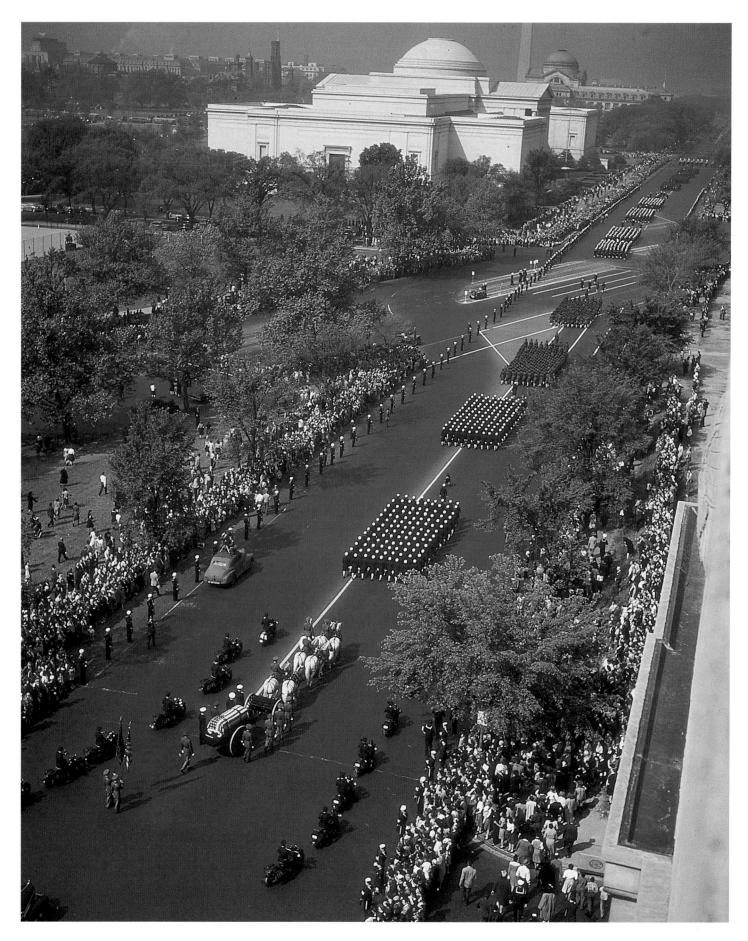

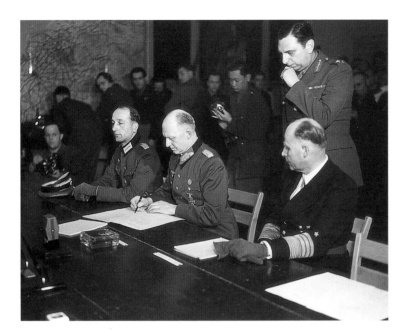

LEFT
General Alfred Jodl signs the act of unconditional German surrender in Rheims, France, on May 7, 1945.

VICTORY IN EUROPE

On April 30, 1945 Hitler and his mistress Eva Braun committed suicide. Two days later on May 2, Berlin fell to the Allies. On May 7, a week after the death of the Führer the Germans surrendered in a modest schoolhouse in Rheims. On May 8 the ceremony was repeated in Berlin to symbolize unity amongst the Allies. It was this day that went down in history as V-E Day. Sadly, Roosevelt did not live to see the destruction of Hitler and his Third Reich, but he had died safe in the knowledge that his cause was won.

BELOW
General Bedell Smith, General Eisenhower's Chief of Staff, countersigns the act of German surrender on May 7, 1945. Left to right: General Sevez, Admiral Burroughs, General Smith, General Ivan Suslapatov, General Carl Spaatz.

LEFT
President Roosevelt's funeral cortege proceeds along Constitution Avenue, Washington, D.C., on April 14, 1945. He had died, aged sixty-three, while sitting for a portrait in Warm Springs, Georgia, two days earlier. His widow, Eleanor, said, "I am more sorry for the people of the country and of the world than I am for us." Churchill echoed these sentiments when he described his death as a "loss to the British Nation and of the cause of freedom in every land."

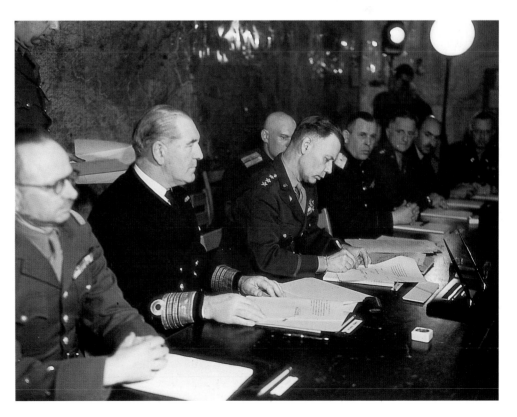

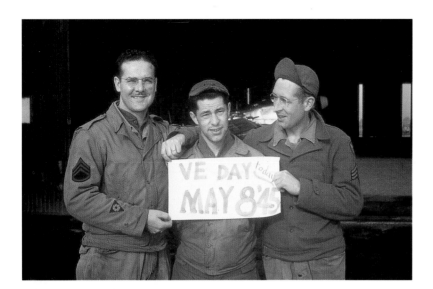

Staff Sergeant Kermit Riem,
Technical Sergeant Roger Fraleigh
and Sergeant Robert Sand, smile for
a commemorative picture at their
air base in Wormingford, England,
May 8, 1945.

General Eisenhower poses after
the unconditional surrender.
L–R: General Suslapatov,
General Morgan, General Smith,
General Eisenhower, Air Chief
Marshal Tedder.

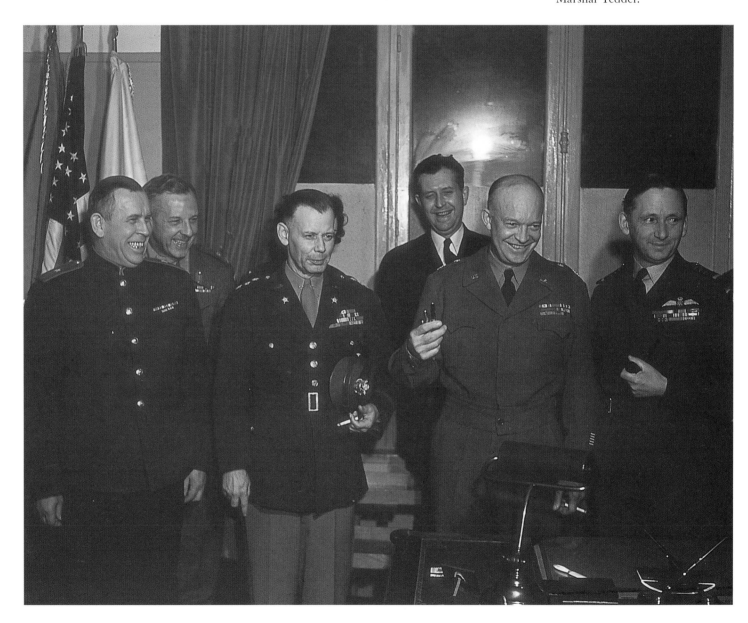

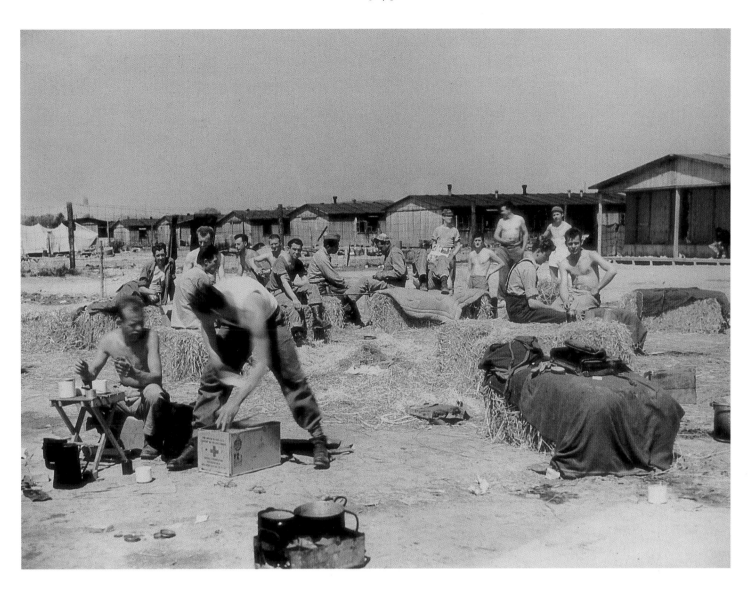

Liberated Allied prisoners of war in a German camp at Moosburg in summer 1945.

A formal portrait of twenty-three-year-old U.S.A.A.F. Captain John T. Godfrey, of Providence, Rhode Island. He destroyed 36 enemy aircraft while serving with the 4th Fighter Group of the 8th Army Air Force. After being shot down over enemy territory, on August 24, 1944, he evaded capture for two days, but was then caught and interrogated near Frankfurt. At first interned in a camp for Allied airmen at Breslau, he was marched with his fellow inmates to Spremberg, east of Berlin. His attempted escape on the march was foiled by freezing temperatures. Subsequently, he was moved to a camp near Nuremberg, which was liberated on April 17, 1945. Godfrey was awarded the Silver Star, the Distinguished Flying Cross with seven clusters, and the Air Medal with three clusters.

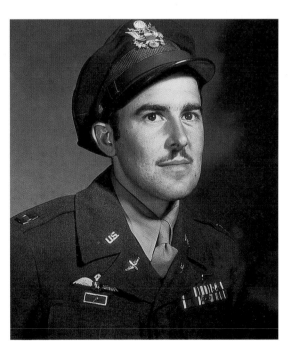

CONCENTRATION CAMPS

As the Allies advanced through Germany, the full horror of the Nazi atrocities was revealed. The American, British and Free French troops penetrated the camps of Buchenwald, Dachau, and Bergen-Belsen, whilst the Russians, approaching from the east, entered the death factories of Lublin-Maidanek and Auschwitz. Although it is impossible to be certain of the exact death toll from Hitler's concentration camps, death camps, ghettos, and labor camps, the Nazis murdered over 10 million people, including an estimated 6 million European Jews.

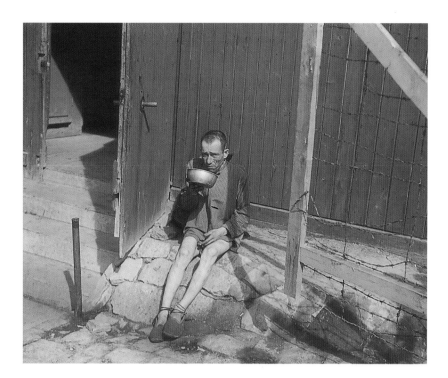

ABOVE

One of over 20,000 liberated inmates of Buchenwald concentration camp, near Weimar, Germany, on April 18, 1945. The camp was liberated on April 11 by troops of the U.S. 80th Division; five days earlier, 15,000 inmates had been forced to leave the camp by their German guards. Though Buchenwald was not an extermination camp, its records show that on average over 200 men and boys died daily of "starvation, beatings, torture, or sickness."

RIGHT

Liberated inmates of Buchenwald chat with G.I.s visiting the camp on April 18, 1945.

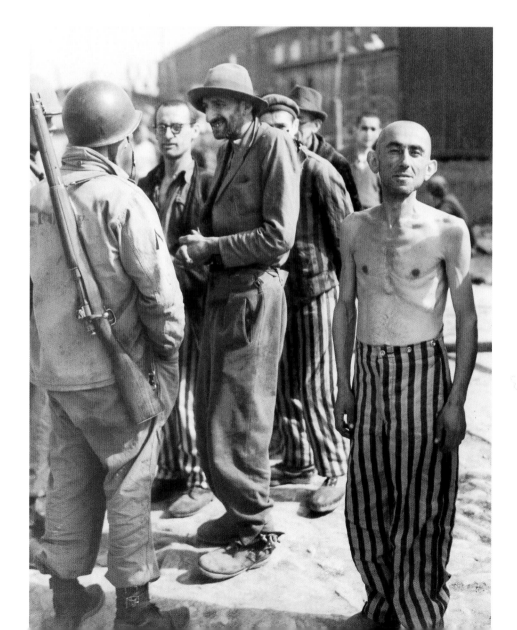

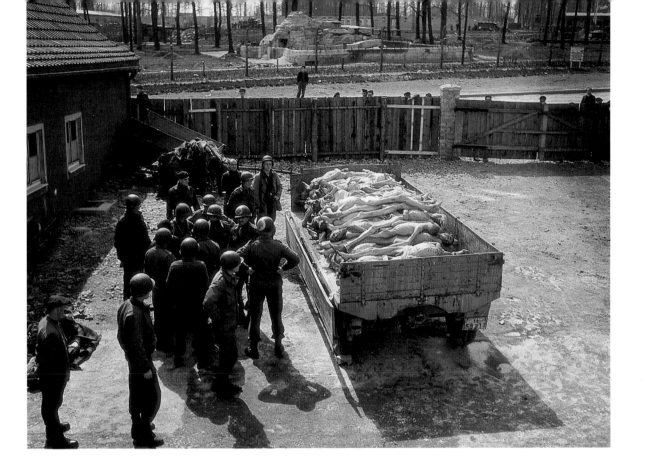

ABOVE

The corpses of some forty inmates of
Buchenwald, abandoned by German guards
in a truck outside the camp crematorium;
they were photographed on April 18, 1945.
The camp was opened in 1938 but, despite
the horrors discovered there, it contained
more "long-term" survivors than many of
the other Nazi concentration camps.

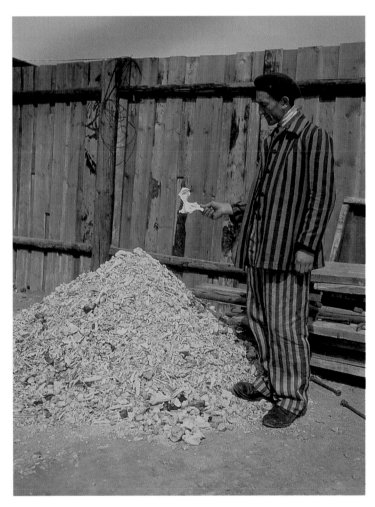

RIGHT

Also on April 18, a survivor of
Buchenwald surveys a pile of bones
shoveled out of the crematorium.
From within the camp, CBS Radio's Ed
Murrow delivered a moving commentary
which revealed to American listeners the
horror of what had happened there.

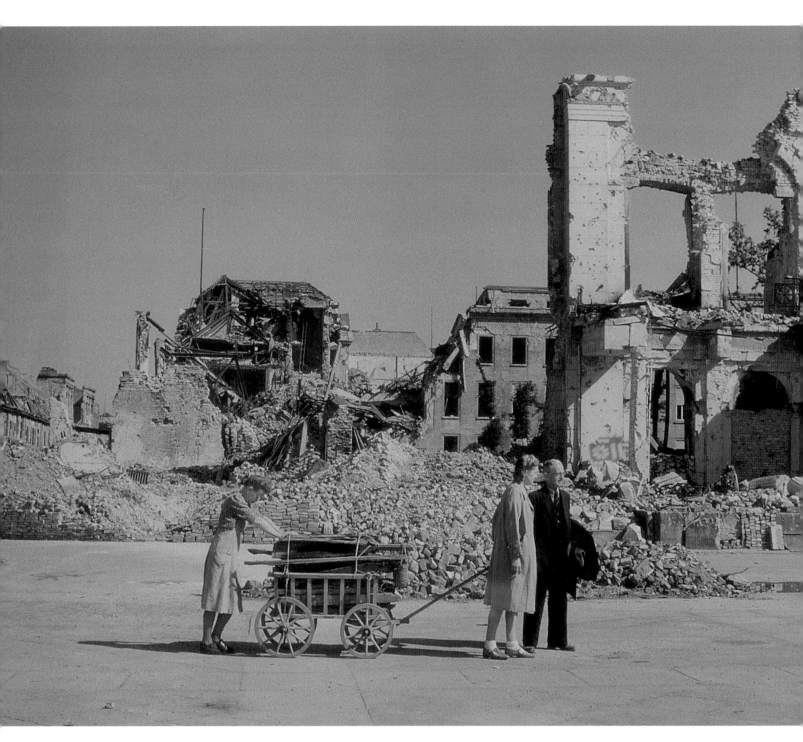

THE RUINS OF GERMANY

Quite apart from the devastation caused by Allied bombing, many German cities and their populations suffered further destruction from heavy fighting during their capture by the Allies in the spring of 1945. This was particularly true of Berlin, which descended into an orgy of killing and retribution as Soviet forces entered the city during the last few days of April 1945.

ABOVE

German refugees pass the ruins of Goebbels' Propaganda Ministry, Berlin, in summer 1945.

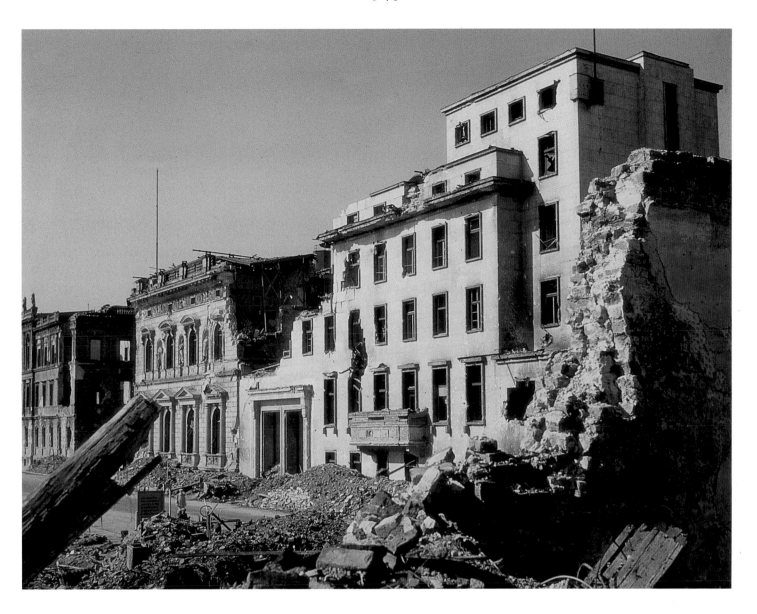

ABOVE

The Reichs Chancellery, Berlin, in summer 1945. Once the stage for many of Hitler's best-known public appearances, and former nerve center of the Reich, it was shattered in combined raids by the U.S. 8th Air Force and the Royal Air Force.

RIGHT

Belgium: as peace fell over Europe in summer 1945, numerous German prisoners remained in captivity while the process of de-Nazification and screening for war criminals continued.

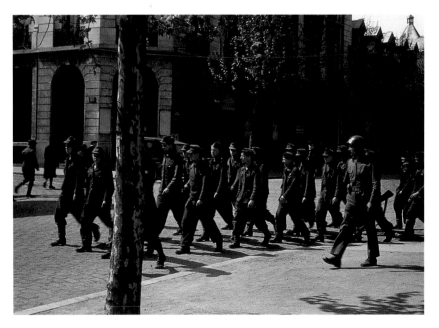

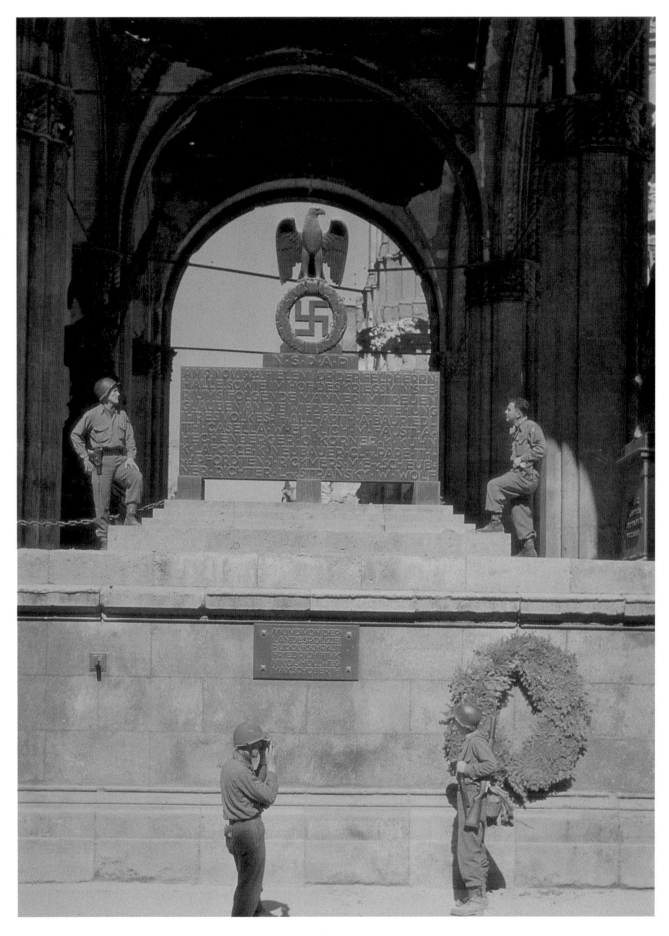

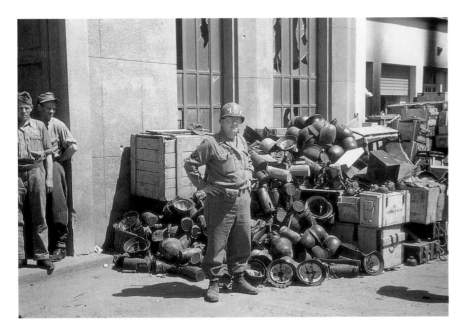

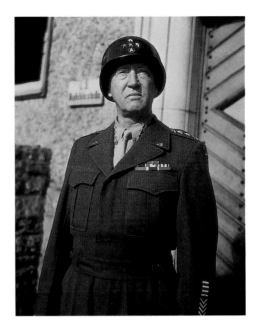

ABOVE

Equipment confiscated from German prisoners of war in Bolzano, Italy, May 1945.

ABOVE

General George S. Patton Jr., photographed in 1945.

LEFT

In summer 1945 G.I.s pose outside the Munich memorial to the fallen of Hitler's 1923 Beer Hall Putsch.

RIGHT

With the aid of Major Paul Kubla, from Elizabethtown, Kentucky, Reichsmarschall Hermann Goering gives a press conference while under arrest in summer 1945. In April, as the Soviet troops encroached on Berlin, Goering had left for his native Bavaria. Hitler misinterpreted a telegram from Goering, wherein he offered to take command of all surviving German forces, as an act of treason and had him stripped of all powers and placed under arrest by the S.S. Following Germany's surrender, Goering was tried at Nuremberg and found guilty on all counts. The day before his planned execution in October 1946, he committed suicide by taking a cyanide capsule, the source of which remains a mystery.

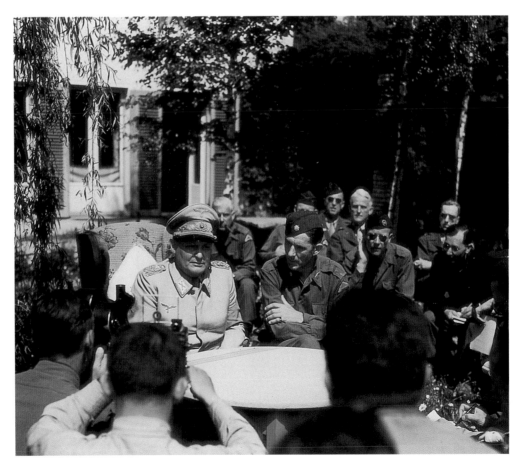

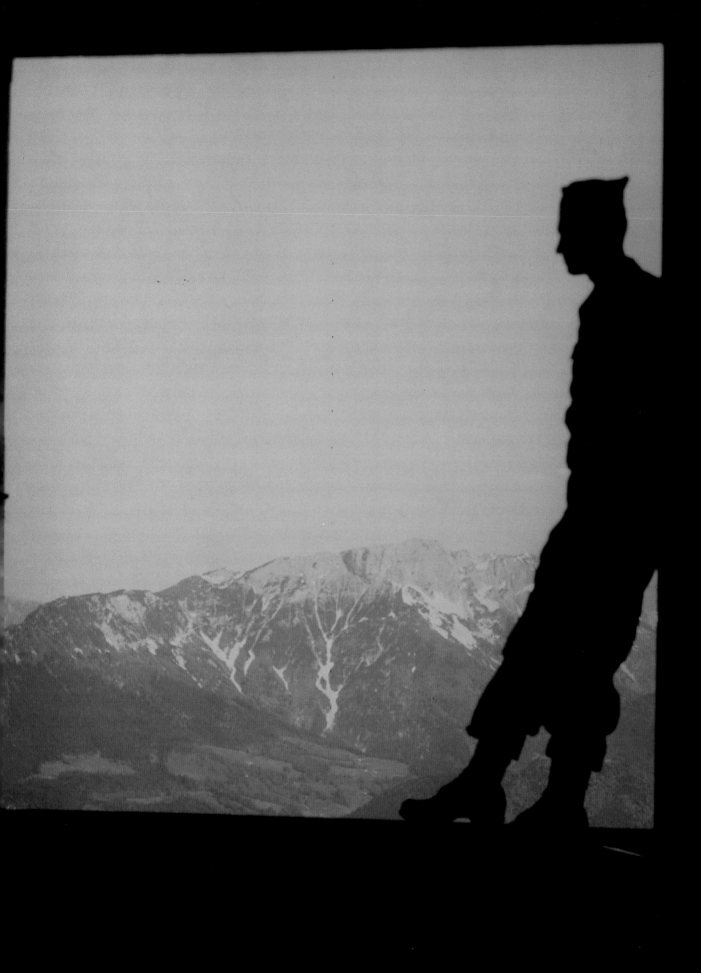

LEFT

A G.I. of the 101st Airborne Division's 327th Glider Infantry Regiment looks out over the Bavarian Alps from Hitler's front window at the "Eagle's Nest," in summer 1945.

RIGHT

Captured German U-boat 858 is brought to anchor at Cape Henlopen, Delaware, in May 1945. After the crew of the Type 1XC submarine surrendered at sea, command was taken by Lieutenant Commander Willard D. Michael, U.S. Navy, who can be seen in the conning tower with a microphone. The U-boat is being escorted by a Sikorski HNS-1 helicopter and an airship.

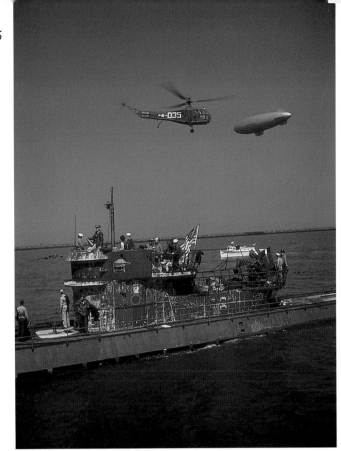

BELOW

Crew members of German U-boat 858 under arrest in May 1945, after being escorted for over a thousand miles to surrender off Cape May, New Jersey.

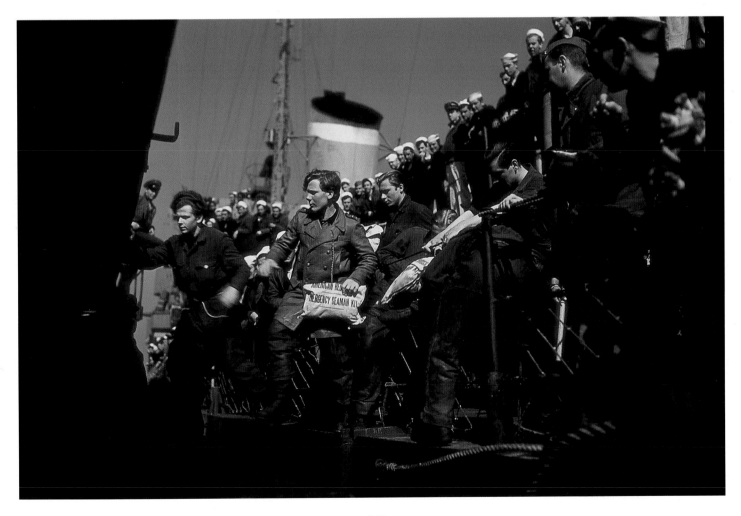

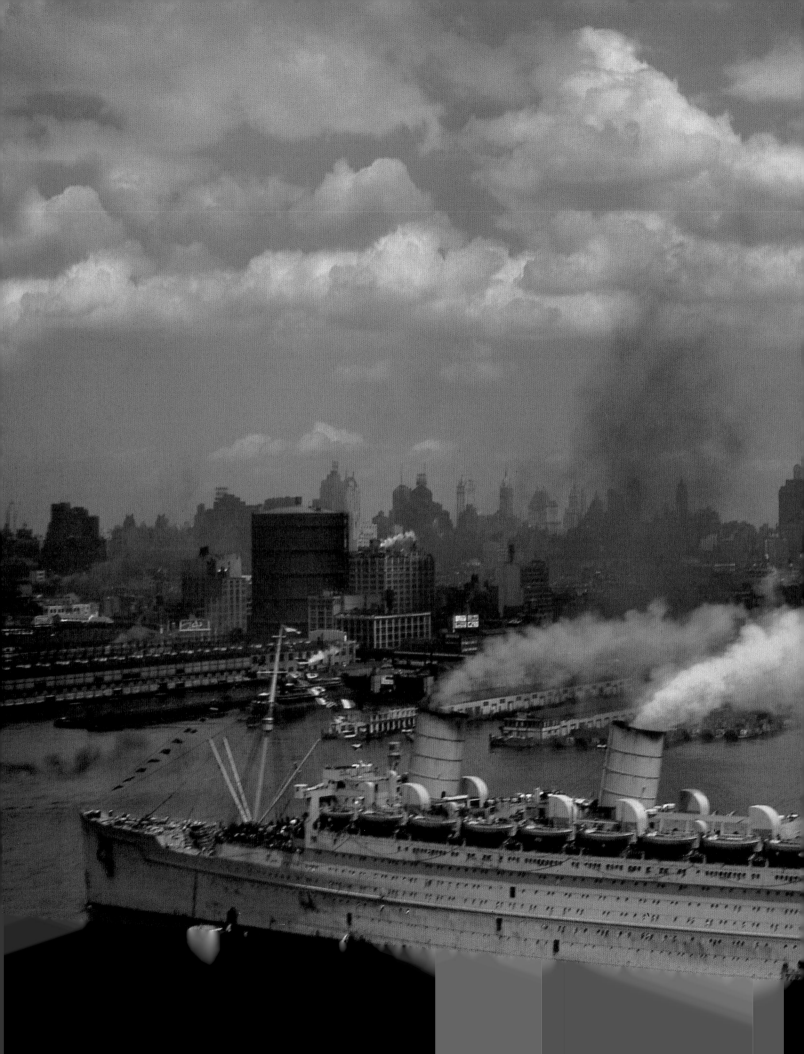

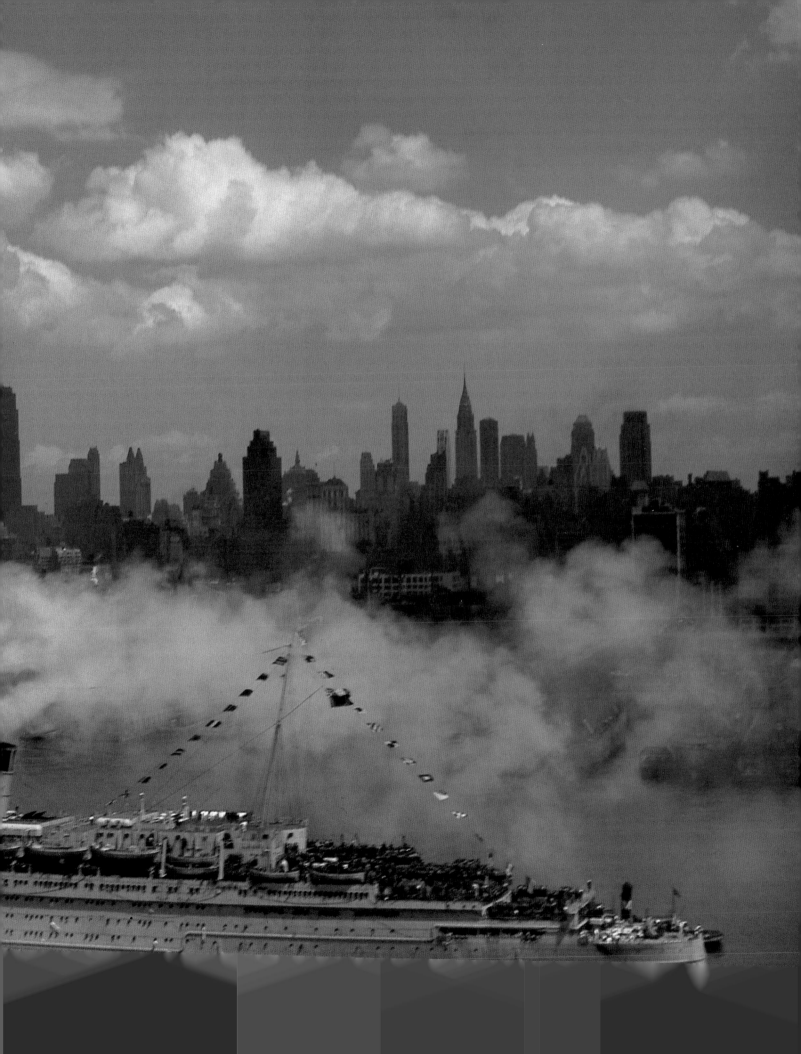

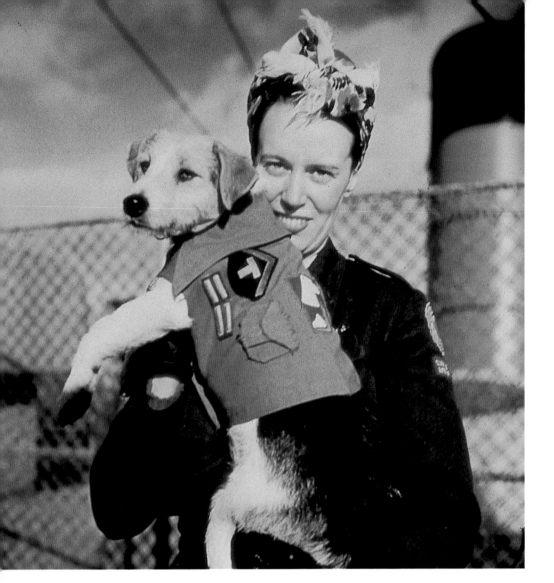

PREVIOUS PAGE
An aerial view of H.M.S. *Queen Mary* entering New York harbor on June 20, 1945. Aboard her were thousands of returning service personnel. In 1942, during one of the many transatlantic crossings she made as a troopship, she rammed her cruiser escort, *Curacao*, which sank, with the loss of 338 lives.

ABOVE

Spotty, for two years the unofficial mascot of I Company, 70th Infantry Division, is seen in the arms of Red Cross nurse Rosaline Palmer, of Menlo Park, California, aboard the *Queen Mary* en route to New York on November 4, 1945. Spotty had been abandoned in Southampton, England, by I Company because they thought he could not be brought to the U.S. Rescued by two nurses, he was reunited with his owner, Private Caputo, of Hammorton, New Jersey, on November 20, 1945 in New York.

RIGHT

Shipboard sweethearts Sergeant Edna McDonald, of Warrenville, South Carolina, and George Zavoda, of Linden, New Jersey, snapped on November 4, 1945, following the relaxation of non-fraternization rules after their second day at sea.

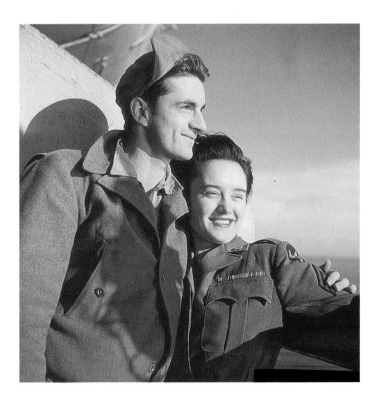

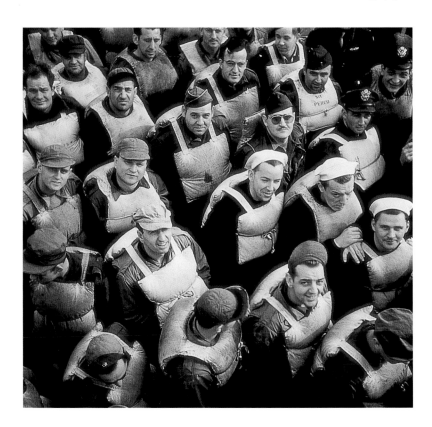

THE WORLD'S POLICEMAN

For most U.S. service personnel, their terms of daily duty overseas brought them into contact with distant culture for the first time. For many Americans of European origin, war service came to represent a significant bridge back to their cultural origins. In foreign policy terms, the millions of Americans who served overseas quickly became symbols of the new role of the United States as the world's policeman.

LEFT

Everyone aboard ship was required to wear a life-preserver for lifeboat drill, which was held daily at 11.00hrs. This drill took place on November 4, 1945.

BELOW

The scene from the deck of a home-ward-bound troopship as it rounds the southern tip of Manhattan, New York.

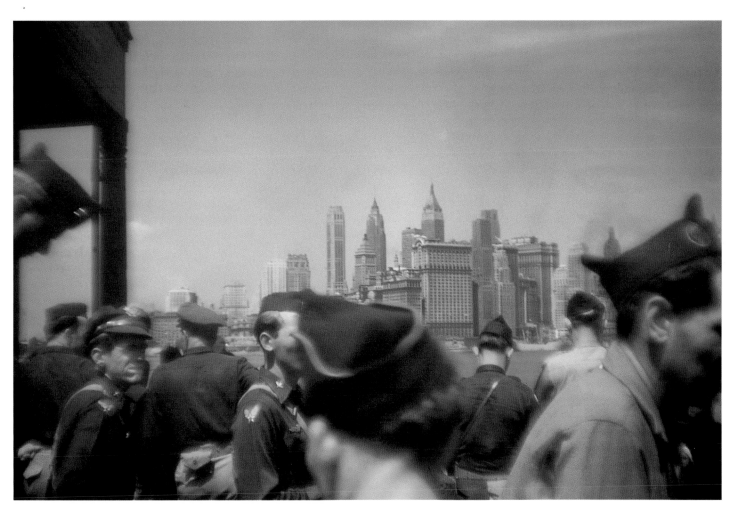

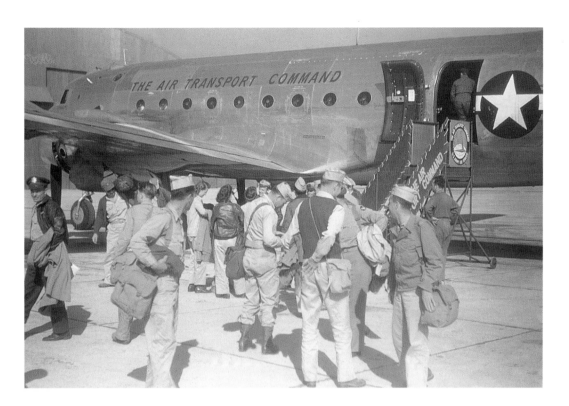

November 17, 1945: Members of the 345th Bomb Group, The Air Apaches, step off their C-54 transport plane at Hamilton Field, California, upon arrival from the Pacific theater. The photographer, a member of the group, had left the United States 30 months and 17 days earlier.

The crew of a U.S. Army tugboat give their personal greeting to troops aboard the *Westminster Victory*.

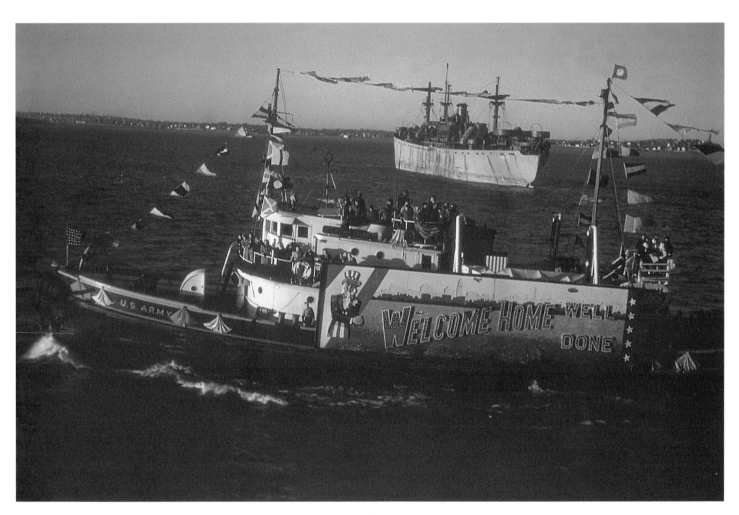

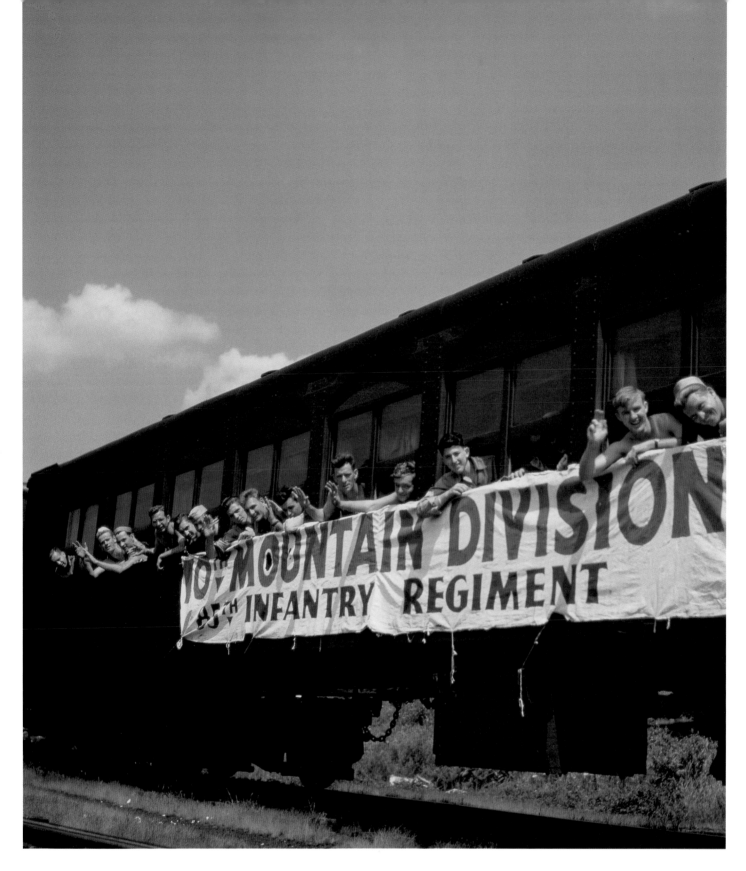

Troops of the 85th Infantry Regiment, 10th Mountain Division,
lean out of carriage windows on their way home in August 1945.
Within twenty-four hours of their arrival at a processing center,
they were aboard trains taking them to regional centers from
where they began a thirty-day furlough.

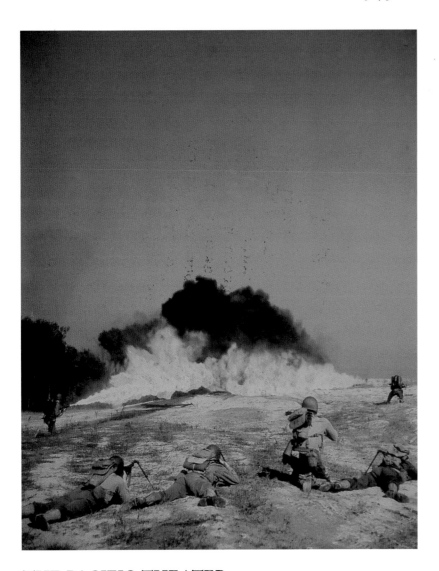

LEFT
Flame-thrower training at the
Edgewood Arsenal, Maryland.

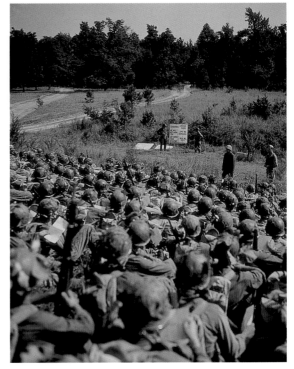

THE PACIFIC THEATER

Victory in Europe was only a partial triumph for the Allies. Many U.S. servicemen faced immediate re-deployment to the Pacific theater to continue the war against Japan after the European campaign was over. In many ways, this was an even more daunting proposition than the battleground of Europe. In Europe, the greater part of the most vicious fighting had been undertaken by the Soviet Red Army. In the Pacific, U.S. forces were engaged in one-to-one fighting over difficult terrain, in a bitter campaign against an equally implacable enemy.

ABOVE
A Japanese-American soldier teaches recruits commands in basic Japanese at Camp McCllellan, Alabama, in July 1945.

BELOW

Troops and a Red Cross dog train in gas masks, in preparation for redeployment to the Pacific theater, in 1945.

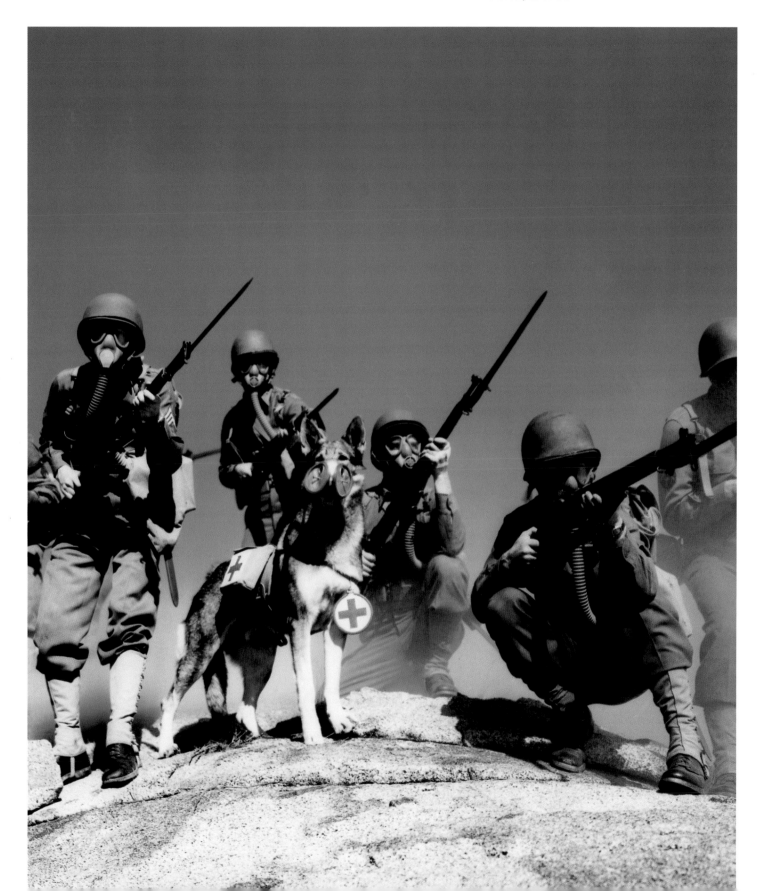

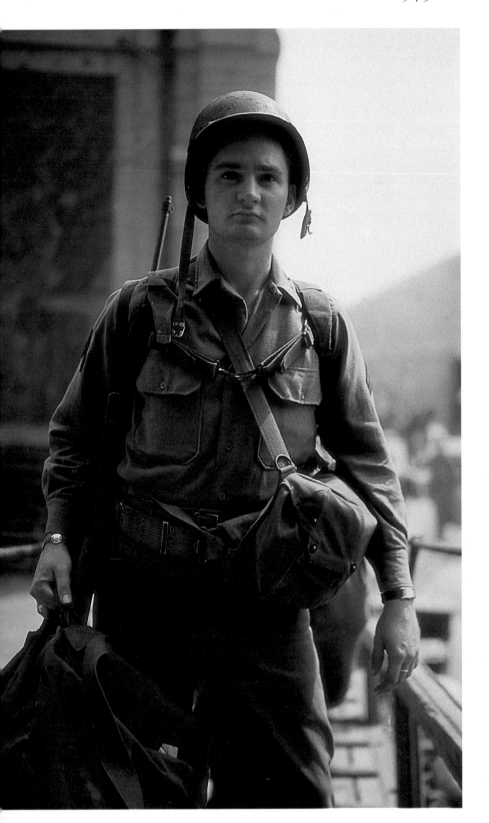

LEFT
Corporal Charles Hannon, from Akron, Ohio, boards a troopship near Marseilles in July 1945, after leaving the Calas staging area with his combat engineer unit for C.B.I. (China-Burma-India theater). He said, "I hope that this trip that we're making will not be a futile one."

BELOW
On November 4, 1945, Staff Sergeant Lester Lanke, from North Judson, Indiana, leaves Europe for an America at peace.

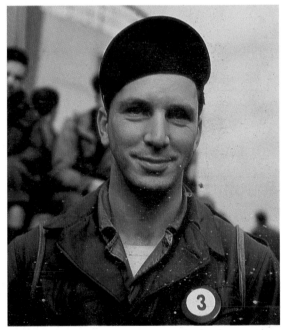

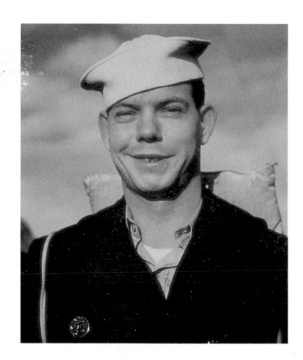

Machinist's Mate 3/c M.D. McCulloch, of Leaksville, North Carolina, prepares to sail to the U.S.A. on November 4, 1945. He hoped to become a postal officer aboard a civilian ship.

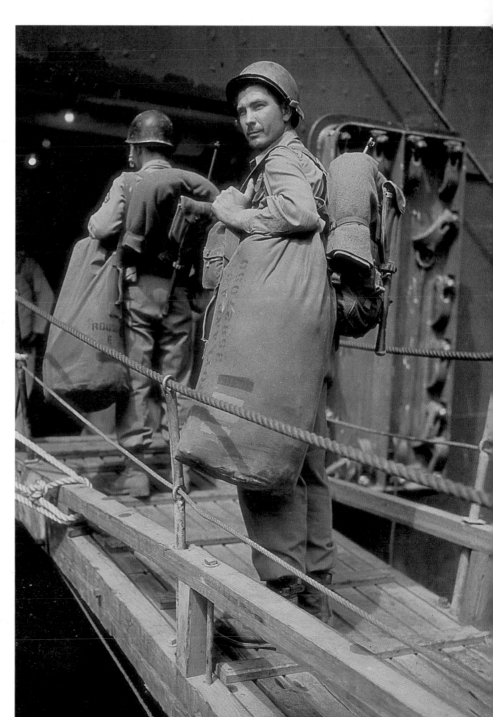

Private Royland Otter, of Madison, Indiana, a combat engineer, boards a troopship in the Calas staging area near Marseilles bound for the C.B.I. theater in spring 1945. He commented to the photographer that, "It would have been nicer to have gone through the States to see my wife and three daughters, but it's too late now."

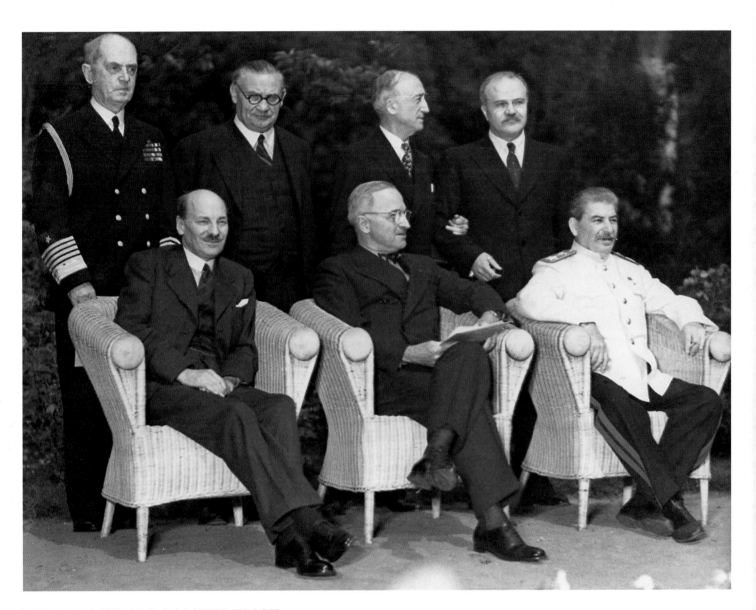

THE POTSDAM CONFERENCE

By the time of the Potsdam Conference in August 1945, the "Big Three" had assumed a very different complexion. President Roosevelt had died four months earlier, to be replaced by Harry S. Truman, and Winston Churchill and his Conservative party had suffered a shock, landslide defeat in the British general election to be replaced by the Labor party under the leadership of Clement Attlee (Churchill's deputy in the wartime coalition government).

ABOVE

At the Potsdam Conference, August 2, 1945. Seated are (L–R) British Prime Minister Clement Attlee, U.S. President Harry S. Truman, and Soviet premier Josef Stalin; standing behind them are (L–R) Admiral William Leahy, U.S. Chief of Staff; Ernest Bevin, the British Foreign Minister; U.S. Secretary of State James F. Byrnes; and Russian Foreign Minister Vyacheslav Molotov.

RIGHT

The mushroom cloud of the first atomic weapons test at Alamogordo in the New Mexico desert, on July 16, 1945. The success of the secret Manhattan Project atomic weapons program was revealed to Churchill at the Potsdam Conference, which was taking place at the time.

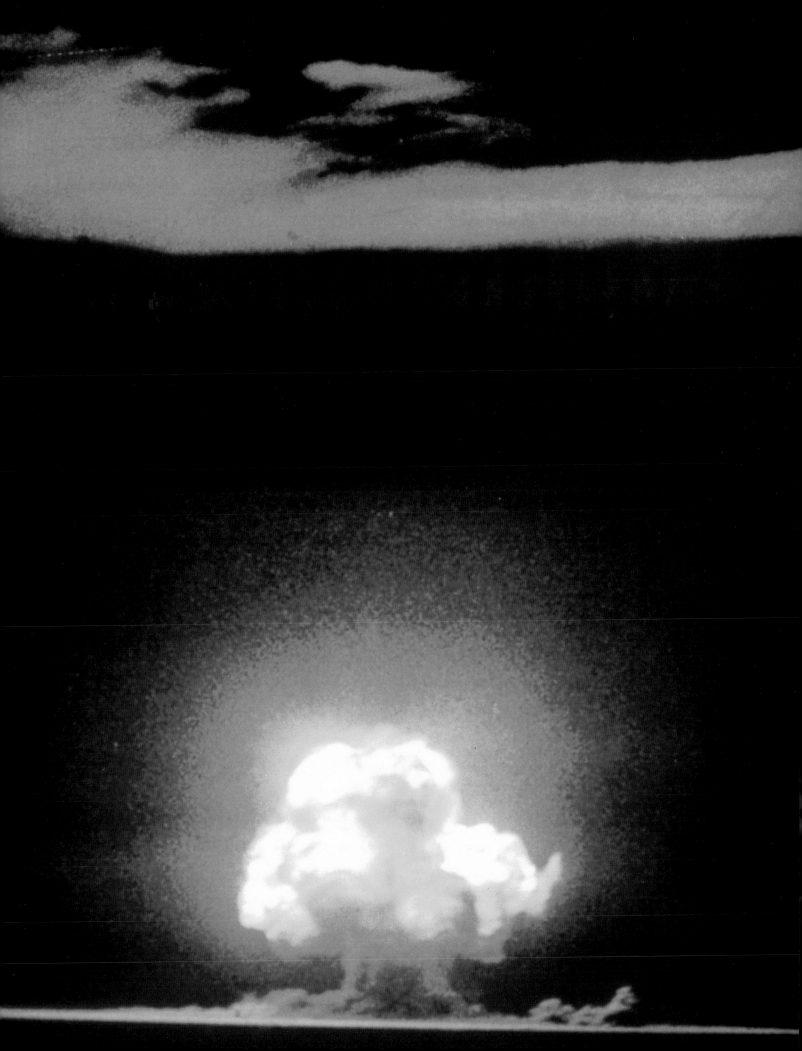

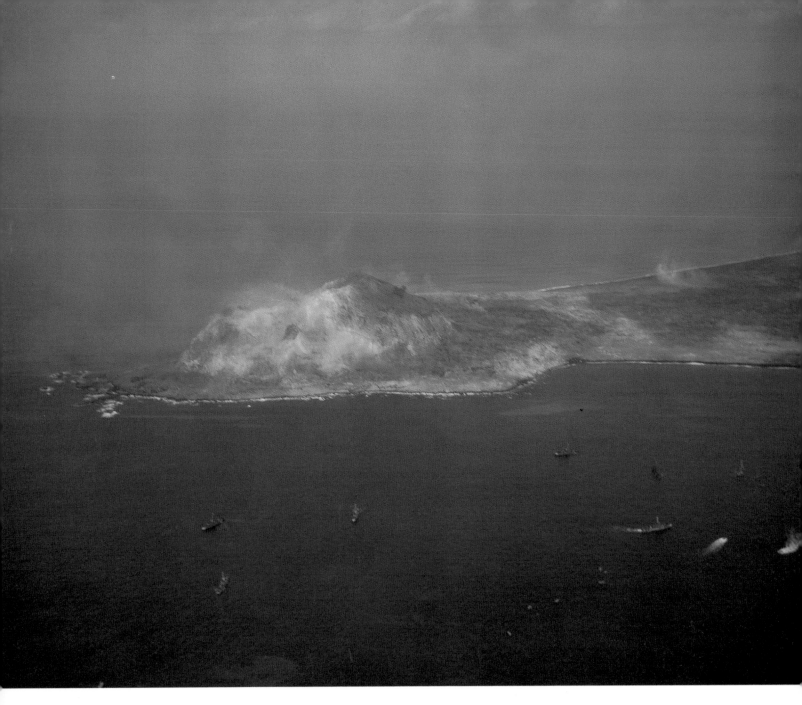

IWO JIMA

Iwo Jima was a key island in the battle for territory in the Pacific. Although only eight miles across, the craggy volcanic terrain was being used by the Japanese as a radar warning station and a base for fighter interceptors and was defended by 20,000 Japanese troops. On February 23, after three days of furious combat, the Marines hoisted the Stars and Stripes on Mount Suribachi and photographer Joe Rosenthal captured one of the war's most famous images. It had taken almost a month of bitter fighting, 20,965 American casualties (including 6,821 dead) to complete the capture of the island.

Aerial view from a reconnaissance aircraft of bombardment and landing operations at the moment of attack on Iwo Jima, on February 19, 1945.

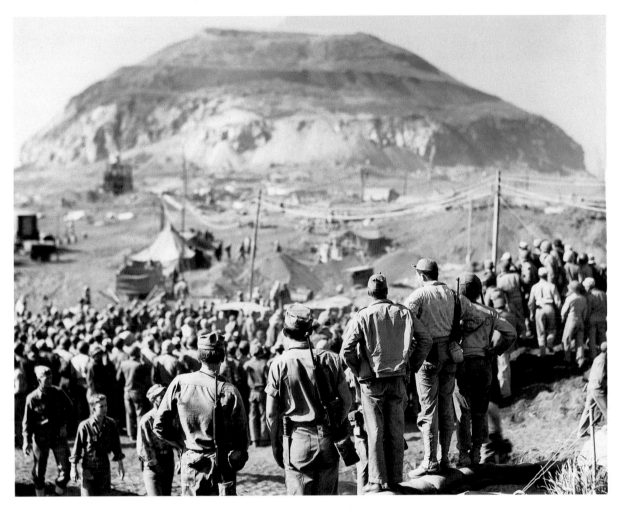

ABOVE

The official flag-raising ceremony on Iwo Jima on March 14, 1945.

BELOW

Marines read mail during a lull in the fighting for Iwo Jima, in March 1945.

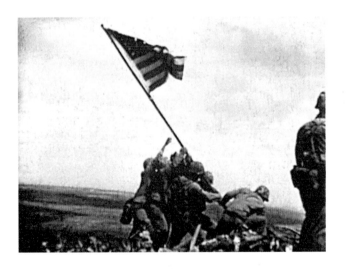

ABOVE

A still frame from the U.S. Marine Corps 16mm Kodachrome motion picture footage of the second flagraising on Mount Suribachi, Iwo Jima Island, February 1945.

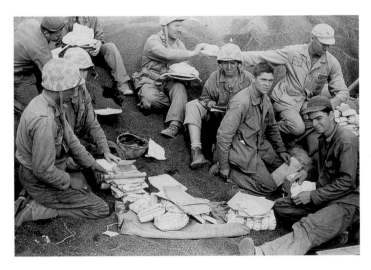

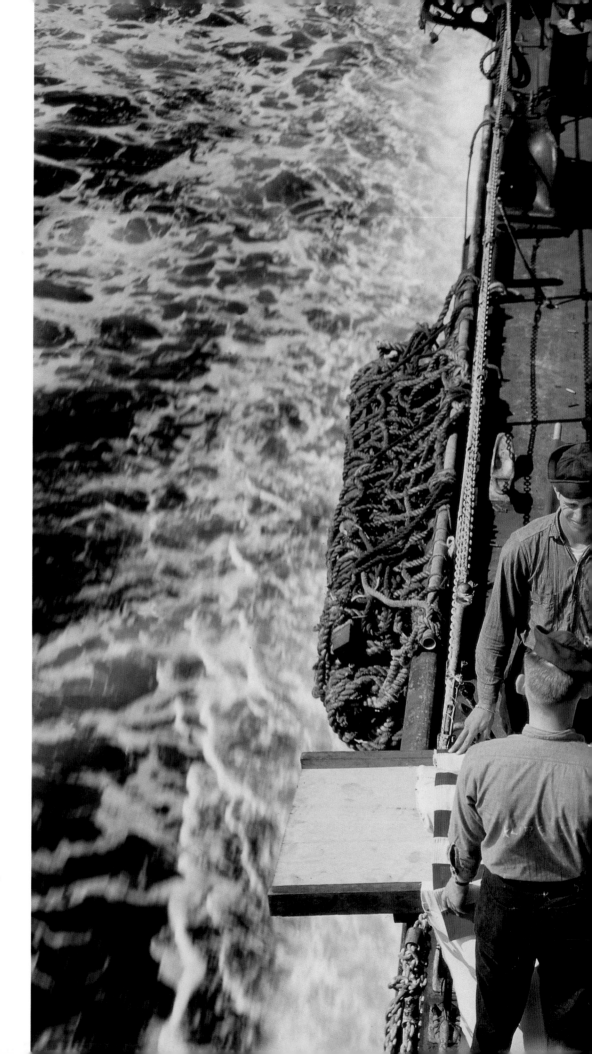

The burial at sea of a U.S.
Marine in late February 1945.
He had been wounded on
Iwo Jima, and died while
being evacuated to Saipan for
treatment aboard the hospital
ship U.S.S. *Hanford*.

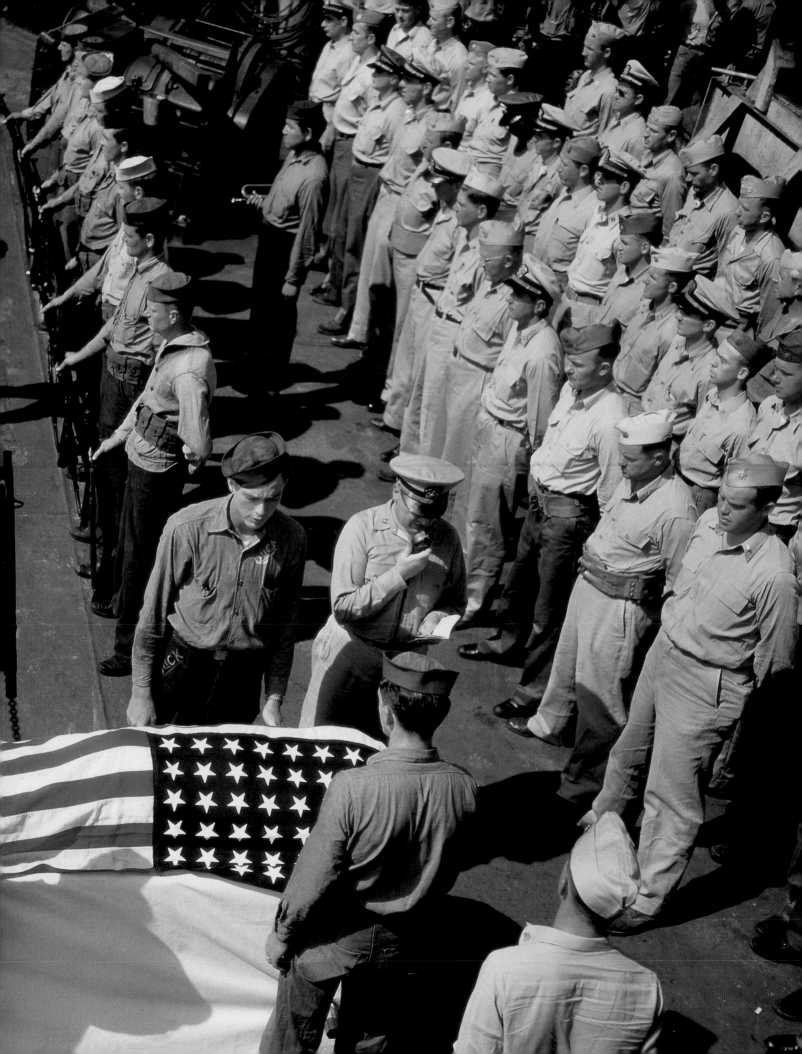

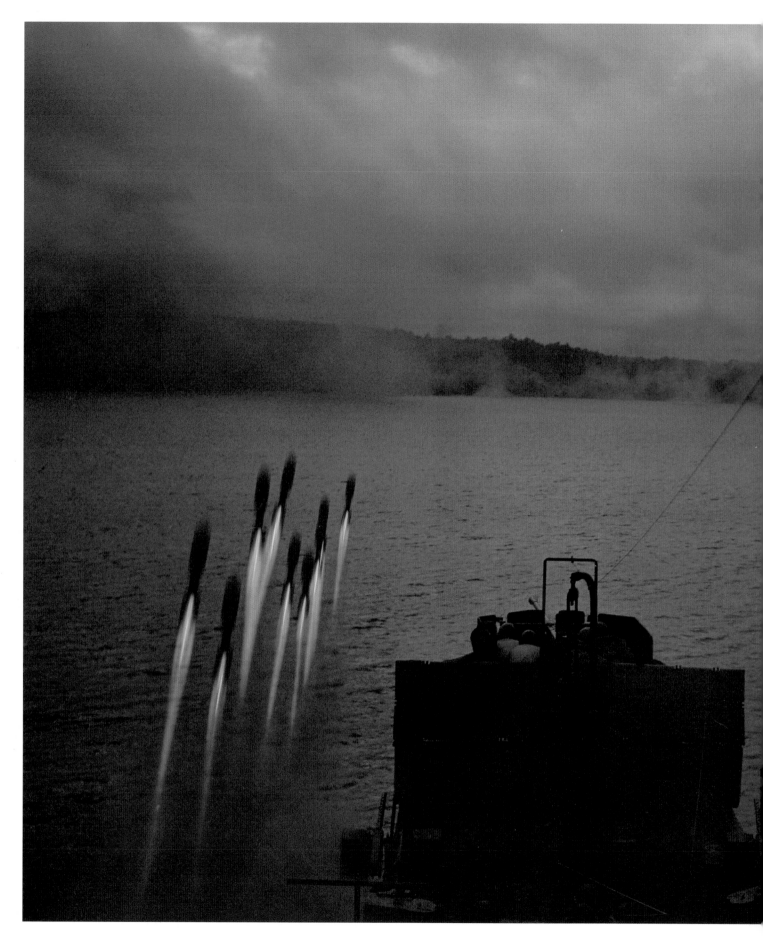

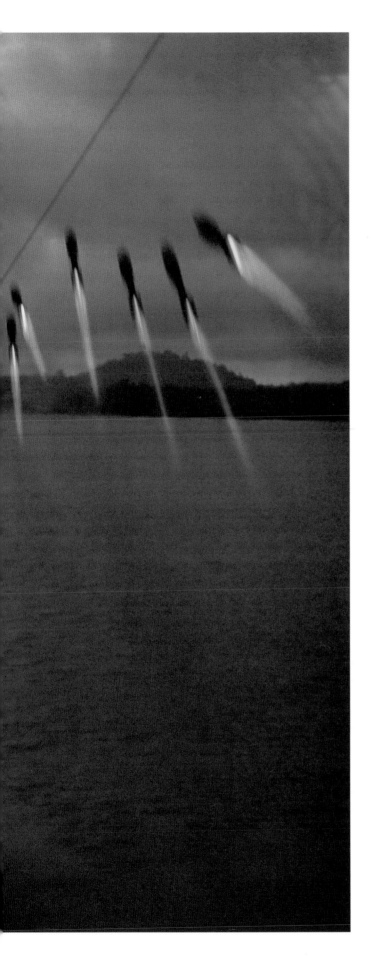

A dawn shot of rockets fired onto the island of Mindanao, in the Philippines, on April 17, 1945.

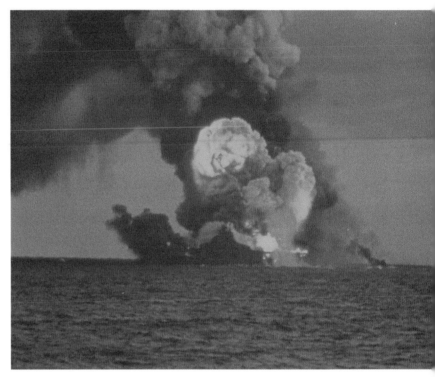

ABOVE
The inland Sea of Japan, on March 19, 1945: a huge explosion occurs aboard the U.S.S. *Franklyn* following an attack by Japanese kamikaze bombers. The *Franklyn* was hit by two 500lb bombs.

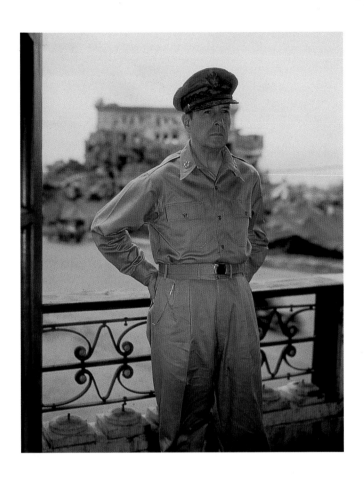

LEFT

General Douglas MacArthur, Supreme Allied Commander Pacific Ocean Area, poses on a Manila balcony in August 1945, having kept his promise to return to the Philippines.

BELOW

Captain Jesús Blanco, an intelligence officer, briefs pilots of the 201st Mexican Fighter Squadron of the Mexican Expeditionary Air Force at their Porac Strip base, Clark Field, Luzon, the Philippines, in July 1945.

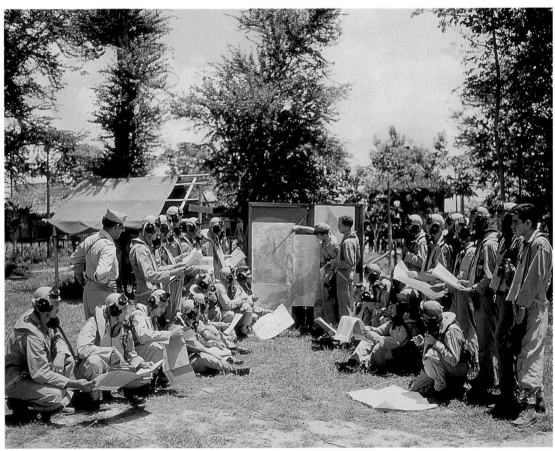

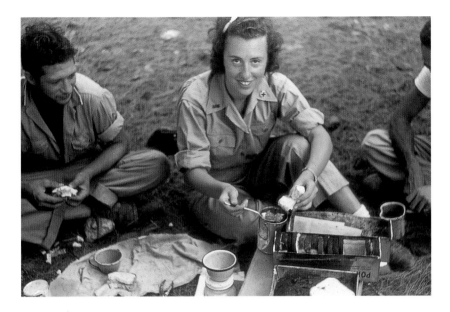

ABOVE

A Red Cross nurse shares a picnic with servicemen on Mindoro, the Philippines.

THE PHILIPPINES

The fighting for control of the Philippines became a psychological fulcrum to the war in the Pacific. When General Douglas MacArthur was forced to abandon the islands in 1942, he vowed to return. It would take three years for him to fulfil his promise, but eventually Manila, and the rest of the country, were liberated. The many battles on and around the islands would be writ large in the accounts of World War II: Leyte Gulf, Coral Sea, Corregidor, Bataan; as would, in equal measure, the stories of infamy and treachery, heroism and courage.

BELOW

Soldiers of the 1st Company, 129th Infantry Regiment, 37th Division, fire their 37mm gun at Japanese positions in Intramuros, Manila, the Philippines.

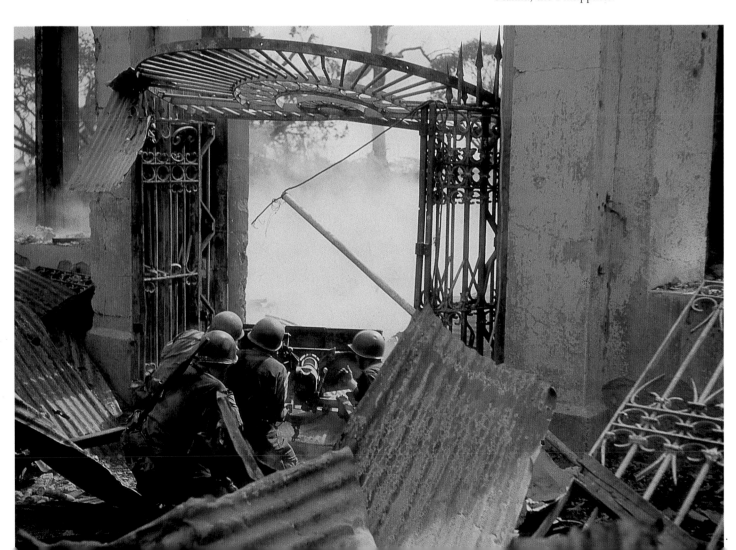

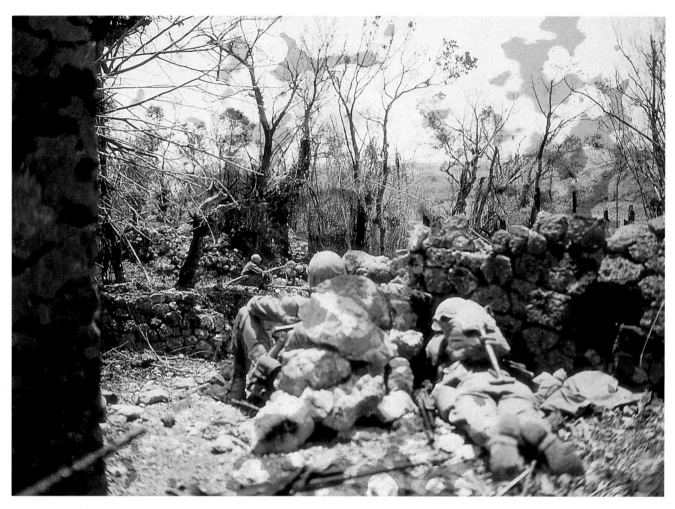

OKINAWA

The U.S. invasion of Okinawa began on April 1, Easter Sunday. The capture of the island was vital to any future invasion of Japan's main islands, lying over 400 miles to the north. The assault can only be compared in scale with the Normandy landings on D-Day. Over half a million troops took part, supported by over 1,200 warships. Japanese resistance lasted for almost three months. The fighting was extremely fierce, culminating in mass suicides by Japanese soldiers and civilians.

ABOVE
Marines advance on Okinawa on May 11, 1945.

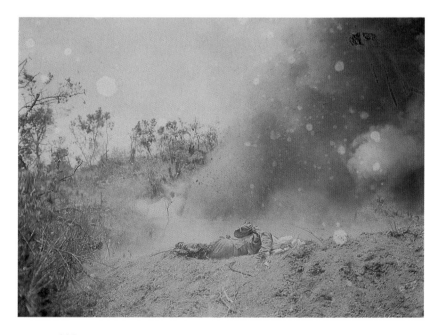

RIGHT
Grenades are used to flush out Japanese troops from underground positions on May 11, 1945.

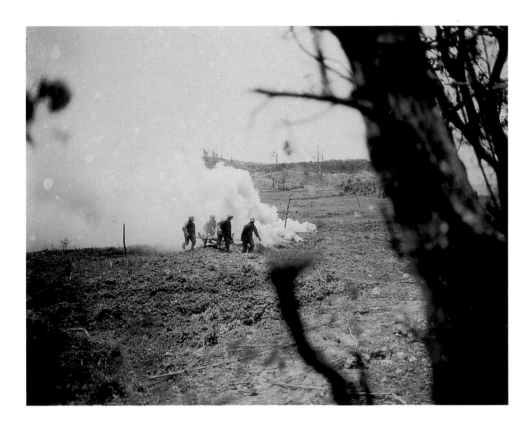

LEFT

On May 11, 1945, Marines bring in a wounded comrade under cover of a smokescreen during the battle for Okinawa.

BELOW

A grim reminder of the human cost of war: grave markers being manufactured in bulk on the Russell Islands in February 1945.

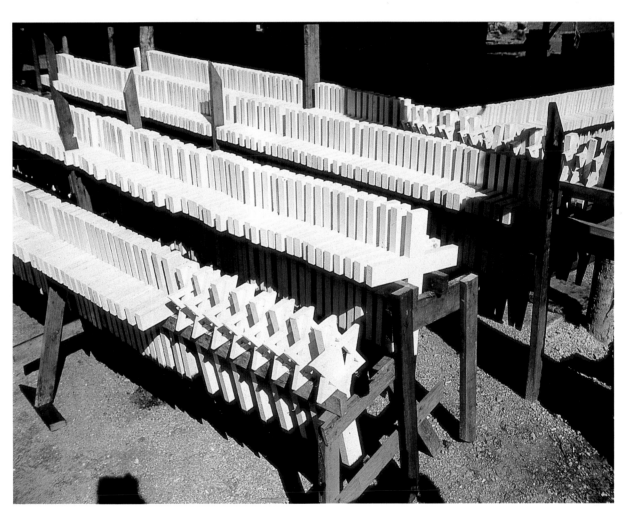

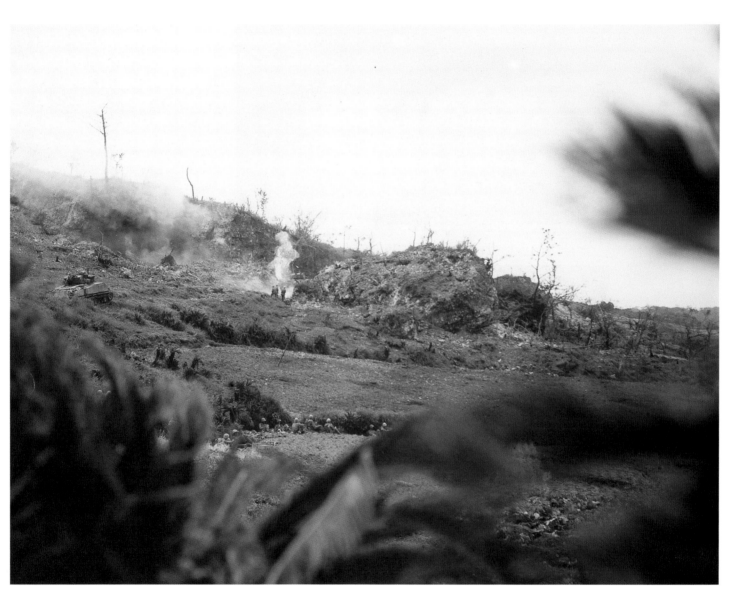

ABOVE

A Japanese ammunition dump
explodes after flame-throwers
were used on it—as on many
Japanese positions—by U.S.
troops in June 1945.

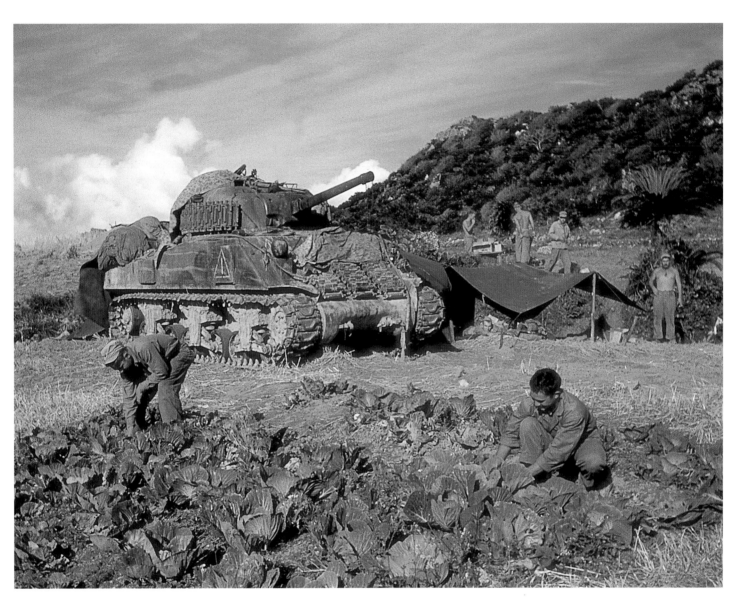

ABOVE

Tanks of 6th Marine Division
are parked overnight on
Okinawa on May 6, 1945.

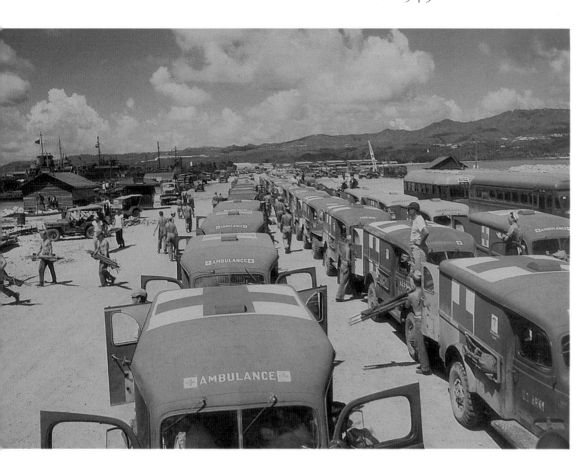

RIGHT
Fleet Admiral Chester W. Nimitz lands, on January 26, 1945, to direct the attack on the Okinawa battlefront.

ABOVE
Ambulances await the arrival of the U.S.S. *Solace* at the dock in Guam on June 4, 1945. The *Solace* was carrying casualties from the fighting on Okinawa.

RIGHT
Seen from the battleship U.S.S. *West Virginia*, the U.S.S. *Idaho* fires a salvo from her 14inch guns at point-blank range onto the island of Okinawa on April 1, 1945.

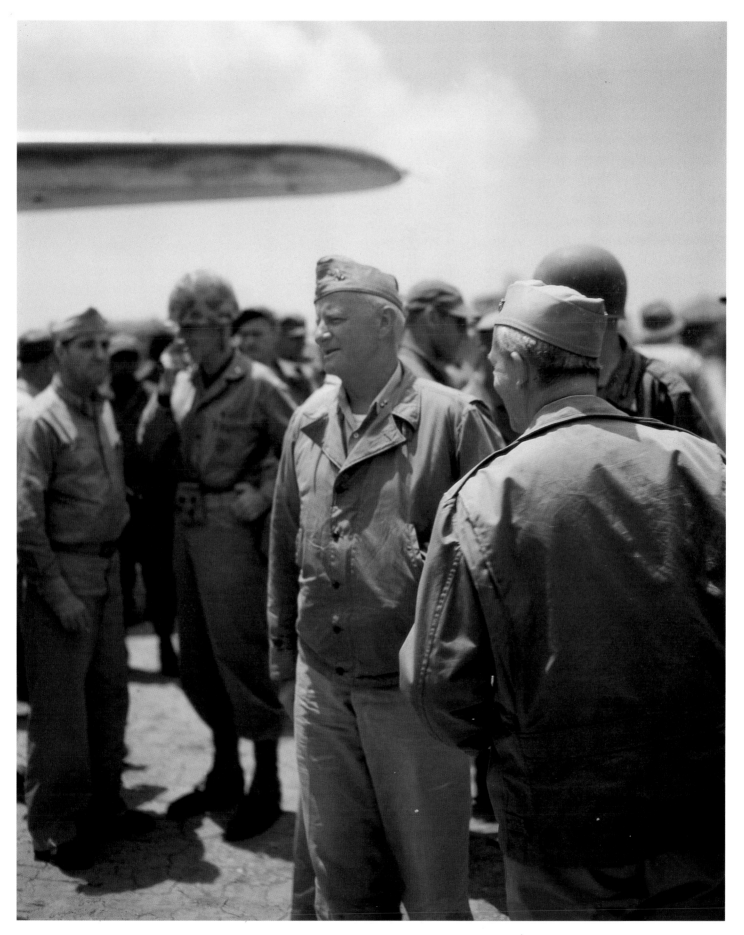

U.S. CASUALTIES

Over 16 million Americans served in the Armed Forces during World War II. 405,000 forces personnel lost their lives during the conflict; a further 670,000 returned home wounded. 140,000 soldiers, sailors and airmen were captured by the enemy and became prisoners of war.

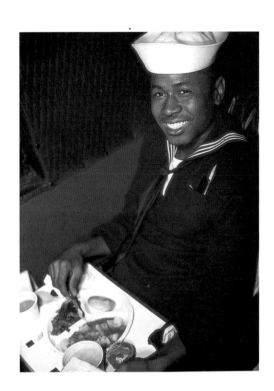

LEFT
Willie Blue of the U.S.N.R. has a hot meal aboard a National Air Transport Service (N.A.T.S.) aircraft. These flights carried wounded and convalescing troops to medical facilities near their homes.

BELOW
The Naval Convalescent Hospital, Santa Cruz, California—formerly the Casa del Rey Hotel—was used for the rehabilitation of injured Navy personnel. Exercising in June 1945, under the supervision of Overton Cheadle, are (L–R) S.N. Fecko, F.R. English, and L.K. Freijt.

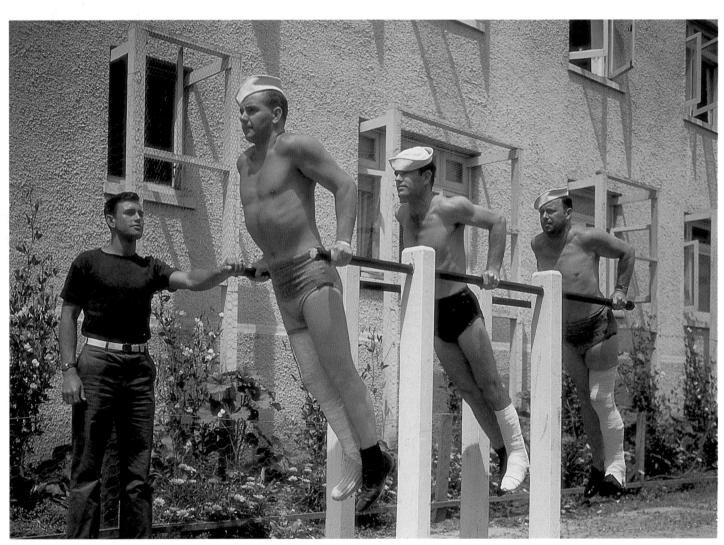

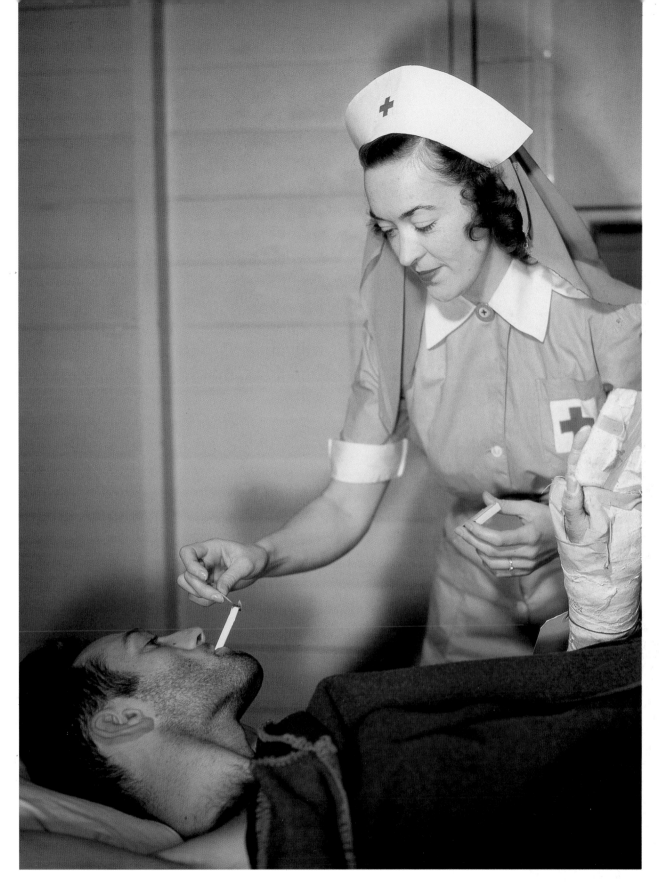

Mrs. R.D. Whitley, wife of Commander Ralph Whitley U.S.N.
(M.C.), a volunteer Red Cross "Gray Lady," lights a cigarette for
Ralph Haynes U.S.N., at the Air Evacuation Center, Naval Air
Station, Patuxent River, Maryland, in 1945.

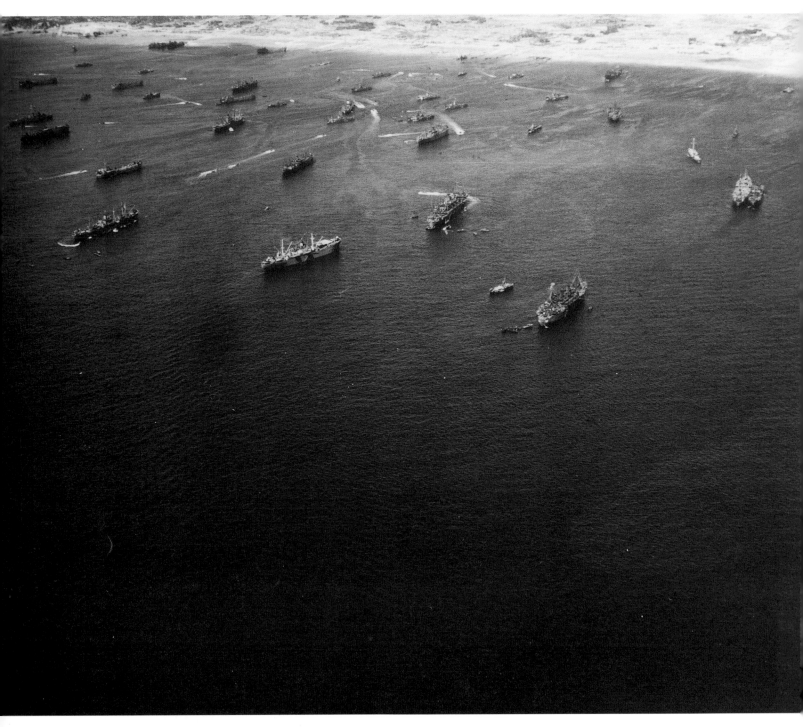

INVASION OF JAPAN

The invasion of Japan's main islands was scheduled for November 1945 on Kyushu (the southernmost island) and on Honshu (the main island), to the east of Tokyo for January 1946. The Japanese army had 53 divisions deployed (nearly 2 million men) half of whom had been mobilized between January and June 1945. The invasion plans were nullified when the dropping of the atomic bombs on Hiroshima and Nagasaki brought the Japanese surrender on August 15. By the time U.S. forces arrived and the war formally ended on September 2, the army had effectively disarmed itself and all Japanese civilians had been instructed to concentrate on peace and national reconstruction.

ABOVE
An aerial view of the invasion armada approaching Japan in August 1945.

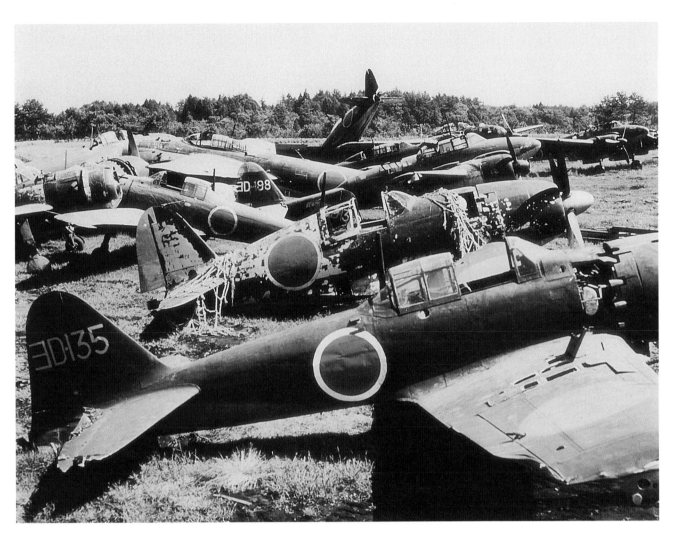

ABOVE

Wrecked Japanese Mitsubishi Zero and Kawanishi fighter planes at Atsugi Airport in September 1945.

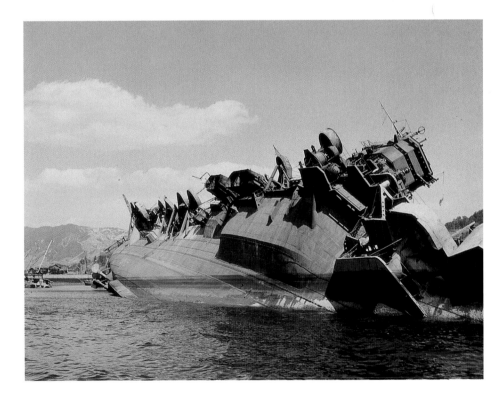

RIGHT

The Japanese aircraft carrier *Amagi* beached in Kure harbor.

HIROSHIMA

Hiroshima was chosen as the first target for the atom bomb mainly because it had not been a target for conventional bombing by the U.S.A.A.F. It was thought that previous bomb damage might reduce the psychological impact on Japan's leaders by diminishing the perceived effect of the devastation by a single weapon. The ancient city of Kyoto was also considered, but was saved by its beauty and heritage value. The centre of Hiroshima was reduced to ashes by the blast and at least 120,000 people died instantly, or within a few days of the blast. Many thousands died in the following months and years as a result of their injuries and the effects of radiation.

BELOW

Hiroshima, Japan, after the dropping on that city of the first atomic bomb on August 6, 1945.

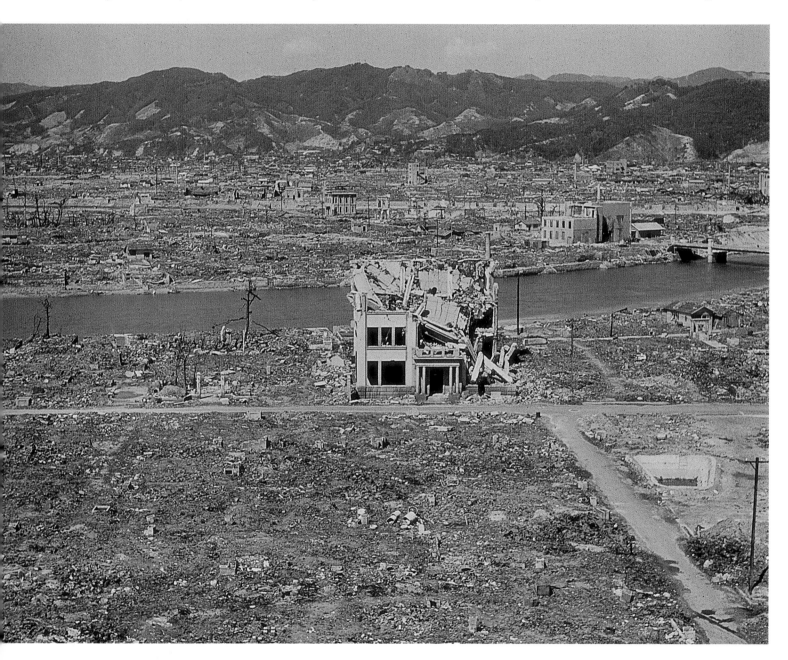

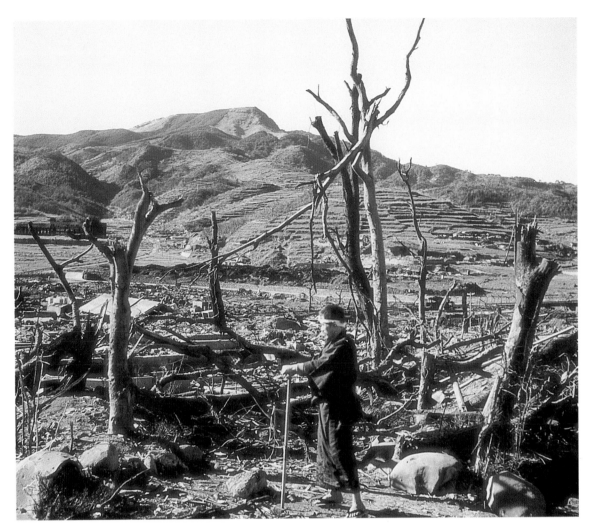

Nagasaki, Japan, which was
A-bombed on August 9, 1945.
In the foreground is Dr. Nagai,
an instructor and X-Ray
specialist from Nagasaki
Hospital. The photograph was
taken on September 8; a few
days later Dr. Nagai died from
the effects of atomic radiation.

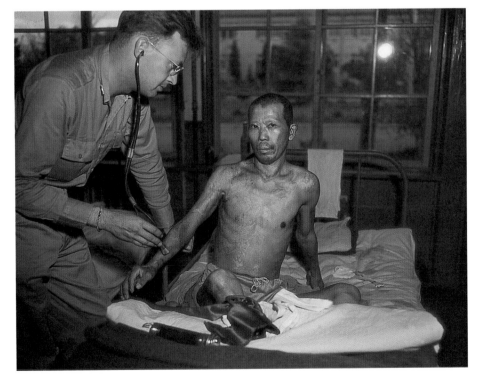

LEFT

A Japanese survivor at
Omura Navy Hospital,
Guam, on October 6, 1945.

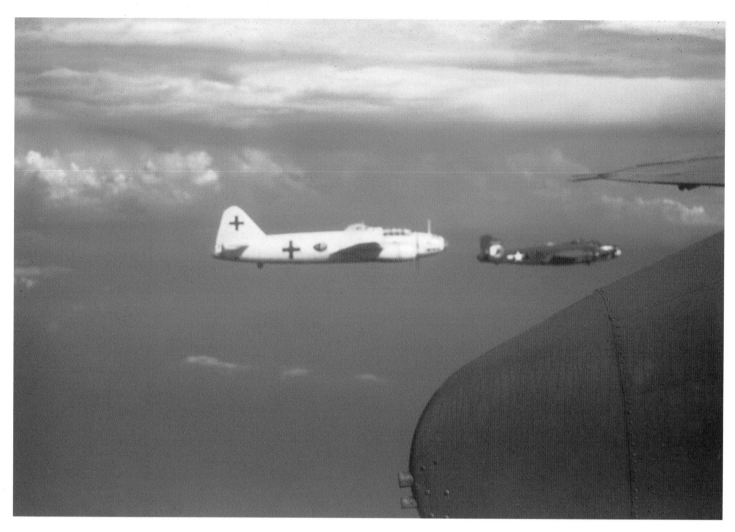

ABOVE

August 19, 1945: Betty Bombers, painted white and bearing a green cross, were used to convey the Japanese emissaries to Ie Shima with an escort of B-25 bombers of the 345th Bomb Group. From there they were taken by C-54s to General MacArthur's headquarters in Manila to make arrangements for the formal surrender and occupation of Japan.

RIGHT

General Douglas MacArthur countersigns the formal Japanese surrender document aboard the U.S.S. *Missouri* in Tokyo Bay on September 2, 1945.

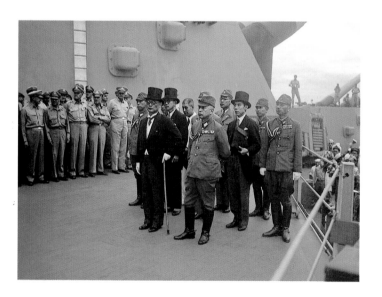

LEFT

The Japanese delegation aboard the U.S.S. *Missouri* in Tokyo Bay for the formal ceremony of surrender on September 2, 1945. Front row: Foreign Minister Mamoru Shigemitsu (left) and General Yoshijiro Umezu, Chief of the Army General Staff. Behind them are three representatives each of the Foreign Ministry, the Army and the Navy. They include Major General Yatsuji Nagai, Army; Katsuo Okazaki, Foreign Ministry; Rear Admiral Tadatoshi Tomioka, Navy; Toshikazu Kase, Foreign Ministry, and Lieutenant General Suichi Miyakazi, Army.

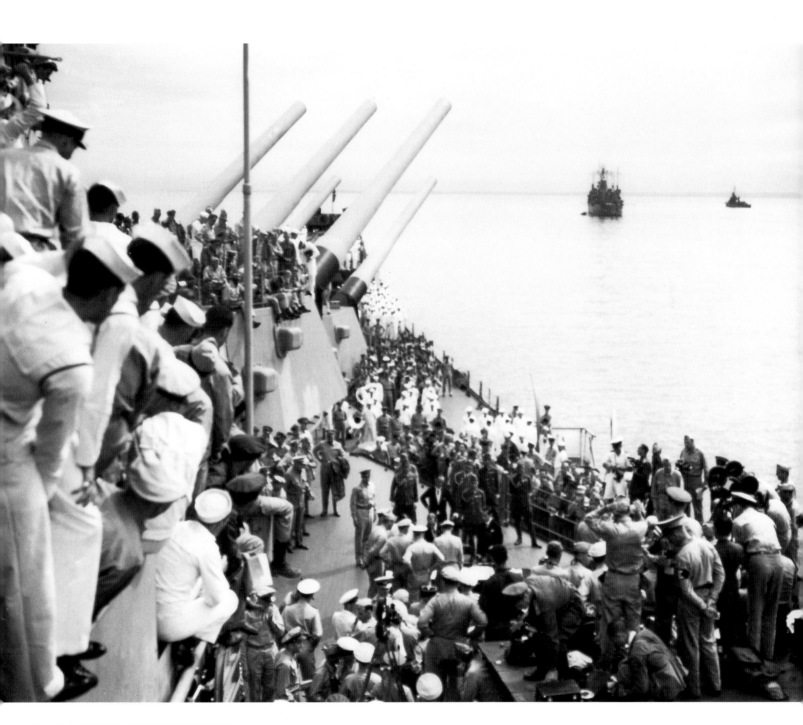

JAPANESE SURRENDER

The Japanese decision to surrender followed a long struggle within the imperial leadership. To the majority of the military, surrender was unthinkable. It was only when Emperor Hirohito and the Japanese population faced obliteration that a 'peace party' formed around the emperor. Hirohito, who had advocated peace from at least as early as 1942, then had sufficiently strong support to take the steps towards surrender.

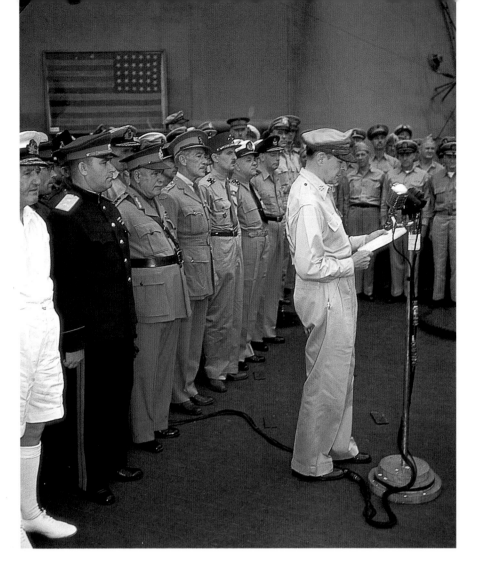

General Douglas MacArthur making a speech aboard the U.S.S. *Missouri* following the signing of Japan's formal surrender. In the background are (L–R) Admiral Sir Bruce Fraser R.N., the British representative; Lieutenant General Kuzma Derevyanko, the Soviet representative; General Sir Thomas Blamey representing Australia; Colonel Lawrence Moore-Cosgrave representing Canada; General Jacques Le Clerc, the French representative; the Dutch representative, Admiral C.E.L. Helfrich; and Air Vice Marshal L.M. Isitt representing New Zealand.

Japanese naval officers, led by Vice Admiral Michitoro Totsuka, surrender at Yokosuka Naval Base to Vice Admiral Robert Carney on August 27, 1945.

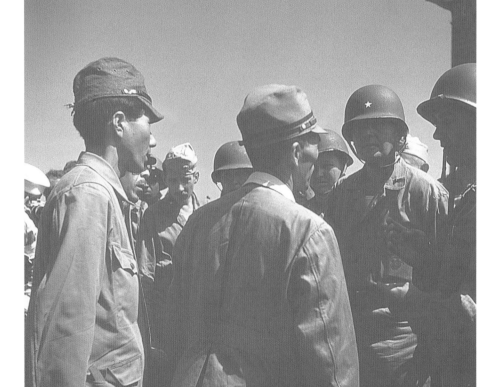

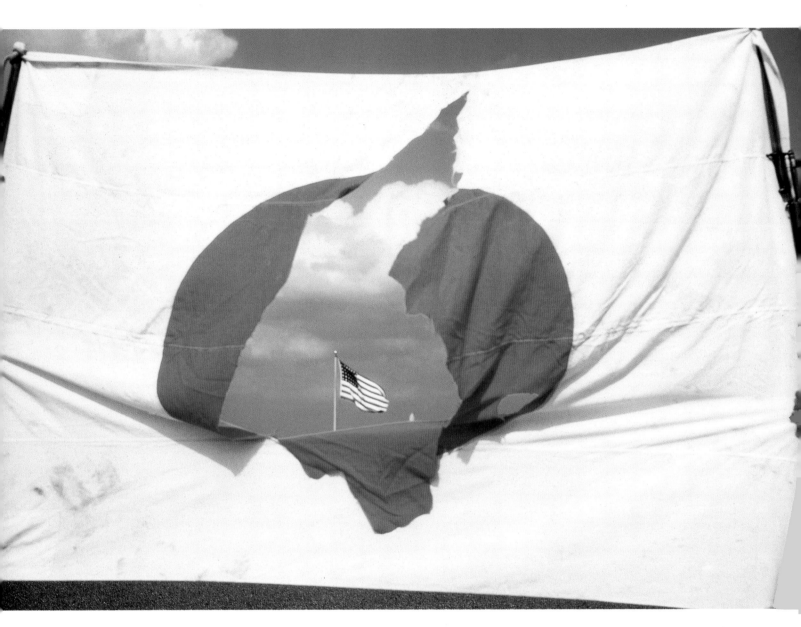

ABOVE

A battle-torn Japanese flag captured in the Solomon
Islands frames the Stars and Stripes, signaling the
liberation of yet another Pacific island.

CHRONOLOGY 1933 – 1945

1933

January 30 – Adolf Hitler is appointed Chancellor of Germany.

February 15 – A gunman, Giuseppe Zingara, tries to assassinate President-elect Franklin Roosevelt. The Mayor of Chicago is hit and later dies.

March 4 – Franklin D. Roosevelt is inaugurated as the 32nd President of the United States.

March 5 – The Nazi party wins 288 votes in the German general election, more than twice the number gained by their rivals the Social Democrats.

March 12 – President Roosevelt's first "Fireside Chat" to the American people broadcast on the radio.

April 19 – President Roosevelt announces the removal of the U.S. dollar from the Gold Standard.

November 17 – The U.S. recognizes the Soviet Union and begins trade.

General

Roosevelt's "New Deal" legislation includes:
– The Agricultural Adjustment Act
– Federal Securities Act
– The Federal Emergency Relief Act
– National Industrial Recovery Act

Germany opens "concentration" camps for enemies of the regime.

In December Prohibition is repealed (21st Amendment).

1934

March 24 – The Tydings-McDuffe Act establishes the independence of the Philippines from the U.S.A. from 1945.

June 29–30 – "The Night of the Long Knives" in Germany. Hitler purges the S.A. and its leader Ernst Röhm, executing many of his rivals.

August 6 – U.S. marines withdraw from Haiti after 19 years of military occupation.

General

Heinrich Himmler takes control of the secret police in Germany.

A Federal Farm Mortgage Corporation is set up to reduce the number of farm closures.

The Fraternal Council of Negro Churches is established to campaign for social change.

Fugitives Bonnie Parker and Clyde Barrow are killed by police in Chicago.

Golf's U.S. Masters is played at Augusta Georgia for the first time.

1935

March 16 – Germany introduces conscription, contravening the disarmament clauses of the Treaty of Versailles.

September 15 – At the Nazi Party's Nuremburg rally, Adolf Hitler proclaims the anti-Jewish "Nuremburg Laws". They restrict Jewish employment, marriage to non-Jews and sexual relations with non-Jews. The swastika becomes the national flag.

October 2 – Italy invades Ethiopia.

General

The National Labor Relations Act outlaws unfair practices by employers and establishes the right to form trade unions.

Storms exacerbate the "dust bowl" in the America mid-west.

More "New Deal" legislation is introduced in the U.S. by Roosevelt, including:
– The Resettlement Administration.
– Rural Electrification Administration.
– The Social Security Act.

James J. Braddock wins the heavyweight boxing title from Max Baer.

1936

March 7 – German troops occupy the de-militarized area of the Rhineland in contravention of the Treaty of Versailles.

July 17 – An army mutiny in Spanish Morocco, led by Francisco Franco, ignites the Spanish Civil War.

November 3 – Roosevelt is re-elected as U.S. president with 523 electoral college votes. His opponent, the Republican Alfred London, wins only 8 votes.

December 11 – Edward VIII abdicates the British throne in the crisis created by his desire to marry Wallis Simpson. His brother becomes King George VI.

General

The Hoover Dam opens on the Colorado river.

1937

April 27 – The German Condor Legion bomb Guernica in the Spanish Civil War.

May 6 – The German airship "Hindenburg" explodes whilst landing in New Jersey. 36 people are killed.

August 8 – The Japanese attack Shanghai in the Sino-Japan war.

December 5 – Japanese troop captures Nanking. Atrocity known as the Rape of Nanking ensues with loss of 250,000 lives.

General

The National Housing Act creates the United State Housing Authority to help make housing more affordable to low income families.

The Golden Gate bridge opens in San Francisco.

Joe Louis wins the heavyweight boxing title.

1938

February 4 – Hitler makes himself Commander in Chief of the army.

March 12 – German troops enter Austria.

September 29/30 – Prime Ministers Chamberlain (Britain) and Daladier (France) agree to allow the German occupation of the Sudetenland (German-speaking region of Czechoslovakia), at the Munich Conference.

November 9/10 – "Kristallnacht" in Germany. Jewish homes, synagogues and shops are looted and burned.

General

A minimum wage (40 cents/hr) is established in the U.S. under the Labor Standards Act.

Hysteria is caused in the U.S. by Orson Welles' CBS radio broadcast of his play, *War of the Worlds*.

1939

January 26 – Barcelona falls to Franco in the Spanish Civil War. His new government is recognized a month later by France and Britain. The U.S. recognizes the Nationalist regime on April 1.

April 7 – Spain joins Italy, Germany and Japan in the Anti-Comintern Pact

May 22 – Hitler and Mussolini sign a 10-year alliance, the "Pact of Steel."

July 16 – The United States revokes its 1911 trade agreement with Japan.

August 23 – The Nazi-Soviet Pact with secret clauses for the carve-up of Eastern Europe is signed.

August 23 – British Prime Minister Neville Chamberlain warns Hitler that Britain will stand by Poland.

September 1 – Germany invades Poland.

September 3 – Britain and France declare war on Germany.

September 17 – The Soviet Union invades Poland from the East.

September 28 – The Polish army offers its formal surrender to the Germans.

November 4 – President Roosevelt amends the 1937 Neutrality Act, allowing Britain and France to purchase arms on a "cash and carry" basis.

General

Albert Einstein writes to President Roosevelt, warning of the dangers of German atomic power prompting an acceleration in atomic research and the beginnings of the Manhattan Project.

Lou Gehrig retires after making 2,130 appearances for the New Yankees.

NBC begins the first regular television service in the U.S.

1940

April 9 – German troops invade Norway and Denmark.

May 10 – Germany invades Holland, Belgium and Luxumburg and outflanks the French border fortifications, the "Maginot Line", by attacking through the reputedly impenetrable Ardennes forest.

May 26–June 4 – Over 300,000 British and French troops, trapped on the beaches of Dunkirk by the German advance, are evacuated in a remarkable recovery operation.

June 22 – France concludes an armistice with Germany. The country is divided into a zone of German occupation in the north and west and an area of French control administered from Vichy.

August 15 – As the aerial battle for supremacy between the Luftwaffe and the British Royal Air Force intensifies over southern England, the R.A.F. shoot down 180 German planes.

September 7 – The first massive bombing raids on London, the "Blitz" begins.

November 5 – President Roosevelt is elected for an unprecedented third term by 449 electoral college votes, to opponent Wendell Wilkie's 82.

General

The French government at Vichy strips Jews of citizenship and bans them from public service.

Nylon stockings, Colonel Sanders "Kentucky Fried Chicken" and the Willy's Jeep are introduced in the U.S.

1941

March 11 – President Roosevelt's Lend-Lease Bill is finally signed. It allows for massive sales of aid to allies whose security is vital to American interests.

April 6 – Hitler invades Greece and Yugoslavia.

June 22 – Operation Barbarossa, the largest invasion force in history, is launched against the Soviet Union as Germany attacks with three army groups.

July 26 – Roosevelt freezes all Japanese assets in the U.S. and levies embargoes on Japan.

July 27 – The German army reaches the Ukraine, deep into the Soviet Union.

August 14 – Roosevelt and Churchill sign the Atlantic Charter.

October 1 – The Germans close in on Moscow. The Soviet government leaves Moscow, but Joseph Stalin stays behind.

November 13 – The U.S. Congress amends the Neutrality Act, allowing U.S. merchants to enter war zones and be armed.

December 5 – Winter tightens its grip in the Russian heartland and after holding two German attempts to capture Moscow, the Soviet Red Army launches a counter-offensive.

December 7 – Japanese imperial forces launch a surprise attack on the U.S. naval base at Pearl Harbor, Hawaii.

December 8 – U.S. and Britain declares war on Japan.

December 11 – Germany and Italy declare war on the U.S..

December 25 – Hong Kong surrenders to Japan.

General

As the German army advances in Eastern Europe, special units begin the systematic elimination of Jews.

Roosevelt establishes the Fair Employment Practices Commission to investigate racial discrimination in employment.

The Mount Rushmore Memorial in Vermont is completed.

1942

January 1 – 26 nations sign the Declaration of the United Nations, forming a coalition against the Axis powers.

January 11 – Japanese forces capture Kuala Lumpur in Malaya.

February 15 – Over 70,000 British and Commonwealth troops are captured as the British garrison surrenders at Singapore.

April 9 – U.S. and Philippines forces surrender on Bataan.

April 18 – Famous "Doolittle Raid" on Tokyo shatter Japanese myth of impregnability of the mainland.

May 4 – Battle of the Coral Sea.

May 6 – Beginning of the Bataan Death March.

June 4 – In the Battle of Midway, U.S. planes sink four Japanese aircraft carriers.

June 21 – Erwin Rommel's Afrika Korps take the vital British stronghold at Tobruk in Libya.

July 28 – The Germans capture Rostov and much of the Northern Caucasus.

August 7 – United States marines capture Henderson Airfield on Guadalcanal and hold it against Japanese counterattacks.

September 13 – The crucial Battle for Stalingrad begins. Leningrad, Moscow

and Stalingrad become the rocks of Soviet resistance on the Eastern Front.

October 23 – The German army suffers its first defeat against British forces at El Alamein in North Africa.

November 7 – In Operation Torch, Allied forces land in Morocco and Algeria under the command of General Eisenhower.

General

U.S. automobile production is suspended to maximise war production. Gasoline and sugar are rationed and "Victory Gardens" are introduced to increase food production.

The War Relocation Authority begins to move over a hundred thousand Japanese Americans from the Pacific Coast into internment camps.

In Chicago, physicist Enrico Fermi creates the first controlled chain-reaction in a nuclear reactor.

1943

January 2 – The German army begins to retreat from the Caucasus.

January 12 – At the Casablanca Conference Churchill and Roosevelt agree to pursue an unconditional German and Japanese surrender.

January 31 – The German army defending Stalingrad surrenders.

May 11 – At the Washington Conference, Roosevelt and Churchill agree on an invasion strategy for Europe. The Mediterranean will come first, through Sicily and then mainland Italy, followed by an invasion in northern Europe.

May 11 – U.S. forces land in the Aleutian Islands.

July 10 – Operation Husky: British and American forces land on Sicily.

July 25 – Benito Mussolini is removed as Italy's Prime Minister and replaced by Badoglio.

September 3 – Italy offers its unconditional surrender, leaving the German army to fight alone in the defense of the Italian Peninsular.

September 9 – Allied forces land at Salerno.

November 1 – U.S. Marines begin to recapture territory in the Solomon Islands.

November 28 – At the Tehran Conference, Churchill and Roosevelt brief Stalin on the plans for the Allied invasion of France.

General

The U.S. congress approves the "Pay-As-You-Go" scheme whereby employers will deduct income tax from salaries and wages.

Race riots break out in Detroit, following large-scale African American migrations to the north

1944

January 22 – U.S. and British troops land at Anzio in Italy.

March 6 – U.S. bombers begin daylight raids on Berlin.

May 18 – German resistance at Monte Cassino finally ends. The defeat allows the Allies to break out from Anzio.

June 4 – Allied forces enter Rome.

June 6 – Operation Overload begins on "D-Day". Allied troops land on five assault beaches in Normandy.

July 15 – U.S. forces capture Saipan in the Marianas.

July 20 – Hitler narrowly escapes an assassination attempt as a bomb explodes close to him at Rastenberg in East Prussia.

August 10 – U.S. forces liberate Guam.

August 14 – Operation Dragoon, Allies land on the French Mediterranean coast.

August 24 – A French armoured unit enters Paris, followed by Charles de Gaulle, leader of the Free French.

September 17 – In Operation Market Garden, U.S. and British airborne troops attempt to seize vital bridges in the Netherlands.

October 25 – Battle of Leyte Gulf: the U.S. navy destroys four aircraft carriers, three battleships, ten cruisers and nine destroyers of the Japanese navy.

November 3 – President Roosevelt wins an unprecedented fourth term with 432 electoral votes to Thomas Dewey's 99.

November 24 – B-29 bombers from Saipan begin heavy bombing raids on Tokyo.

December 16 – The Germans launch a counter-offensive, in the Ardennes, the "Battle of the Bulge."

General

An international conference at Dumbarton Oaks, Washington DC establishes the structure of a future United Nations.

A conference at Bretton Woods, New Hampshire establishes the International Monetary Fund and the World Bank.

1945

February 4 – The Yalta Conference begins: the Allies prepare their plans for a post-war settlement.

February 19 – U.S. Marines attack Iwo Jima, fierce fighting ensues.

February 23 – Marines capture Mount Suribachi on Iwo Jima.

March 26 – Iwo Jima is secured.

April 1 – U.S. forces begin their attack on Okinawa, the largest of the Japanese Ryuakyu islands.

April 12 – President Roosevelt dies at the age of 63. He is succeeded by Vice-President Harry S. Truman.

April 28 – Benito Mussolini and his mistress are shot by Italian partisans.

April 30 – After marrying his mistress Eva Braun, Adolf Hitler commits suicide in his bunker in Berlin.

May 2 – Berlin surrenders to the Soviets.

May 8 – After the formal German surrender, Victory in Europe Day is declared.

July 4 – MacArthur announces liberation of the Philippines.

June 21 – U.S. achieve victory on Okinawa.

July 16 – Atom bomb successfully tested in New Mexico.

July 17 – The Potsdam Conference begins.

July 26 – Winston Churchill loses the British general election. The Labour Party wins by a landslide. Clement Attlee becomes Prime Minister.

August 6 – The U.S. drops an atomic bomb on the Japanese city of Hiroshima.

August 8 – The U.S. drops a second atomic bomb on Nagasaki.

August 14 – The Japanese announce their unconditional surrender.

September 2 – Japan signs a formal surrender abound U.S.S *Missouri*.

General

The foundation of U.N.E.S.C.O., the United Nations Educational, Scientific and Cultural Organisation.

SELECTED BIBLIOGRAPHY

–Ambrose, Stephen, *D-Day* (New York, 1994)

–Bradley, James, *Flags of Our Fathers* (New York, 2000)

–Dear I. C. B. (ed), *The Oxford Companion to the Second World War* (Oxford, 1956)

–Pimlott, John, *The Viking Atlas of World War II* (London, 1995)

–Smith, Carl, *Pearl Harbor* (Oxford, 1999)

–Sulzberger, C.L., (updated by Stephen Ambrose), *American History New History of World War II* (London, 1997)

–Taylor, James, *Encyclopedia of the Second World War* (New Jersey, 1999)

–Williams, Hal R; Breen, T. H.; Divine, Robert; Fredrickson, George M. et al, *America Past and Present* (New York, 1999)

–Weinberg, Gerhard L.A., *World At Arms: A Global History of World War II* (Cambridge, 1994)

INDEX

Page numbers in *italics* refer to captions to illustrations.

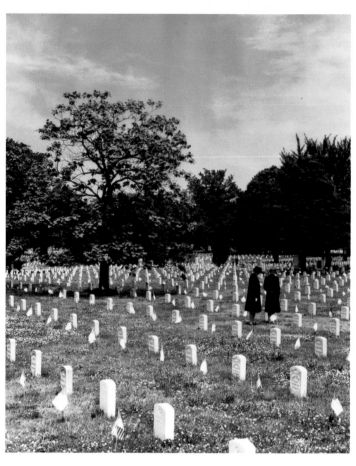

PICTURE CREDITS

Key: National Archive (NA), Library of Congress (LoC), Ethell Collection (EC), Imperial War Museum (IWM)

Front cover NA, 111-C-741 1 NA, 111-C-218 3&4 NA, 342-FH-3A-49530-K-KE 2293 4&5 NA, 111-C-3209 6 NA, 127-GW-1365-106294 9 NA, 342-FH-3A-49651-K2751 10/11 NA, 342 FH-4A 22098-K-KE-4004 12 Peter Stackpole/Timepix/Rex Features 141334 13 Charles Fenno Jacobs/Timepix/Rex Features 114749 14 *above* Library of Congress LC-USF35-238 34185 14 *right* LoC LC-USF35-585 34169 15 LoC LC-USF35-33 33833 16 LoC LC-USF35-91 33874 17 *below* LoC LC-USF35-276 34281 17 *right* LoC LC-USF35-176 34399 18 *above* LoC LC-USF35-311 34090 18 *right* LoC LC-USF35-212 34209 19 *above* LoC LC-USW36-803 35006 20 *left* EthellCollection/Fred Hill 20 *right* LoC LC-USF35-23 33871 20 *right* LoC LC-USF35-520 34411 21 *above* LoC LC-USF35-266 34271 22 *above* BPK F3916 b 23 *below* Hugo Jaeger/Timepix/Rex Features 812126 23 *left* BPK F3833 b 24/25 Hugo Jaeger/Timepix/Rex Features 810037 26 *above* Hugo Jaeger/Timepix/Rex Features 812138 26 *left* Hugo Jaeger/Timepix/Rex Features 815477 27 (26 *right*) Hugo Jaeger/Timepix/Rex Features 815560 28 *above* Hugo Jaeger/Timepix/Rex Features 809977 29 *above* Hugo Jaeger/Timepix/Rex Features 813813 29 *below* Hugo Jaeger/Timepix/Rex Features 813761 30 *above* Hugo Jaeger/Timepix/Rex Features 1173297 30 *right* Hugo Jaeger/Timepix/Rex Features 814111 31 *above* Hugo Jaeger/Timepix/Rex Features 814099 31 *left* TimePix 814140 31 *right* Hugo Jaeger/Timepix/Rex Features 814064 32 *above* Hulton-Getty HJ 4950 33 (32 *right*) Hulton-Getty HJ 4964 34 *below* EC/Henry Beck 35 *above* Eric Schaal/Timepix/Rex Features 144867 35 *right* Eric Schaal/Timepix/Rex Features 115651 36 (37 *left*) Dmitri Kessel/Timepix/Rex Features 116911 37 *above* Charles Fenno Jacobs/Timepix/Rex Features 14676 1 37 *below* Dmitri Kessel/Timepix/Rex Features 115602 37 *left* Charles Fenno jacobs/Timepix/Rex Features 146982 38 *above* IWM TR 9 38 *right* IWM TR 89 39 *below* IWM TR 90 40 *above* EC 40 *below* EC/Fred Hill 41 *below* EC 41 *right* EC/Henry Beck 42 *above* EC/Fred Hill 42 *right* EC/Fred Hill 43 (42 *right*) ECl/Henry Beck 44 *above* EC/Fred Hill 45 *above* EC 45 *right* EC 46 *below* NA, 342FH-4A-21690-K671 46 *left* Robert Y Richie/Timepix/Rex Features 121285 47 *above* Robert Y Richie/Timepix/Rex Features 121349 47 *right* NA, 342FH-4A-22031-K1679 48 *below* NA, 111-C-5904 49 (48 *right*) Hulton-Getty JE 0633 50 *below* Hulton-Getty JE 0641 50 *right* Hulton-Getty JE 0636 51 *below* LoC LC-USF35-550 34414 52 NA, 80-GK-13328 54 EC/Althouse 56 *right* NA, 80-GK-13849 57 *left* LoC LC-USW36-787 35014 57 *right* LoC LC-USW36-786 35013 58 *above* LoC LC-USW36-8 35084 58 *left* NA, 80-GK-383 58 *right* LoC LC-USW36-229 35103 59 *above* LoC LC-USW36-830 35424 60 *above* LoC LC-USW36-561 34655 61 *below* LoC LC-USW36-331 35278 61 *left* LoC LC-USW36-384 34948 62 *below* LoC LC-USW36-78 34888 62 *left* LoC LC-USW36-387 34899 63 *below* LoC LC-USW36-118 35349 63 *left* LoC LC-USW36-418 34971 64/65 LoC LC-USW36-128 35356 66 (67 *left*) NA, 111-C-3022 66 *right* NA, 111-C-120 67 *above* LoC LC-946 67 *left* NA, 111-C-956 68 *above* LoC LC-USW36-1058 35469 69 *above* NA, 111-C-3463 70 *below* EC/Stitt 70 *right* NA, 342-FH-4A-22035-K0626 71 *above* EC/Crowder 71 *below* EC 72 (74 prev page) LoC LC-USF35-288 34251 74 *above* LoC LC-USW36-175 35210 74 *right* (75) LoC LC-USW36-51 34871 76 (77 *left* 3) NA, 111-C-3229 77 *below* NA, 111-C-3748 77 *left* 1 NA, 111-C-201 77 *left* 2 LoC LC-USW36-171 35207 78 *left* Bob Leavitt/Timepix/Rex Features 154248 79 *above* Hulton-Getty HJ 4905 79 *below* Hulton Getty 80 *above* NA, 80-GK-15250 81 *above* NA, 80-GK-387 82/83 NA, 342-FH-3A-49542-K-KE 2417 84 Lofman/Timepix/Rex Features 159049 85 EC 80-GK-2479 86 (87 *left* 2) NA, 111-C-465 87 *below* LoC LC-USW36-295 35371 87 *left* 1 LoC LC-USW36-839 35442 88 *above* NA, 80-GK-15010 88 *right* Lofman/Timepix/Rex Features 156482 89 *above* Lofman/Timepix/Rex Features 156469 90 *above* NA, 111-C-2175 90 *left* NA, 111-C-35 91 *above* NA, 80-GK-14010 92 (93 *left* 2) NA, 80-GK-15092 93 *left* 1 NA, 80-GK-15601 93 *right* NA, 80-GK-2750 94 *above* NA, 80-GK-13307 94 *left* NA, 80-GK-38058 95 NA, 127-GW-1243-067705 96 *above* NA, 80-GK-14381 96 *right* NA, 127-GW-1243-067707 97 NA, 127-GW-1243-067701 98/99 (100 Prev Page) NA, 80-GK-16053 100 *above* NA, 80-GK-16216 101 *above* NA, 80-GK-13969 101 *right* NA, 80-GK-15350 101 *right* 1 NA, 80-GK-13270 101 *right* 2 NA, 80-GK-13244 102 *left* IWM TR1427 104 *above* EC/Sloan 104 *left* EC 105 imperial War Museum TR1624 106 NA, 342-FH-3A-49545-K-KE 2422A 107 EC 108 NA, 80-GK-14053 109 *left* IWM 109 *right* EC 110 *above* Air Force Museum 110 *right* EC/Pealey 111 EC/Crowder 112/113 EC/Stitt 114 NA, 342-FH-3A-49711-K2196 115 *above* NA, 111-C-4622 115 *below* NA, 80-GK-14055 116 Popperfoto 117 NA, 342-FH-3A-49500-K-KE 1074 118 NA, 111-C-1127 119 *left* EC/Henry Beck 119 *right* EC/Henry Beck 120 *below* NA, 111-C-276 120 *left* NA, 111-C-1311 121 NA, 111-C-175 122 *above* NA, 111-C-1918 122 *right* NA, 111-C-137 123 NA, 111-CPF-104 124 NA, 111-C-759 125 *left* 1 NA, 111-C-675 125 *right* NA, 111-C-598 126 NA, 111-C-2024 127 NA, 111-C-1917 128 *left* NA, 111-C-896 128 *right* NA, 111-C-650 129 *left* EC/Fleury 129 *right* EC 130/131 NA, 111-C-1087 132 EC 134 *left* NA, 111-C-3099 134 *right* (135) NA, 111-C-505 136 (137 2nd *left*) NA, 111-C-2818 137 *left* NA, 111-C-266 137 *right* NA, 111-C-475 138 (139 2nd *left*) EC/Robert Sand 138 *left* NA, 111-C-1266 139 *below* NA, 80-GK-1181 139 *left* NA, 111-C-1078 140 NA 111-C-741 141 *above* NA, 111-C-1258 141 *right* NA, 111-CPF-1248 142 NA 342 FH 203 3A 49726-K2166 143 NA 306 SUB HIS 0007 144/145 *left* Hulton-Getty JI 6510 146 *above* NA, 342-FH-3A-49743-K2268 147 *above* NA, 342-FH-3A-49948-K 2558 147 *right* NA, 342-FH-3A-49614-K 2351 148 *above* NA, 342-FH-3A-49603-K- 3913 149 *left* EC 149 *right* NA, 342-FH-3A-49602-K- 2618 150 (1512nd *left*) NA, 342-FH-3A-49659-K2146 151 *below* EC 151 *left* EC 152 *above* NA, 111-C-919 152 *left* NA, 111-C-580 153 *above* NA, 111-C-2162 154 (155 1st *left*) NA, 111-C-565 155 *right* NA, 111-CPF-159 156 *above* NA, 111-C-1932 156 *right* NA, 111-C-313 157 *above* NA, 80-GK-13782 158 *above* NA, 111-C-1767 158 *below* NA, 111-C-1894 159 (158 *right*) NA, 111-C-2158 160 *left* NA, 111-C-1455 160 *right* NA, 111-C-1431 161 *left* NA, 111-C-1515 161 *right* IWM TR 1854 162 *left* NA, 111-C-2191 162 *right* NA, 111-C-446 163 *below* NA, 111-C-3186 164 *above* Hulton-Getty JI 6477 165 *above* IWM TR0099 165 *left* NA, 111-C-2227 166 *left* NA, 111-C-2209 166 *right* NA, 111-C-2194 167 *left* NA, 111-C-2348 167 *right* NA, 306-SUB-HIS-0003 168 NA 111-C-714 169 (168 1st *right*) NA, 111-C-323 NA 111-C-713 170 *above* NA, 111-C-1125 170 *left* NA, 111-C-2573 171 2nd *above* NA, 111-C-562 171 *above* NA, 111-C-850 171 *left* NA, 111-C-2676 172/3 NA 80 GK 4510176 173 *below* NA 306-SUB-HIS-0128 174 top NA 342-FH-3A-49460 174 *below* EC/Robert Sand 175 NA 80-GK-15926 176 *right* NA, 80-GK-1293 180 *right* Ethell 182 *right* Ethell 184 *left* Ethell 189 NA, 111-C-801 175 NA, 80-GK-15926 176 *below* NA, 111-C-1349 177 *above* NA, 127-GS-0166-092315 178 *above* NA, 127-GW-1365-086897 178 *right* NA, 127-GW-1365-086912 179 *above* NA, 127-GW-1365-086935 180 *above* NA, 127-GW-1365 086593 180 *below* EC/Hollandia 181 *below* NA, 127-GW-1427-094055 181 *left* NA, 127-GW-1427-094062 184 *above* NA, 111-C-260 182 *above* EC 182 *below* EC 183 NA 342-FH-3A-49409 184 *left* EC 185 *below* NA, 80-GK-14451 185 *right* NA, 111-C-5926 186/7 NA, 80-GK-4760 190 *above* NA, 111-C-551 191 *above* NA, 111-C-545 192 NA 342-FH-3A-49737-K3264 193 NA 342-FH-3A-49649-K2468 194 NA 342-FH-3A-49677-K3914 195 *above* NA, 342-FH-3A-49887- KE3254 195 *right* EC 196 *left* NA, 111-C-1260 196 *right* NA, 111-C-1233 197 *above* NA, 111-C-3286 197 *right* NA, 111-C-959 198 *above* NA, 111-CPF-908 199 *below* NA, 342-FH-3A-49464-K3516 199 *left* NA, 111-CPF-1084 200 *above* NA, 342-FH-3A-49801-K3537 200 *left* NA, 342-FH-3A-49832-K4111 201 (200 *right*) NA, 111-C-4652 202 *above* NA, 306-SUB-HIS-0008 203 *above* NA, 306-SUB-HIS-0005 204 (205 2nd *left*) NA, 111-C-2563 205 1st *left* NA, 111-C-2333 205 *below* NA, 111-C-2324 206 *below* NA, 111-C-2337 206 *left* EC/Robert Sand 207 NA, 342-FH-3A-49852-K3468 207 *right* NA, 342-FH-3A-49675-K3640 208 *above* NA, 111-C-1071 208 *right* NA, 111-C-1069 209 *above* NA, 111-C-1244 209 *right* NA, 111-C-1243 210 *above* NA, 342-FH-3A-49806-K3560 211 *above* NA, 342-FH-3A-49805-K3559 211 *right* EC/Henry Beck 212 (213 *left*) NA, 342-FH-3A-49877-K3456 213 *above left* EC/HSB 213 *above* NA, 111-C-3214 213 *right* NA, 342-FH-3A-49839-K0092 214 (215 *left*) NA, 342-FH-3A-49870-K3419 215 *below* NA, 80-GK-14622 215 *right* NA, 80-GK-3319A 216/217 (218 previous page) NA, 80-GK-5646 218 *above* NA, 111-C-1786 218 *left* NA, 111-C-1779 219 *below* EC/Wyglen 219 *left* NA, 111-C-1770 220 *below* EC/Eppstein 220 *left* EC/Wyglen 221 *above* NA, 111-C-3359 222 *above* NA, 111-C-423 222 *left* NA, 111-C-2823 223 *below* NA, 111-C-3405 224 *below* NA, 111-C-1771 224 *left* NA, 111-C-2375 225 *left* NA, 111-C-1776 225 *right* NA, 111-C-2376 226 *left* NA, 111-C-1860 227 (226 *right*) NA, 111-C-2926 228 *above* NA, 80-GK-2965 229 1st *above* NA, 127-GW-0353-116322 229 *above* NARA 127-G-4077 229 *below* NA, 127-GW-0352-124547 230 *right* NA, 80-GK-3170 232 *above* NA, 80-GK-4343 233 *above* NA, 80-GK-5007 234 *below* NA, 111-C-1569 234 *left* NA, 111-C-4621 235 *above* EC/Fred Hill 235 *below* NA, 111-C-805 236 *above* NA, 127-GW-0693-124201 236 *right* NA, 127-GW-0693-124202 237 *below* NA, 127-GW-1198-111675 237 *left* NA, 127-GW-0693-124208 238 NA 127-GW-042-0693-124481 239 NA 127-GW 120478240 2nd *right* NA, 80-GK-3829 240 *above* NA, 80-GK-5629 241 (240 1st *right*) NA, 80-GK-5192 242 *below* NA, 80-GK-14578 242 *left* NA, 80-GK-14592 243 *above* NA, 80-GK-13295 244 *above* NA, 342-FH-3A-49449-K4151 245 *above* NA, 342-FH-3A-49444-K-KE-6021 245 *right* NA, 342-FH-3A-49447-K6024 246 *below* NA, 342-FH-3A-49431-K-KE6013 247 *above* NA, 342-FH-3A-49434-K-KE 6016 247 *left* NA, 127-GW-1473-137963 248 *above* EC 248 *left* NA, 111-C-2719 249 *above* NA, 111-C-4626 250 *left* NA, 111-C-2717 250 *right* NA, 80-GK-6218 251 *above* NA, 80-GK-3749 254 NA, 111-C-4634 256 NA, 111-C-5930

Every effort has been made to acknowledge correctly and contact the source and/or copyright holder of each picture, and Carlton Books Limited apologises for any unintentional errors or omissions which will be corrected in future editions of this book.

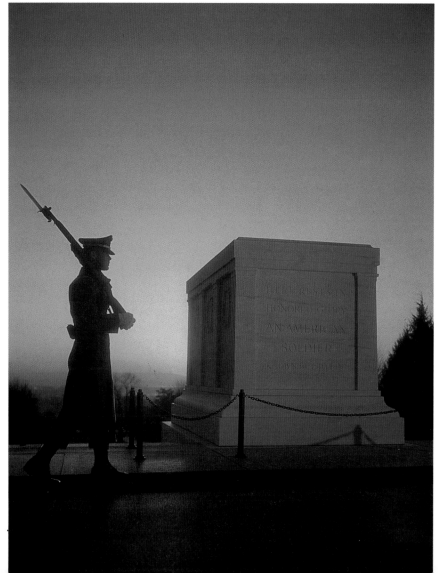